NOETA

NO ETA

THE PIONEERING DAYS OF
SKYDIVING

Dick Fortenberry

iUniverse, Inc.
Bloomington

No ETA
The Pioneering Days of Skydiving

iUniverse books may be ordered through booksellers or by contacting:

iUniverse
1663 Liberty Drive
Bloomington, IN 47403
www.iuniverse.com
1-800-Authors (1-800-288-4677)

ISBN: 978-1-4620-2642-5 (pbk)
ISBN: 978-1-4620-2644-9 (clth)
ISBN: 978-1-4620-2643-2 (ebk)

Printed in the United States of America

iUniverse rev. date: 07/05/2011

ACKNOWLEDGEMENTS

I would like to thank some of those who helped
make this possible.
Sandy Layman, with all of her secretarial skills.
Rich Benjamin and his organizational and computer skills.
Jerry Bourquin and his contribution of pictures.
And my wonderful wife, Linda, who, without her support,
none of this would have been written.

Preface

I was standing on the tail gate of the C-130-E Hercules at 30,000 feet. No one had ever jumped from this altitude without a stabilizing chute. We would be the first to do it "Free-fall". There were seven of us from the United States Army Parachute Team. We were breathing supplemental oxygen from bailout bottles strapped underneath our reserve parachutes. The Air Force Flight Surgeon was nervously walking between us looking for signs of hypoxia, or any other reason to scrub the jump. I looked out at the horizon of the El Centro desert and could actually see the curvature of the earth. The parachutes on our backs were out dated Air Force survival chutes with a stencil on them stating "CONDEMED. NOT FOR PERSONEL USE". Our "automatic openers" were set for 1,800 feet.

The "GO, NO GO" light turned from red to green and we stepped into the void. It was 29 April, 1960.

Chapter 1

"Holy shit, what now?" I would find that this phrase would follow me around like a wounded water buffalo and play a big part in my next two careers. It covers such areas as "What the . . . ! Where the . . . !, Why the . . . !, and How the . . . !, and is usually uttered when, in aviation terms, you run out of airspeed, altitude and ideas all at the same time. Only one other phrase emits more total frustration and in some cases, finality, and that's "Oh Shit!" But on this day, December 28, 1960, I was trying to figure out why my parachute was tilting so badly and why I was hanging at a 45 degree angle in the harness! Just a few seconds before, I had been filming Danny Byard in a 120 mph freefall over Sicily Drop Zone, Fort Bragg, North Carolina with an 8 millimeter movie camera strapped to my helmet. At 2,200 feet, I pulled my ripcord to open the parachute. Instead of the normal, steady, 3 to 4 "g's" we experienced during the opening shock, I felt two separate jolts. Now I was watching, with some concern, as my parachute was going through stages of opening and closing. I figured that I had a 50/50 chance (a lot of things I do don't add up) of hitting the ground during the open phase. I also figured that this meant I had a 50/50 chance of hitting the ground like a sack of you know what. I didn't like the odds!

What led up to this predicament occurred about three months prior when Loy Brydon, a fellow member of the Special Warfare Center Sport Parachute Club, and myself, found out that the Air Force had 300 B-12 type survival parachutes that they were going to cannibalize. Loy and I got in his pickup, hired a U-HAUL trailer and headed for Augusta, Georgia where this dastardly deed was to take place. We convinced these Air Force cannibals that we had a thousand uses for the outdated parachutes at Fort Bragg, and "No Sir, we would never consider jumping them!" So we loaded up our booty and headed back for Bragg, arriving exhausted but ready to start our "unauthorized" research and development program.

There were three Sport Parachute Clubs at Fort Bragg; the Special Warfare Center, which was mostly Special Forces, the 18th Airborne Corps and the 82nd Airborne Division. The sport was in its infancy with very little governing as nobody knew what the hell we were doing, including us. What was normal procedure or policy had probably been discovered that day. We were hungry for adventure, thirsty for knowledge, Gung Ho and rearing to go and we had 300 beautiful, outdated, obsolete and illegal parachutes to do it with. And of course, Loy and I being the straight shooters we were, divided the bounty equally between the other two clubs, 75 parachutes for each of them and the rest for us! So much for straight shooters, this was a golden opportunity and we were not going to let it pass.

The B-12 survival parachute was the mainstay for the Air Force and the Army in the early 1960's. It was made up of a #8 nylon webbing harness, nylon pack tray with thin steal ribs inside and four flat bungee cords on the closing flaps. The canopy was 28 feet in diameter with 28 suspension lines attached to four 3 foot risers that connected the whole thing to the harness by two cape wells. The nylon material between the suspension lines were called gores and went from the skirt, or bottom, of the canopy to the apex.

To get a basic idea of how it worked, the gores were neatly folded, the skirt evened up (this was critical), the canopy was then folded into a long fold, (which was the width of the pack tray), the suspension lines were then stowed into the pack tray with rubber bands, and the canopy accordion folded on top of the lines. A spring operated pilot chute was attached to the apex and was positioned on top of the canopy. The pack tray was then closed and secured by four pins that were attached to a ripcord cable with a handle on the end. When you pulled the ripcord handle, the pilot chute would come out and act as an air anchor. As the parachutist fell away from the pilot chute, the canopy would extend, the lines play out and the parachute would open, (hopefully), and the body ceased to be a projectile and became a passenger.

The basic design worked well, but a few modifications had been introduced by various individuals. The most notable of these changes was to put a sleeve over the canopy, stow the suspension lines onto the sleeve and attach the pilot chute to the apex of the sleeve. This slowed down the opening process and resulted in a much reduced opening shock. It also cut down on the malfunction rates. (Forgot to mention those, didn't I?).

Okay now, we can't just be floating around at the will of the wind, can we? No telling whose back yard, chimney, swimming pool or barbecue party we may end up in, not to mention highways, byways, trees and telephone wires. The later happened to a friend of mine resulting in a burn so severe that his arm was useless for the rest of his life. Anyway, to counter the effect of the wind, the parachute must be steerable. This meant a forward speed (I use that term sparingly) and a turn rate. The original design was simply to cut out the "gore" directly behind the canopy and add a "guide line" to each side of it allowing you to redirect the out rushing air and making a 360 degree turn somewhere between sunup and sundown.

The next modification was the one that affected my current dilemma. A "D" ring had to be added in order to attach the reserve parachute to the front of the harness. To do this, the harness had to be unthreaded through two sets of "friction adapters" which were used to adjust the size of the harness, much like a seat belt. The theory is that the harder you pull, the tighter it gets (kind of like asking the boss for a raise), unless you push the friction adapter upside down, then it can be easily adjusted or even unthreaded. To prevent this from happening accidentally, the end of the webbing was widened, or rolled, and stitched so that it would not physically fit through the adapter opening. Well, that morning I put a set of "D" rings on my newly acquired, outdated, obsolete, illegal, "No I wouldn't dream of jumping it"; harness and forgot to roll and stitch up the end of it!

Are we getting a picture here? During the opening, the butterfly snap of the reserve chute that hooks into the "D" ring got wedged under the friction adapter that holds it all together and it all went "FFFLLIITTHTHTH"! The whole left side of the main lift web came unthreaded. The cape-well which connected the left half of the canopy to the harness was now about six feet higher than it should be and the only thing holding it there was the diagonal back strap that, "Thank God, or either the Pioneer or Erving Parachute Company" was rolled and stitched. This accounted for the opening and closing of the parachute and the weird angle that I was hanging. My first thought was to activate the reserve chute, but the only thing keeping me in the, now defunct harness, was a little strap from the reserve to the left side of the harness saddle that kept the reserve from flapping around in freefall. So far so good! I elected to keep what I had and climb the diagonal back strap which pulled the cape well back to a somewhat level position. This righted the canopy but it was in a slow turn and heading for the woods to the west of the drop zone. I would have to hold the back strap with one hand (kind of like doing a one arm pull up) and use my other hand to steer the canopy with the guide line. Now I'm getting tired. Great! I've got another thousand feet to go and my arm is giving out. At about two hundred feet, I thought "I can't hold on any more!" I took a quick look at the ground and said, "Oh yes I can!"

The landing was hard, but I didn't notice. I just lay there exhausted until John Hollis, our First Sergeant, came over and said "What the hell happened?" I said "Hi John. I'm just going to lay here and wait for the first snow to come and cover me up!"

Now you might ask yourself, "why would anybody want to jump out of a perfectly good, functioning, airplane?" For as many Sport Parachutists (I prefer that to Sky Divers) as there are, you will find almost as many answers. For me it started back in the early to mid 1950's when I was attending Elementary School in Banning, California, where I grew up.

Banning was a small town right in the center of the San Gergonio pass that runs from Palm Springs to San Bernadino, Riverside and ultimately the Los Angeles area. In those days, Routes 66, 99 and every other major thoroughfare leading into L.A. from the East came right through the middle of town on Ramsey Street. The first traffic signal you hit coming from Palm Springs or Indio, trying to reach millions of destinations on the other side of it was the one at the intersection of Ramsey Street and San Gergonio Blvd.; I used to marvel at the power that light commanded. I could drive up on "Z" Mountain (so named because of the pattern it made going up the side of it toward Idyllwild) on Friday evenings and watch head lights stretched bumper to bumper for 20 miles and just imagine all of the swear words, arguments, high blood pressure and stress that one little light could command!

One block west of that awesome light on Ramsey Street was the Fox Theater; the holder of many of my adolescent memories; first date, first time I held hands with a girl, and first time I made a real ass of myself, but we won't go into that. My best friend, Bobby Sanford, and I used to play guitars and sing on the stage during the intermissions. One day I was watching a newsreel between features and they showed a new sport being conducted in a little town called Lille, France. It showed these guys jumping out of an airplane and falling almost out of sight before opening their parachutes. I was hooked. I didn't know how, where or when, but I was going to do that. It wouldn't come until November 8th, 1958.

I'm not real big on fate, but I have to admit that a number of events would transpire in a sequence that would pretty well dictate the rest of my life.

I was born in Coleman, Texas, to Mildred Ernestine Haney Fortenberry, wife of Richard Franklin Fortenberry, my mother was only sixteen. Shortly after that, we moved to Southern California, where, at 18 years old, my mother was killed in a car accident. The circumstances leading up to this tragedy have always been sketchy. All I was ever told was that she was leaning against the passenger side door when it came open. She fell out and broke her neck. I was also told that I was standing in the front seat between her and my father when it happened.

My father listed his occupation as "Preacher" but because of this and other failings in his life, he became a chronic alcoholic, and could never really accept the responsibility of a child. I was imparted to my Grandparents, Baxter and Jesse Fortenberry, when I was two and a half years old. They had already raised nine children of which they out-lived five, but they gladly took me to raise. They were affectionately known to everyone as "Mamaw and Bampaw" and were, without doubt, the most wonderful and loving people on the face of the earth! But, in 1956, when I was 18, Mamaw died, leaving an enormous void in everyone's heart, especially Bampaw!

After the mourning period was over, we tried to get on with our lives, but I began to feel like I was an unnecessary burden on Bampaw, which he assured me I wasn't, but I decided to quit high school and move on.

With an incomplete education and no skills, I decided to join the Army, which would give me three years to figure out what I should do with the rest of my life. I went to the recruiter and got the papers for Bampaw to sign.

Now, Ted and Ray, (my dad's twin brothers) had always been like second fathers to me. They taught me the little necessities of life, how to drive a truck, how to drink beer and how to fight! And boy could they fight! They said "Well Terrell, it's probably the best thing for you to do right now. It'll give you the chance to learn a trade. Maybe you can join the Corps of Engineers and learn to drive a Cat (short for Caterpillar) or Grader or something. By the way, what did you sign up for?"

Wait 'til I drop this one on them! "Well, I decided to join the Paratroopers." There was a collective pause, and then ... "You what! You dumb S.O.B. You'll get yourself killed. What did you do a dumb ass thing like that for? Bampaw, don't sign those papers."

Bampaw just looked at me and saw something in my eyes that made him turn to Ted and Ray and say, "Listen boys, did I ever tell you not to ride those wild horses, or do any number of the dang (Bampaw never swore) stupid things you've done in your lives? Leave Terrell alone, he's old enough to make his own stupid decisions." I said "thanks Bampaw, I think."

So Bampaw signed the parental release and the next thing I knew I was in Ft. Carson, Colorado, knee deep in snow, 17 degrees below zero, and marching 21 miles off bivouac.

One of the good things that happened to me in Basic Training was that I met my lifelong friend, James Garvey. Jim was Gung Ho to the core and had volunteered for a newly formed organization called "The Special Forces Group." In later years we would just refer to it as "Group." Jim was maybe 6 feet 2 inches tall, weighed around 175 pounds, of which maybe a half ounce of it was body fat, and gave off the demeanor that if he got shot today, he wouldn't fall until sometime next week. The first thing Jim wanted to do when he met me was whip my ass! For some reason I have that effect on a lot of people, but to know me is to love me! Anyway, we became close buddies and he began to try and persuade me to volunteer for Special Forces with him. I said "Not only no, but hell no." These guys were trained to jump behind enemy lines, survive off the land, eat pulsating snake hearts and conduct Guerrilla Warfare. Not for me dude! Besides, I had heard that no one from our Basic unit was going "Airborne" so I had already gone to personnel and signed up for the elite *Mountain Cold Weather Command*; it sounded like an exciting alternative.

Well, piss me off! After the first four weeks of basic training, two of our class went to the 101st Airborne Division, *The Screaming Eagles*, so, I marched right back to personnel and signed up again for Airborne Training. This got to the short and curlies of some of the training NCO's so they decided that if I could pass their Physical Training Test, I would be allowed to go Airborne. Little did I know, but I was soon to learn. The test took place at 2100 hours (9:00 PM) with just me and them. The weather was knee deep snow, in sub-zero temperature. The uniform for the event was boots, fatigue pants and Tee shirt for me, and winter coats for them. "By the book," I had to do the prescribed number pull-ups, sit-ups, pushups, squat jumps, run a prescribed distance in a prescribed time plus a few things I think they just made up. These exercises were done one after the other with no rest in between. I think the only reason I passed was that I was so fucking mad that I wouldn't give them the satisfaction of watching me fail! But what happened next was, I guess, their way of getting even!

"Holy shit, what next?" I said as I looked at the orders. Jim couldn't wait to break the news to me. Personnel, with a little help from a couple of NCO's I was intimately acquainted with, decided to fix my ass. Myself, Jim, and one other guy came out with orders assigning us to the 77th Special Forces Group, Fort Bragg, North Carolina. I think I was the only G.I. ever assigned to Group that didn't volunteer for it. It turned out to be the best mistake the Army ever made for me!

We arrived at Fort Bragg, North Carolina in the spring of 1958. Looking back almost 53 years and trying to describe what it felt like is not difficult. I can picture it as if it were yesterday. Well, maybe day before yesterday. I was a nineteen year old, snotty nosed Private First Class, dressed in an "Ike" jacket and brown shoes, getting ready to set the world on fire. I had absolutely no idea of what to expect, but I was sure ready to find out. I was also in awe of all the guys walking around with "Bloused Boots," (their pant legs tucked into the top of their jump boots), The parachute and glider patch on their hats, the patch on their shoulders saying AIRBORNE like a giant advertisement for America's young gladiators ready to defend against all aggressors and uphold the traditions and honor of those who went before. And especially those coveted silver wings on their chests. During WWII, the Germans called them "Devils in Baggy Pants." Now it was my turn!

Jim and I reported in to FB 1, which was a training team under the supervision of 1st Sergeant Doug Hodge, who was sitting there casually devouring a pulsating snake heart. Just kidding. Reporting in along with us was the most unlikely candidate for a Special Forces Operator I could ever imagine, David Crocco!

How do I describe Dave Crocco? He was about 5 feet 9 inches tall, weighed about 125 lbs. and looked like if he sneezed, he would disappear. David had a constant look of surprise mixed with bewilderment on his face; the look that says "You gotta be kidding!" But we would find out through jump school, S.F. training and our next fifty some odd years friendship, that 5 feet and 120 lb. of Dave Crocco was Heart and the rest was all Guts.

The rest of FB 1 was Sgt. Bonier, 3rd Army heavy weight boxing champion, Sgt. Rocky Niesom who, I think, they let out of the stockade because he was too mean, and a collection of men picked for their unique, for lack of another description, talents.

In 1958, Special Forces consisted of only around 400 Officers and men. It was a fresh, new concept which would eventually be the Field Agents for the Special Warfare Center.

In our training we were taught to infiltrate behind enemy lines, link up with local resistance fighters or indigenous personnel for the purpose of total disruption through sabotage, assassination, social disorder and anything else we could think of. We pretty well had free reign. We also had to be able to survive off the land, be cross trained in at least two other skills so if one operator got compromised, another could take over his duties. I picked demolitions and foreign weapons. But first, all of us FNG's had to go to jump school.

For the next three weeks, we would go through some of the most rigorous physical and mental training of our young lives. The first day was designed to weed out the weak and faint hearted as rapidly as possible so they could get on with the business of reshaping our bodies and minds. This was accomplished by subjecting all of us to a five mile run. All the while, the instructors are making you drop out and "Get Ten" pushups, then catching up with the class only to have another instructor get in your face with a piece of paper yelling "Come on and quit. All you have to do is stop and sign this paper, you pansy! You know you can't make it! Quit!" Compared to these guys, my two NCO pals back in Basic were amateurs.

Well, I didn't quit, I passed out. I don't even remember falling. I was up in the back of a First Aid truck with a bloody nose and skinned knees. I tried to get out and continue, but the medics wouldn't let me. I was devastated, I had no second plan. If I couldn't be a Paratrooper I had no idea what I wanted to do, or could do. The rest of the day was a blur. The next morning we were informed that those of us, who wanted to try, could take a PT (Physical Training) run. This consisted of sprinting at full speed for four minutes, walking two minutes, sprinting four minutes, walking two minutes and sprinting four minutes then it was over. There were about twenty-five of us who had failed the five mile run the day before. About ten or twelve of those quit right there; the rest of us lined up. I noticed that there was a jeep full of instructors going with us. In the first four minute sprint we lost about a third of the students. During the two minute walk, I watched as the tired instructor got into the jeep and a fresh one took over. On the next sprint we lost all but three of us. I had no idea of how much the next four minutes would influence the rest of my life. All three of us made it, but I don't think I had another ten seconds left in me. At that moment though, I knew I wouldn't fail Jump School.

Through the use of many training devices such as aircraft mockups, the thirty-four foot tower, the three foot platform, the suspended harness and many more, we would learn how to uniformly, safely and willingly, jump out of a perfectly good airplane. This being 1957, that airplane would be a C-119 "Flying Boxcar" which reminded me of a bumble bee, in that, aerodynamically a bumble bee can't fly, but he doesn't know that so he flies anyway. In between all of this learning, we would do about a million pushups, sit-ups, and squat jumps.

Every morning started out the same; the "Daily Dozen" (which were 12 exercises designed by the military to strengthen every muscle you have), then we did a mile run.

Dave Crocco didn't know for years how much he helped get me through those runs. When I would start getting tired and have doubts as to whether I could finish the run, I would pick out Dave and tell myself "I can run as long as that little scrawny bastard can run."

Three instructors always stuck in my mind; Bill Edge (who would later be on the *Golden Knights* with me), Blood Burns and a Japanese instructor named Tomosato. Tomosato could do pushups with one arm faster and longer than I could with two. Blood Burns was a colored Instructor that, when he got nose to nose with you and opened his mouth, you swore he was going to swallow you. His hands were so huge that when he saluted his wrist was about half way to where my elbow would be. And he had a great, if not some times morbid, sense of humor. Bill Edge was about 5' 10" tall and 175 pounds of romping, stomping airborne hell! And I was assigned to his platoon! I once saw him kick a Colonel in the ass who had fallen out of a run and told him "Now get up and run. If you can catch me, you can kick my ass!" At graduation, that Colonel went up to Sgt Edge and said "Sergeant, that was the best kick in the ass I ever had," and saluted him. As my friend Saul says "That's the kind of guy that could fall into a barrel of shit and come out smelling like a rose."

Jump week arrived and we were all filled with a sense of anticipation and apprehension not to mention a little fear. Anyone who says he's not afraid to make that first jump is either lying or crazy. We would make one jump a day for the next five days to qualify for those coveted silver wings. This had to be done without breaking anything, which would cycle you back through the entire course.

For some reason, I was beginning to have second thoughts. I had dreamed about this for years and now at the moment of truth, I was faltering. We had already lost over half of our class in the two prior weeks of training. I wondered if I was the only one with any doubts. Well, I would go ahead and "chute up" but I wasn't going to jump out of any airplane. The "Riggers," those guys trained to pack the parachutes, were on hand to help us put them on and to see that it was done right. All the straps that held you in the harness snapped into a single release button and was held in by a safety pin, not to be confused with those used on diapers. It was a forked device that went under the release button so that it couldn't be pushed accidentally. Not a cheerful thought! Well, I'll go ahead and get on the aircraft, but I'm not jumping out.

The Jump School instructors also acted as "Jumpmasters" on the airplanes. They would make sure that we did everything just like we were trained. We had heard stories that if you didn't jump, these jumpmasters would kick you out. They assured us that was not the case. They said they would just pull us out of the door and that would be that. "Works for me!"

We climbed into the C-119's and strapped ourselves into the webbed harness seats. I still remember the smell of oil, aviation fuel and the odor of every other paratrooper that had "Sweated out" a jump in this airplane. "Well, I'll go through the take-off, but I'm not jumping out of this airplane."

We took off for the longest, and the shortest, airplane ride of our lives, headed for Sicily Drop Zone, Fort Bragg, North Carolina. I began to look around me to see if anyone was as apprehensive as me. What I saw was what we would, years later, in Vietnam, refer to as the "Thousand yard stare." That's approximately where your eyes focus when they are open but not looking at anything in particular. Some people refer to it as day dreaming. Well, this is just the opposite.

In times of fear or apprehension, your life is passing before your eyes. Not flashing as they say, but passing in kind of a slow motion. It's more reflective. You think of the things you wish you had done, regret some things you did. You make resolutions, you think of the girl back home and you want to tell your mother you love her one more time. You tell your dad you understand everything he tried to instill in you, even though you don't. Wishing you had asked a certain woman to marry you, and in some cases, regretting you did. And sometimes, wondering if you will see the next sunrise. It's all there in the "Thousand yard stare."

Accompanying the "stare" is usually a lot of yawning, and today I noticed that I couldn't keep my mouth closed.

The first two days of jump week would be individual tap outs. That's where each student has the opportunity to shuffle up, stand in the door and watch the earth passing by 1,250 feet below and wondering what stupid assed decision got you in this predicament. Now your life can flash before your eyes. Then the jumpmaster slaps you on the butt and yells "GO!" But, I'm ahead of myself.

Approaching the Drop Zone, the jumpmasters go through a series of commands that prepare us for the jump. "GET READY!" All yawning stops! "STAND UP!", but I'm not jumping out of this stupid airplane!" "HOOK UP!" Attach the static line of the parachute to the anchor line cable of the airplane. This automatically opens the parachute as you fall away from the airplane, which ain't gonna' happen because I'm not jumping out of this stupid airplane! "CHECK YOUR EQUIPMENT!" Recheck the front of your equipment and the back of the guy in front of you. "SOUND OFF WITH EQUIPMENT CHECK!" The last guy in line, or more commonly called a "stick", yells "10 OK" and taps the guy in front of him who yells "9 OK" and taps the guy in front of him who yells "8 OK" and on down the line until everybody is OK except me because I'm not jumping out of no stupid airplane! "STAND IN THE DOOR!" "OK, but I'm not . . . . "Goiiinnnnngggg!" "Holy shit", what did I just do, and why did I do it!

The first thing you notice is the rush of air from the aircraft propellers, referred to as 'prop blast', then the opening shock of the parachute which is actually a nice 2 or 3 "G" tug. Hands up to spread the risers and make sure you have a fully deployed canopy, and then the silence. It wasn't as much of a silence as it was stillness. You could hear everything from the wind whistling through the suspension lines to people talking on the ground; it was awesome to say the least. Next comes the ground rush and the adrenaline starts pumping again in anticipation of the landing. A perfect PLF and the first jump is history!

Have you ever noticed how people react when they have been through something really scary and survived it? Well, picture about 150 nineteen year old students with a few "old timers" of twenty-one thrown in and the occasional ancient old fart of twenty-five, all talking at once, back slapping and chest thumping relief with everyone describing his own personal interpretation of the experience. It was a mad house.

All but one student, who broke an ankle, completed jump week. I was recommended as honor graduate by Sgt. Edge, but awarded runner up. That was fine with me, because I wasn't going to jump out of the damn thing in the first place!

It was May 31, 1957. We had the coveted silver wings on our chest, the glider and parachute patch on our hats and AIRBORNE on our shoulders. We were ten feet tall and bullet proof!

Chapter 2

For the next two years, from June 1957 until the summer of 1958, we would learn to survive in some very hostile environments. We would learn how to live off the land (an interesting prospect given that I hadn't learned how to live out of a grocery store yet), and how most foreign weapons were assembled and operated; also demolition skills from making booby traps, to blowing up bridges, (all the little niceties you can put on your resume). My Demolition instructor was SFC Ray Love, who was one of the eighty or so soldiers selected to start the original Special Forces Group. We learned communications to include Morse code, hand to hand combat, (at that time we didn't call it martial arts), infiltration methods from sky, ground or sea. The medics were trained not only on how to treat wounds and illnesses with normal medicines and drugs, but also herbs, roots, plants and, I think sometimes, even voodoo and witchcraft! They were also trained in amputations and child birth.

We spent months on individual specialty training then went to a "team" where we integrated these skills with those of the rest of the team to form a cohesive combat group that could operate behind enemy lines, totally independent of the normal routes of communication and logistics. One enjoyable spin off of all this was that, occasionally, we got to practice these skills during field exercises against the 101st and 82nd Airborne Divisions. On one such occasion they had to call off the exercise because our Special Forces Team had stolen so much equipment and so many firing pins out of artillery pieces that if a national emergency came about, such as war, two Divisions would already be partially neutralized. We captured a Battalion Command Post and during a convoy ambush, accidentally destroyed some valuable equipment sending a few people to the hospital. All in a days work, but we had to give it all back and say we were sorry. Well, we gave it all back any way!

I feel the need to elaborate a little more on the capture of the command post and the ambush.

Number one, we didn't actually capture the command post, we went one better. Most sound sleeping is done between midnight and sunrise, so we waited until about 0200 hrs (for you civilians, that's 2 a.m., for the Marine Corps, that's when the big hand is on 12 and the little hand is on 2), and sneaked into the Battalion Headquarters. First, we had to neutralize the guards. This wasn't difficult except that we were not allowed to physically knock them out, but they weren't exactly sure of that. After what we did, I'm not sure they hadn't rather have been knocked out. We made them take their boots and socks off and used one of their old stinky socks to gag them with, then tied them to a tree. Next, two of us were elected to go into the camp armed with machetes and little notes which we pinned on the collars of their fatigue jackets. But, I wasn't satisfied with that; I tied their boot laces together in knots so that if they did try to chase us, it would be pretty damn uncomfortable. Now, for the fun part! The two of us lined up at the end of the rows of tents with our machetes at the ready. A nod of the head and away we went, screaming like banshees, down the middle of the Company Street, cutting the lines to the tents so that they would collapse on the occupants. Can you imagine waking from a deep sleep to a blood curdling noise and then having your house fall on your head? As they emerged from the rubble putting on their fatigue jackets, they began to look at each other trying to figure out what the little piece of paper on their collars said. It was a simple message. "LAST NIGHT, YOUR THROAT WAS CUT!"

Not only did this nullify the command decision making process, but when word got out, rumors began to fly and morale dropped like crazy. It was even rumored that "Those Special Forces Bastards killed someone."

As for the ambush, we intended to isolate the convoy by dropping trees in front of the lead vehicle and behind the last vehicle. Now, to drop the trees exactly where we wanted, we placed a cutting charge of C-4 plastic explosive at the base of the tree and a "kicker" charge at the top to direct where it fell. Well, on the front tree, the "kicker" charge malfunctioned and the tree fell much slower than intended, and as a result, right on top of the truck. There were a couple of broken bones and a whole bunch of pissed off paratroopers, but no one was seriously injured. These things happen when you try to introduce realism into a training environment.

Sometimes we would spend days in the field living in whatever kind of shelter we could make or find. After any kind of operation, we would have to move our "Safe House". Sometimes we would move just because we had been there too long. We wore civilian clothes, grew beards and knew most of the bootleggers within a twenty five mile radius. A man had to relax occasionally.

At the time, it was one big, boisterous camping trip; but we knew in the back of our minds that it could become deadly serious at any time.

A lot of our infiltrations were accomplished at night by parachute. During this period of time, I had acquired an admiration for the "Rigger" Detachment. These were the guys who packed and maintained all of the parachute equipment used by the 77th Special Forces Group. They were the 'experts'. My friend Saul told me to be careful how I use that phrase because an expert is a guy who can put his mouth over a mule's ass and blow his bit out! But these guys signed their names to every parachute they packed in order to display the confidence they had in their skills and the parachutes they gave us to jump. They were at the marshalling area before every jump to issue the parachutes, help adjust them and to make sure that everything was exactly right before we got on the airplane. And, if there was an empty seat, they would almost fight to see who got it. They used to love to jump! This, in turn, instilled a tremendous amount of confidence in all of us. I wanted to be one! So in the summer of 1958, Jim Garvey, Dave Crocco and I shipped off to Fort Lee Virginia where the Army conducted its 'Aerial Delivery' School.

Rigger School was divided into three parts; the first month was Packing (we referred to it as 'pack and unpack'). We learned to pack every parachute the Army owned, from the twenty-four foot reserve parachute worn during troop drops, to the 100 foot in diameter cargo chutes used to deliver everything from jeep trailers to tanks. We would pack the rig, have it inspected by an instructor, then unpack it and do it all over again. One of the more common knots we had to tie was a 'surgeons knot with a locking knot'. Simply, it was a double over hand wrap with a square knot on top. Now, as you all know, a square knot is tied by wrapping right over left, left over right; Right? Any other way, for instance, right over right or left over left is . . . ., all together now; A GRANNY KNOT. Well, the penalty for tying a Granny Knot in Rigger School was to take 100 five inch strips of #5 waxed cord home with you that night and tie each one into a surgeons knot and locking knot. The next day, the instructor may inspect any or all of the knots, if one was a granny knot, you got 200 strips of #5 waxed cords that night, or he may not even look at them. He might just throw them in the trash can. For some reason I was never willing to take the chance! At the conclusion of 'Pack and Unpack', we packed our own parachutes, including the reserve, and went up to jump them. It was a nice confidence builder.

One funny incident occurred during this jump. Well, anyway it was funny to the rest of us who didn't have a whole lot to cheer us up at the time. One of the students landed in a tree. Landing in a tree is no big deal, but getting out can be a little tricky. The main parachute snagged in the top of the tree and left him hanging about twenty feet in the air. Now there are a couple of ways to get down! One is to start swinging back and forth until you can grab the tree trunk, branch or just any part that will hold your weight. After this is done, you pull the safety pin out of the harness release button and push it. Then merely climb down out of the tree. The second method is, if you're not successful in getting a grip on the tree, get a grip on the harness somewhere then release one side of the reserve parachute and pull the ripcord handle. Pull all of the suspension lines out of their retainer bands and the parachute is hanging upside down underneath you. Now, you hit the harness release button and climb down the reserve parachute taking care not to end up inside of it because I'll guarantee you the only way to get out is with a knife! Well, the fun part I was talking about was that this dude forgot rule number one, get a grip on the harness! He hit the release button and fell twenty feet breaking his ankle. The bad part was that he got recycled to the class behind us and had to do the whole damn thing all over again.

'Rig and De-rig' was what we called the 'Aerial Delivery' month. We would put jeeps, trucks, tanks and whatever on platforms mounted with shock pads and, depending on the weight of the "thing," up to as many as (four) 100 foot diameter parachutes and drop them somewhere over Virginia. Usually, Blackstone Army Airfield until the class ahead of us 'Streamered' (the parachutes didn't open) a 105 millimeter Howitzer Cannon onto the runway. It was kind of a neat sight, sticking barrel first into the runway. Again, it didn't take much to amuse us!

Maintenance month was a little boring in that the main thing we learned was how to sew. Sewing in its self is not bad if done in the privacy of your own home, behind closed doors. But no. the Army made us do it in front of everyone, including each other. How humiliating and disgusting watching a bunch of bad assed paratroopers setting around darning parachutes, or anything for that matter. But learn we did. When we completed the course, we could operate every sewing machine in the Army inventory, repair any damage to a parachute or harness, tailor our own cloths or sew someone's shirt sleeve shut who had earned your wrath. I never knew a sewing machine could be used as a weapon until Rigger School.

Sometime during all of the packing, rigging and sewing, I managed to get tattooed! (Thank God Mamaw wasn't alive to see this). Five of us got together and talked each other into it because we would never have done it on our own. It's kind of like sex. Guys need to talk about it and compare it. We were smart enough to know that this would be with us for life, so it had to be done right, by a professional. Did you ever see a professional tattooist? I wouldn't sit next to one in a dark movie, but here we were, ready to let one mark us for life! Well, we were smart (I substituted that word for lucky), we found a tattoo artist who just did it as a hobby, he charged us five bucks a piece but I'm serious, he was an artist. He owned his own wine vineyards and winery, "and some mighty fine wine I might add." He showed us samples of his work and gave us advice on where to have the tattoo placed. For instance; on the forearm it will be seen more often. If you're in doubt, the upper arm where it will only be seen when you are in a bathing suit or want it to be seen. The work was all free hand, no stencils to trace. We all picked the same design, a set of Paratrooper Wings with the parachute descending into a red fire. On top was U.S. and underneath was PARATROOPER. To this day, I've never really regretted it. It reminds me of a youthful daring and the freedom of choice I had in those days. It was a good deal too. We each got a $5.00 tattoo and drank about $10.00 worth of "some mighty fine wine."

Like I've said, I'm not big on fatalism, or where the stars happen to be during a certain event, or Karma. I'm even a little skeptical about the Bible and "Organized Religion." Let's face it, before the Bible was written, the stories were told and retold over countless camp fires for years, each time taking in the tellers interpretation, exaggeration or deletions. I know today that I can't get the same, correct, information in an office memo if it goes through more than two hands! Then it was written over and over again, and translated into more languages than I can count. In each translation, more interpretations, exaggeration and deletions had to take place. I do feel in my heart that there is a 'Supreme Being' out there. Some people call Him or Her Allah, Buddha or any number of names. I refer to him or her as "God." There has to be! All of this couldn't have just happened; also, I don't believe that God is the mean, vengeful, wrathful God that I was raised to believe. I prefer to think of Him or Her as a loving, forgiving God, with a sense of humor. If you have ever felt yournew born child's hand gripping your finger, you know what I mean by love. Anytime I feel guilty, sad or any number of negative feelings, I pray to my God and I feel better. As far as having a sense of humor, did you ever watch a 'Gooney Bird,' the 'black-footed Albatross', try to take-off or land? The Gooney Bird is a great big bird on little teeny legs. His body is so close to the ground that he can't flap his great, long wings enough to get airborne without the help of a real strong head wind. You can distract him, by whistling or making a commotion, to the point that he will fly right into an obstacle. But the real humor is watching him land. Every landing is a controlled "Crash." They roll end over end, or their legs collapse and they just slide to a stop on their chins. And, they always get up with this look on their face as if to say "I meant to do that."

Anyway, someone out there has been watching over me all my life and I have been blessed in many ways. Sure, there has been heartache, pain and sorrow, but I just chalk that up to life and go on to the next step.

The next step after "Rigger School" was an assignment to the 77th Special Forces Rigger Detachment with Captain Kovack commanding. The Detachment was supervised by the best thing that ever happened to a soldier, First Sergeant John T. Hollis. John T. was a First Sergeant from the "Old School." He worked us hard, but as long as we did our jobs and kept our noses clean, he would go to bat for us in almost any situation. God knows he kept Garvey and me out of trouble enough.

One time, Slaybach (one of the other riggers) and I took Jim Garvey all the way to Columbus, Ohio, on a three day pass. Way out of limits! On the way back to Bragg, Slayback ran into a tree in Blue Field, West Virginia. All of a sudden, out of nowhere, there were police, ambulances, tow trucks and people all over the place. The people ogled, the police checked our licenses, and the medics checked our bodies and the tow truck hauled our car away. The next thing we knew, police, ambulances, tow trucks and people were all gone, leaving Slaybach and I standing on the side of the rode in the rain, trying to decide whether to "shit or go blind." Neither made any sense and the whole situation was so ridiculous that we started laughing uncontrollably. After a while we collected ourselves, stuck our thumbs out and started hitching.

By morning it was obvious that we were not going to be back in time for roll call, so I mustered up what courage I had and called John T. I think his exact words were "You dip shits!" But he said that he would cover for us until roll call the next morning. If we weren't there by then, we could "Grab our ears and pull our heads down between our legs and kiss our ass goodbye!"

The other terrific thing about John T. was that if you crossed him some way, he wouldn't court martial you or put you on extra duty, he would take you out behind the packing shed and "Pin your ears back." And then it was all forgotten.

Danny Byard was one of the Riggers but also had the extra duty as Company Clerk. Danny would, through the years, become one of my closest friends and confidante, as he would be too many others. I never met a person who didn't like and respect Danny Byard. Some thirty three years later, after Danny's death, Colonel William P. Grieves related a story to me that summed it all up. He and Brigadier General Joseph W. Stilwell, the son of General

"Vinegar Joe" Stilwell of the WWII Burma campaign, and architects of the Strategic Army Corps (STRAC) Parachute Team, the forerunner of the *Golden Knights,* were brain storming one day; he said they were sitting in General Joe's office randomly discussing everything from Military Strategy to Philosophy when the General said "I'm going to say one word, and when I do, write down a name on a piece of paper and so will I." General Joe then said "Gentleman." Colonel Bill wrote down a name and he and the General both turned them over at the same time; both had written down Danny Byard.

My personal assessment of Danny has always been that "If he had two cents between himself and starvation, he would spend one penny on a loaf of bread and the other on a flower to look at while he ate it." I thought the world of Danny Byard.

Although freefall jumps were forbidden in the Armed Forces at this time, Sergeant Fred Mason had already gone down in history as the first U.S. Military jumper to compete in World Competition. Jumping under the sanction of the National Parachute Jumpers and Riggers Association (NPJR), Fred was the lone representative of the United States when France hosted the second World Parachuting Championships in 1954. The NPJR was formed by Joe Crane in 1948 and was an affiliate of the National Aviation Association (NAA). In 1955, Jacques Istel was a delegate to the Commission of International Parachute Championships. He was a Naturalized Citizen of the United States and vowed to get the U.S. more involved in Sport Parachuting. He began to campaign in 1956 and drew the interest of a few civilians and college students. He worked along with Joe Crane promoting the idea of a complete U.S. Parachute Team and trained anyone who could participate. In 1956,

Jacques Istel led the first United States Team in the Third World Parachuting Championships in Moscow.

All of this wasn't getting me any closer to making a freefall, and I was beginning to make threats of getting a B-12 parachute, finding a farmer with a Piper Cub, or something, and making the jump. Danny would get me off to the side and talk me out of it. He used such logic as "It's going to be legalized any day now and if you go out and get hurt, it might wreck it for everyone." So I would go back to making all of the static line jumps I could as a "Rigger."

The news came around April of 1958; Freefall Sport Parachuting was legalized, but would be done under the strict supervision of Military sanctioned Sport Parachute Clubs. In order to get these Clubs going, the Army contracted two civilian instructors from a company named Parachutes Incorporated, (PI). Enter Jacques Istel and Lewis Sanborn.

The year before, the NPJR had changed its name to The Parachute Club of America (PCA), with Joe Crane as its President. It was still under the supervision of the National Aviation Association and was also sanctioned by the Federation Aeronautique Internationale (FAI), the international governing body for all world aviation records and sporting events. Shortly after that, Jacques and Lew established the first U.S. based commercial parachuting centers in Orange, Mass. and Hemet, Calif.

The Army decided on an elite cadre of paratroopers picked from Fort Bragg, N. C., Fort Campbell, Ky., Fort Benning, Ga. and Germany. I, damn it, wasn't one of them! But the training would be conducted at Fort Bragg and the Special Forces Rigger Detachment was chosen or volunteered, I don't know which, to provide Riggers to pack their parachutes. The volunteer Riggers were promised five static line jumps on the new steerable parachutes as an incentive. Well, it was a start.

The cadres of jumpers to be trained by PI were: Colonel Conine, Capt. James Kovach, Capt. Peterka, Capt. Hill, SFC Ralph Palmer, Sgt. Danny Byard, Sgt. Linwood Pate and maybe one other, I can't recall. The Rigger support would come from Sp-4 James Garvey, Sp-4 David Crocco, Sp-4 Skip McFarland and myself.

I had heard stories of Jacques Istel and Lew Sanborn, the legendary "Skydivers" who pioneered the sport in this country. My friend Saul always told me "Never be a pioneer, they're the ones with the arrows sticking out of their asses". But here I was, standing in the shadow of legends on the threshold of a new era in aviation history. If I sound awe struck, I was! I had yet to see a live freefall but the anticipation was like waiting for Christmas morning.

My first impression of Jacques was mixed. I was well aware of his credentials but he didn't look the part. He looked and acted more like a business man than a pioneer. And if there were arrows sticking out of him, I sure couldn't see them. He was constantly directing people, organizing, making schedules and timetables. If there were any jagged edges on Jacques, the French accent erased them.

Lew, on the other hand, had an air of confidence about him and a ruggedness that said if he wasn't doing this, he would be trekking the Himalayas, rowing the Amazon, sledding to the North Pole or some other trivial adventure. You also knew, instantly, that you could trust him; when he shook your hand, it was as if to say "You are my friend until you prove otherwise."

The first thing they did to build confidence and enthusiasm in the students was to put on a demonstration. They boarded the Army L-20 Beaver and climbed to 12,500 feet over Sicily Drop Zone and jumped. I heard someone say "They're out," but I couldn't see them, and in those days, I had eyes like a hawk. I kept looking and looking but a strange thing happened. Before I saw them, I heard them! It was a clear, calm day and I could hear the air rushing by their bodies as they fell at 120 miles per hour straight down. Finally, I heard "Craaack, Craaack," and there they were, two bright red parachutes at 2,000 feet. In 60 seconds, they had fallen 10,500 feet, just 60 feet less than 2 miles. That's it (Slobber)! I'm hooked (Drool)! Gotta do it (Blubber)! Where do I sign (Froth)!

Each student started with five static line jumps in the Spread Eagle position or French Cross as it was commonly referred to. The static line was attached to the cable containing the four pins holding the pack-tray closed. A dummy ripcord with a red flag attached was in the ripcord pocket. The student would leave the aircraft, count to three and pull the dummy handle while the static line pulled the pins. It was pretty realistic. After five successful dummy pulls, the student made his first free-fall. Everything was the same except that the pins were now attached to the ripcord and, trust me, psychologically it makes a difference.

Over the next month, they would make a prescribed amount of successful free-falls in increments of 5, 10, 15, 20, 30, 45 and 60 second delays. To me, successful meant not hitting the ground at 120 mph. But they had to perform certain maneuvers like alternating 360 degree turns. No big deal by today's standards, but remember, those guys had arrows sticking out of their backsides. They used no instruments like stopwatches and altimeters until they went past 15 seconds. On a still day you could hear them counting at the top of their lungs, ONE THOUSAND, TWO THOUSAND, THREE THOUSAND, FOUR THOUSAND, etc. I even heard one stop counting at TEN THOUSAND, and start over again. I thought to myself, "This could get interesting," but he stopped counting and pulled. On the ground, I asked him what happened. He said "I sneezed and lost count and started over again then realized this ain't gonna work, so I just pulled!" He may not be a rocket scientist, but he knew that 25 seconds divided into 4,500 feet didn't compute.

After graduation, they all went to their perspective units and started the first Sport Parachute Clubs in the United States Army. Me? I only got one jump out of the whole deal. Lying bastards.

The Special Warfare Center Sport Parachute Club was originated with John Hollis, Danny Byard, Ralph Palmer, Ray Love, Jim Garvey and yours truly as its original Board of Directors.

Little did I know what a turn my life was about to take!

CHANGE

Any real change implies the breakup of the world
as one has already known it.
The loss of all that gave one an identity,
the end of safety. And at such a moment, unable to see
and not daring to imagine what the future
will now bring forth,
one clings to what one knew,
or thought one knew, to what one possessed
or dreamed that one possessed.
Yet it is only when persons are able, without
bitterness or self-pity, to surrender a dream
they have long cherished or a privilege they have long possessed
that they are set free—for higher dreams,
for greater privileges.
All people have gone through this,
go through it, each according to their degrees,
throughout their lives.
It is one of the irreducible facts of life.
author unknown

Chapter 3

I have to jump a little ahead of myself here; in fact I'm jumping 32 years ahead. It is January 20, 1995, and as I sit here having an emotional problem with my computer, my wife, Linda, just placed an envelope in front of me. It's addressed to me with a return address to MIKE & REBELLIOUS. In the envelope are a two page letter and some pictures. One picture is of a beautiful sunset taken from the bow of a boat. On the back it simply states "A trade wind sunset at 46 degrees west". My God! The man is half way across the Atlantic Ocean, by himself, in a 57 foot Sloop that he had built in Lagos, Nigeria. I'm going to print his letter in its entirety, whether he likes it or not; it's just too beautiful not to. He can always come up here to Virginia and take it out of my hide.

Mike and Rebellious

14 January 1995

Dear Dick and Family;

I have attempted to write a little as the trip progresses as a means of sharing it with you.

The departure from Dakar was delayed a bit. I found that the bottom of the boat had become too badly fouled to make the Atlantic crossing with, and in such a very short time. It had only been about a month since I did it in the Gambia, but the barnacles and weeds had grown terribly fast. I had to make reservations for the use of a slipway for cleaning and a coat of bottom paint.

On the 18th of December Rebellious went back in the water at 0930 and we quickly departed the anchorage at 1330 to prevent any African barnacles to gain a foothold. The island of Gore was passed at 1500 with the Madeleins abeam at 1630—the last of Africa!

Good breeze and fine weather was the rule to Cape Verde. Anchor was down at Port de Praia at 0130 in the morning of the 21st of December—60 hours from Dakar.

At 0200 on the 23rd of December we departed Port de Praia. At 1500 that day we were abeam the island of Fogo which is a very impressive 9282 ft volcano. A few settlements with mining activity around the base, but not a green thing in sight—a real moonscape.

At 1800 passed the island of Brava, the last of the Cape Verdes and the last land I will see until Tobago. At sunset a school of porpoise played around the boat for about an hour cutting across the bow, I guess playing "chicken" to see who could come closest without getting hit—what beautiful animals.

25 December—Merry Christmas all. A quiet night with a light breeze and clear sky. I have flying fish on the deck almost every morning now, and it has become my breakfast fare. Is this seagoing "manna", I wonder?

1st of January 1995, Happy New Year all—Rebellious made good 131 miles today. The best she has ever done.

From the 3rd on N. E. wind force 4-5 and sea state to match have been the rule, with good daily runs including another record breaker 155 miles. I have finally gotten used to the downwind rolling motion. I thought that I had everything secured and rattle free, but Rebellious has made things rattle that I did not even know was on board.

Days have been wonderful and nights spectacular. I have learned a lot more star names and locations; I have a simple book on astronomy that is my companion each night until I get tired. I am more confident of my celestial navigation now as my noon fix works out to within 4 miles of the G.P.S position.

The wonderful part of this trip has been the serenity; the peace and solitude. The sea is full of life. I never tire of watching the flying fish do "body bank shots" off one wave after another to gain momentum. The porpoise are always around. I see other fish around the boat that I cannot identify.

This now has the overall effect that the closer I get to Trinidad; the resentment is building against this solitude being interrupted. I have no urge to press on sail to speed arrival.

11th of January—Wind and weather was much the same until the 7th when the wind backed to the S. E. This brought afternoon and evening showers with light breeze. This light breeze lasted until noon on the 9th and then went calm. Have been motoring since. This certainly is not the forecast trade winds for January. Should see the southeast end of Tobago this evening.

12th January—0045 sighted the island of Tobago in the moonlight. 0600—abeam Scarborough light and Trinidad in sight ahead. 1720, entered the "Dragon's Mouth" and at 1930 at anchor at Peakes Marina.

Total distance sailed anchor to anchor was 2251 miles in 473 hours for an average of 4.75 Knots per hour. I suppose this is relative slow, but it certainly was a lovely trip.

I am just starting to get my land legs and looking around a bit. At first glance this is a lovely place. Hope you enjoy the pictures. Sorry, no disasters to tell about this time. I think single handing is the best.

So long for now, will write more when my mail gets here.

Love to all,
Mike

The reference to no disasters was in response to his last letter. While "Shaking it out" along the coast of Africa, he was de-masted in a gale and almost lost his arm to gangrene from barnacle cuts. I wrote him back and said that it sounded like he was having a hell of a good time! Michael J. Gordon is what legends and ballads are all about. He's made from the same clay as Daniel Boone, Davey Crockett, Wyatt Earp and Admiral Byrd. Maybe seasoned with just a little larceny, and more integrity in his little finger than most men have in their whole body.

Mike Gordon and I met in 1963. He was the 1st Sgt. of the 623rd Maintenance and Parachute Repair Company at Fort Bragg. He also did almost all of the aircraft maintenance and repairs for the Fort Bragg Flying Club, plus, he flew Skydivers on the weekends in a Cessna 195 that he had built from the remains of two wrecked aircraft that he salvaged.

By this time, I had pretty well established myself in the Sport Parachuting community by winning a position on the 1960 and 1962 U.S. Parachute Teams. Mike wasn't impressed!

The XVIII Corps Sport Parachute Club also had a Cessna 195, and as I had just gotten my private pilot's license, I was looking to build a little *"free"* flying time. I cornered Mike working on N-1545D, his 195, and asked him if he would check me out in it. I think his comment was something to the effect of "Does the expression fat chance mean anything to you?" The next day when I asked the same question, he said something like "What part of *No* don't you understand?" The next day when I asked him, he said "I don't have time." The next day when I asked him he said "God you're pesky!" The next day when I asked him, he rolled his eyes back in his head and said "Alright, damn it, I'll make you a deal. If you can get permission from the 18th Corp. Club to use their aircraft, (N-1003B) and when I get time, I'll see if you can fly it!" "Hot Damn!"

Well, I knew the President of the 18th Corps Club pretty well, and as he was a private pilot also, I promised to check him out after Mike checked me out. This ought to be interesting, the blind leading the blind.

About a week later, the day after Christmas, (it seemed like forever), Mike "found the time." He took me out to one of the old dirt strips that the Army had placed around Fort Bragg as emergency landing strips. I quickly found out that I didn't know shit about flying! Number one, I had been flying mostly Piper Cubs and Cessna 140's. Although they were both "tail draggers", main landing gear in front with a small wheel on the tail, the 195 was much more airplane. It had a radial 300 horsepower Jacobs engine with a constant speed propeller and a whole lot more torque. When you flared for a 3 point landing, the engine cowling rose up in front of you and blanked out all forward visibility; leaving you blind accept for looking out the side. The same was true with taxiing. You had to keep weaving back and forth, looking out of the sides to see where you were going. Point number two, I had exactly 105 hours and 30 minutes flight time. Just about enough to think you know it all and get into trouble.

Mike humbled me in a hurry. At first I felt like a total idiot, but then I started to get the "feel" of the aircraft, when Mike saw this, he began to rebuild my confidence by giving me harder tasks. He taught me the proper techniques in flying Skydivers and getting maximum performance out of an airplane without abusing it. He taught me some of the pit-falls of flying in general and this aircraft in particular. "You never stop flying a Cessna 195 until you park it, turn it off and walk away. Then turn around and see what it did behind your back!"

Four hard days later, I was ready to fly my first lift of jumpers. Boy, what a rude awakening. I had never flown the airplane fully loaded; four jumpers with equipment, 1,000 pounds and full fuel. First, the airplane would not accelerate. Anyway, not at the rate I was used to. I felt like one of those Gooney Birds I talked about earlier. I tried to force her into the air, but that was one of the pit-falls Mike had told me about. "Let her seek her own flying speed." So I waited. Finally, she said "OK, I'm ready," and I eased her off the ground. But she didn't climb like a trail horse on its way back to the barn. She was laboring under this burden that had been placed on her. If I let the manifold pressure drop an inch, she would slow her ascent by 50 feet a minute as if to say, "Come on pilot, work with me on this, maximum effort by you, maximum performance by me; together we can do it." So we became a team. I got to where I could feel every protest she made, and I would respond with what she expected of me. Hey guys, does this sound familiar?

With fairly calm winds, we would land in one direction; pick up a load of jumpers and take off in the opposite direction. It was a time and money saver. I flew 8.5 free hours that first day. I don't know how many times I went up and down, but I was exhausted at the end of the day. It was a happy exhaustion.

Catastrophe struck the next day, only my second day as a "Jump" Pilot.

A "Full Bird" Colonel named Seay flew in from Fort Leavenworth, Kansas. He had heard how well organized our clubs were and wanted to jump with us. The first lift consisted of Colonel Seay, his Aide and Sgt. Sam DeLuca, a very experienced jumper from one of our clubs. We also had a "low level" student. We went up to 3,600 feet and dropped the student for a ten second delay and then began our climb to 12,500 feet for a sixty second delay. The three of them were going to do relative work; that's where you fly around in close proximity to each other, making contact and maybe a three man star.

I started the final approach so as to be level at 12,500 feet at the exit point. I throttled back and Sam began to give corrections in 5 degree increments to position the aircraft exactly over the exit point. He gave me the cut signal indicated by a slicing motion across his throat with his finger. I cut the engine and watched the Colonel go, followed by his Aide and Sgt. Sam DeLuca. A hard right bank and I could watch them during the first part of the fall. Everything seemed normal so I got busy flying the airplane. I could usually beat the jumpers to the ground.

I landed to the North on Sicily's dirt runway and taxied to the end where four or five jumpers should be waiting, geared up and ready to go. The President of the Corps Club was there to meet me. He simply said "Dick, you might as well park it, the Colonel went in." It didn't hit me what he meant. I said "Hey, just because the Colonel left doesn't mean we can't continue jumping." He said. "No, you don't understand, he didn't leave, he went in; he didn't open, he didn't even pull his ripcord." When that sunk in, it was a definite "Holy shit!"

As expected, jumping was suspended for the rest of the day. The investigation continued for days but no obvious cause was found. Sam DeLuca reported that he and the Colonel were holding hands until a little before 3,000 feet when they let go to separate for the "opening". Sam said that he gave the Colonel the OK sign and the Colonel responded with a "thumbs up." Sam opened and the Colonel just kept going. What a bummer.

It didn't take long for the "D.Z. humor" to start. A couple of days later, one of the jumpers asked me if I was sensitive about the incident. I told him not really. I was sorry it happened but I didn't know the Colonel personally. The jumper said that they found out during the autopsy it was suicide. I asked how they could determine that. He said "It seems the Colonel was pregnant and didn't want his wife to find out." Well, on to more pleasant things.

Little did Mike and I know that a friendship had begun that would not only continue through our respective military careers, but see us working together on numerous flying jobs in civilian life. But I'll cover that later. As for now, let's get back to the Fort Bragg Flying Club.

As I mentioned, Mike did all of the maintenance work for the Club which was located at Brown Strip (named for the color of the dirt, how original), on the North East corner of Fort Bragg. Well, Mike's house was just about a mile up the road where he had a large garage converted into a hangar/workshop. Most of the routine maintenance he did at the Club hangar, but for major jobs, he would take the wings off and secure the tail wheel to the back of his pickup and haul it down the road to his house.

I had seen pictures of some of the airplanes Mike had striped down and rebuilt from the ground up. Some of the fabric work and paint jobs approached artistry.

As Mike had a full-time responsibility to the Army, all of this took place after 1800 hours on weekends. What better place to learn the inner workings of an airplane and what held it all together? So, I started just hanging around his workshop; after a few days of "How does this work?" and "What does this do?" and "What's this?" and "How did you do that?" Mike said "Hold it, damn it. If you're going to hang around and be a pest, make yourself useful!" At first, it was cleaning up the hangar and fetching things. But before long I was right in there with grease up to my elbows. I couldn't put into a book how much Mike taught me. It was marvelous to anchor a crank shaft onto a work brace and start building an engine around it, watching the pieces fit together like a huge metal puzzle, and then a few days later hang it on an airplane and watch it come alive.

We would take a J-3 Piper Cub, or any fabric aircraft, and strip it down to bare wood and tubing, repair all damage such as corrosion, and then rebuild it. Mike taught me how to lay out the fabric and cut it to the proper measurements and then, how to stitch it together on the wings and fuselage, much like an old sail maker. Now, if you think those Parachute Rigger Instructors were hardnosed about surgeon's knots and locking knots, you should have seen Mike inspect my stitching before he would let it pass on one of his airplanes!

Then we would hit the dope. Don't get excited, it wasn't that kind of dope, but man, it was toxic. After covering the wings or the fuselage with aircraft fabric and stitching it all together, you had to dope it. This is a concoction that shrinks and hardens the material to where it's almost like metal, and it takes a lot of dope to do this. The fumes could get horrendous, especially in the winter when all the doors and windows were closed. They could also be dangerous if breathed to long. Our safety mechanism for this was Mike's German Shepard named King. We would keep King in the hangar with us, and when he started baying and howling like some drunk walking down an alley, Mike would say, "it's time to get out of here."

During the rebuilding of one of the Flying Clubs J-3's, the Club President, Major Lucas, stopped by Mike's hangar to "Shoot the breeze." During the visit, he made the mistake of looking at the Cub and said "It'll never hold together." I looked at Mike and thought "Uh Oh," Mike just barely glanced at him and let it go. But two weeks later when Mike delivered the airplane to the club, I knew something was in the wind.

He pulled it up to the gas pump with his pickup, took the tail out of the bed and parked the pickup. When he walked back, he had a parachute on his back. Mike was just finishing fueling the Cub when Major Lucas walked up and asked what he was doing? Mike Said "I'm going to test fly your airplane for you." The Major asked "What's the parachute for?" Mike said "Regulations." The next ten minutes were hilarious and entertaining to say the least.

Mike climbed in and started the engine. He let it warm up sufficiently, then, with the heel brakes on, revved it up. It couldn't go anywhere because of the brakes but the prop wash had sufficient force to lift the tail off of the ground.

Mike sat there in front of the gas pumps with the tail about three feet off the ground and checked the magnetos. There were a number of students and a couple of instructors on the flight line. You could hear their interest starting to peak as the murmurs and whispers started. Major Lucas said "What in the hell is he doing?"

In the next instant, Mike let off the brakes and took off in about 100 feet on the taxi way. The Major yelled "Holy shit!" Mike went straight up into a hammer head turn and straight back for the taxi way, and the Major. If the Major had stayed standing, the Cub may have hit him. But when I looked at him, I don't think he could have gotten his nose any deeper into the dirt. Mike pulled up to complete a loop then came out of the top of the next loop in an Emmelman. From there, he continued to do a series of loops and rolls and a few maneuvers I had never seen. At one point, he disappeared behind a row of trees and I wondered if he had gone too far, but he shot out from behind them going straight up. He then came by the Club house so low that the wheels were rolling in the tops of the trees knocking pine cones onto it. All this time, the Major is having kittens. Another series of loops, gaining altitude in each one, and the "test flight" was over. Mike came in for a picture book landing, got out; walked up to the Major and said "I think it'll hold together!" The Major was a color I've never been able to describe, but he never said a word. Mike threw his parachute into the back of his pickup (he never got high enough to use it) and drove off. Hey, it made my day.

There was one other historical incident that Mike contributed to at Brown Strip. The Fort Bragg Flying Club decided to host an Air Show but didn't have sufficient funds to attract big named talent. They did, however, hustle up some pretty good, local talent.

Major Lucas approached Mike to see if he could contribute something, assuming it would consist of flying an airplane. But Mike got in contact with an Army Pilot friend stationed at Simmons Army Air Field and worked out a little different routine.

Come Air Show day, no one had yet seen what Mike's contribution was going to be, so everyone was a little surprised when he showed up dressed in mechanics coveralls. His pilot friend was sitting in one of the Cubs with the engine running when Mike walked up and began a pre-flight inspection of the aircraft. At a point when Mike was in front of the airplane, the pilot pushed the throttle forward and the airplane started its take-off roll. The wing strut hit Mike in the belly. He hung on and they took off with him dangling outside of the airplane on the wing strut.

When they came back around for a low level pass in front of the spectators, Mike had climbed up on the engine cowling and was riding it like a horse only backwards with the prop at his back and him facing the windshield. He had a rag out and was washing the windshield! The next low pass they made, he had climbed back underneath the wing strut and with a wrench, to the wheel off the aircraft. And, of course, he had to put it back on. After a few other shenanigans, they came in and landed to a hearty round of applause. The Major had his fingernails chewed down to the quick and vowed to never, ever, have open dialogue with Mike Gordon again.

So why was I surprised to read "A trade wind sunset at 46 degrees west?"

Chapter 4

In most Parachute Clubs today, you can put your money down in the morning, train all day and make your first free fall jump by late afternoon. Not so in 1958.

It was a Parachute Club of America regulation that you had to make five static line jumps while successfully demonstrating your presence of mind by pulling a "Dummy" ripcord handle with a red flag attached to it. You also had to demonstrate your ability to maintain a face to earth, stable, body position. Upon completion of all this, you could make your first freefall which was supposed to be a five second delay, which was counted out loud by the student jumper. The adrenaline rush was usually so high that most students got three seconds at the most, and some were lucky to let go of the airplane before pulling the ripcord. I was no exception.

In 1958, it was very difficult to arrange for aircraft to jump out of. First of all, Sport Parachuting or Sky Diving, as it was being called, was conducted on the weekends and the pilots were assigned on a volunteer basis. Not too many were willing to give up their weekends to accommodate a bunch of stupid jerks hell bent on killing themselves. Second, airplanes cost money to operate and it was like pulling hens teeth getting someone to authorize the expenditure.

As a result, it took me from 9 June to 3 October to make the required five static line jumps. In fact, I made my last static line jump representing the Special Warfare Center Parachute Club in an inner service competition on Yomoto Drop Zone, Fort Campbell, Kentucky. It was an accuracy event and I landed 99 yards from the target! With the antiquated equipment and lack of experience, I was lucky to hit Kentucky!

Over a month would pass before I would get that first freefall out of the way.

November 8, 1958, a chilly, clear, sunny, beautiful day. My log book reads: location, Sicily D.Z., Ft. Bragg, N. C., Aircraft Type L-20, Jump-master, S. Wichowski, License number C-89, and back Chute Type, 28 ft. blank gore with sleeve (serial number 44221), Chest Chute Number 6124.

As Jim Garvey and I had done on so many other occasions, we would make our first free-falls on the same day.

Jumping in itself wasn't any big deal any more. I was a veteran of about thirty troop (military) jumps by now, but the adrenaline was starting to pump. I looked at my parachute and focused on the ripcord handle. This was no "dummy" handle with a silly red flag attached to it, this one was real. It was alive. Attached to it was a long, thin cable running through a metal tube called cable housing. At the end of it was (four) 2 inch pins that were securely placed through four eyelet's that protruded through four grommets that held the two flaps of the pack tray closed. Inside that small container was a carefully packed twenty-eight foot diameter, candy striped, Air Force survival parachute with a stamp on it stating "CONDEMNED", and a solemn promise that "No Sir! We would never consider jumping them."

With the adrenaline pushing the "Red Line," I would have no problem pulling the pins out of the grommets (If they hung up, I would probably pull the pack tray inside out) but never the less I did something that would become a habit for years to come. I "armed" the pins by pulling them out about a quarter of an inch.

Getting "chuted up" was kind of a ritual. It gave me time to reflect, to calm down, clear my mind, and later, during the rigors of National and International Competition, time to rehearse in my mind what I was to accomplish in the air. It was a magic time because it belonged only to me; it was the Cave Man preparing for the hunt, the Knight putting on his armor, the Gun Fighter strapping on his holster, or the Race Car Driver being strapped into his car or the Dragon Slayer preparing for confrontation.

This was what I had been waiting for ever since that moment in the Fox Theater in Banning. It was finally here.

After "Chuting Up" we climbed aboard the DeHavelin L-20 "Beaver" and took off.

Climbing to jump altitude was always a slow process and, again, gave you time for reflection. There was no door on the aircraft so you could feel the wind rush and the temperature decrease as we gained altitude. The final approach was started at about 5 miles from the exit point with the aircraft still climbing to the jump altitude of 2,200 feet. The winds were out of the Southwest at about 5 miles an hour so the opening point would be just inside the tree line. I would be the first student out and watched as Sgt.

Wichowski gave heading corrections to the Pilot. I heard the engine throttle back and knew that we were at jump altitude. Sgt. Wichowski gave a final heading correction and called to the pilot "Cut." The pilot pulled the throttles back to idle so the prop blast wouldn't blow me off the step and Sgt. Wichowski shouted "GET IN THE DOOR!"

Here it was; all of the waiting, planning, training and anticipation over. I climbed out on the step being careful not to let my foot slip inside of it, and grabbed onto the wing strut. I could see the earth 2,200 feet below and nothing but air in between. I vaguely remember the shout "GO!" and jumped up and off of the step, pushing off of the strut with my hands. "HOLY SHIT," I was in freefall! ONE THOUSAND, TWO THOUSAND, THREE THOUSAND, FOUR THOUSAND, hand on the ripcord (no dummy flag this time), FIVE THOUSAND, pull! I could feel a slight thump as the bungee cords pulled the flaps on the pack tray open. In my mind, I could visualize everything happening as planned. The pilot chute crabbing air and acting like an anchor, the sleeve with parachute straightening out, the suspension lines deploying and releasing the locking flap allowing the parachute to slide out of the sleeve, and that beautiful 'G' force called "Opening Shock." A look up showed that I had a good parachute, then silence.

Out of the 1,500 jumps I would make in my career, I would always marvel at how quiet it was right after opening.

Sgt. Wichowski had given me a good spot, but between my "marveling," "goo gooing" and "gaa gaaing," by the time I was at a thousand feet, there was no way I was going to land any closer than 100 yards to the target; but right now I didn't care, I was in heaven!

The landing was nothing special and I had a long walk back to the packing area. When I got there, everyone shook my hand and congratulated me. Then someone asked where my ripcord was? "Oh Shit!" I had committed the cardinal sin and let go of it when I pulled. It cost me the one and only case of beer I would ever have to buy for that dumb trick! Don't get me wrong, I would buy many more cases of beer for pulling dumb stunts, but not for that one.

As I stated before, I had been hooked on the idea of Sky Diving for a long time, but there were other reasons that had developed after arriving at Fort Bragg. One was the fact that a nineteen year old paratrooper with a lot of free time can get into a lot of trouble on Hayes Street in Fayetteville, North Carolina. I mean a lot of trouble; I was no exception, so I figured this new sport would keep me off the streets and out of trouble.

Another reason was that over the next year or so I would meet some legendary people who were pioneering the sport in the civilian field. One of the people I met was Bobby McDonnell from Buffalo, New York. We first met in August of 1959 at St. Catharine's, Canada, it was the first major parachute meet I had ever competed in. Again, I was pretty awe struck. I also got to meet and compete against the well known Canadian parachutist, Darrel Henry. I surprised myself and everyone else by winning 3rd place overall.

Loy Brydon had made a name for himself as a Sky Diving pioneer out in Snohomish, Washington, but had recently re-enlisted in the Army and was stationed at Bragg. Jim Pearson, who started jumping in Buffalo, New York with Bobby McDonnell, was also lighting up the sky out on the West Coast. There was "Batch" Pond and the whole Pond family (most notably, Nate Pond) jumping up in Connecticut. Steve Snyder in Valley Forge, Pa. Steve was a whiz kid who had graduated from one of the Institutes of Technology and would later become quite rich and famous for designing, patenting and marketing some of the best safety devices in aviation, including some of the automatic openers used in a lot of the military ejection seats.

Charlie Hillard was in Fort Worth, Texas, kicking up a storm in Sky Diving and Aerobatic Flying. Charlie would go on to win the 1972 World Aerobatics Championship along with Mary Gaffney. He also became the lead pilot with the "Red Devils" Aerobatics team and later on, the "Christian Eagles." The last parachute jump I saw Charlie make was on Yomoto Drop Zone, Fort Campbell, Kentucky, I believe it was October of 1958. He had a brand new, baby blue, 1.6 ounce rip-stop nylon parachute. There was only one tree on Yomoto. Right smack in the center of the D.Z., and Charlie was hanging right in the top of it! Charlie was recently inducted into the Aerobatics Hall Of Fame, a well deserved honor. He was one of the best Aerobatic Pilots who ever lived, an exceptionally nice guy and great representative of the sport.

Dave Burke, Bob Singclair, Lew Sanborn, Jacques Istel, George Bosworth, Lyle Hoffman, Walter Fair, Floyd Hobby, and George Stone, they were all out there doing their "thing." I had no "delusions of grandeur", all I wanted was a chance to jump with these guys and maybe even enter a parachute meet with them. That way I could, later on, say "I ran with the Big Dogs!"

Well, it wouldn't take too long, it couldn't. There were so few parachutists in the United States that you were bound to run into them sooner or later.

Two major events happened to me in 1959; I married my first wife and won the East Coast Parachute Championship in Orange Mass.

You noticed I said my first wife. I have been fortunate enough to have had two wonderful wives as my companions during two totally different periods of my life.

In April of 1959, I married Lucille Engle. Lucille was from Warren, Ohio and had followed her brother into the Army. She was a WAC (Women Army Corp.) who had also been bitten by the parachuting bug and was a member of the 18th Airborne Corps Sport Parachute Club and became the first woman to make a parachute jump at Fort Bragg. Lucille was my companion through the glory years of parachuting and the turbulent years of Vietnam. We were together for 17 years in which she bore me three wonderful children, Theresa Anne, Diana Lynne and my only son, Richard Chanc. After I got out of the service we began to grow in different directions. Both of us were at fault and neither one to blame. During my years of parachute meets and demonstrations, and being on the "road" she had to become pretty independent. Then there were 38 weeks of Army Flight School, punctuated by two weeks at home followed by one year in Vietnam, home for six months and then back to Vietnam.

Where wives married to normal husbands who were there to rely on during family crises, she had to handle it alone, all of this made Lucille very independent. Then the "Dragon Slayer" comes home and says "I'm back, I'll take charge" and she can't turn over the reins, as I said, neither one to blame. We were divorced in September, 1976.

The other major event that changed my life forever was a one day accuracy event held in Orange, MA, open to anyone who had a parachute license and sanctioned by the Parachute Club of America. I was there representing the Special Warfare Center Sport Parachute Club, along with Danny Byard, John Hollis, Ralph Palmer and Ray Love. We arrived straight from the Meet in St. Catharines, Canada, and I, for one, felt pretty "Hot!" The event would only be four jumps for accuracy; you could throw out your worst jump and score the best three.

My first jump was measured at 23 feet 9 inches, not bad in those days. The next was 6 feet and 11 inches. Then I got cocky and my third jump was 49 feet 10 inches. Well, I learned a good lesson about concentration that day, but I figured I had blown the competition. My last jump was 10 feet 4 inches; a good jump, but there were some "Big Hitters" left to go, all I could do was sweat it out.

When they tallied it all up at the end of the day, I had won my first major Parachute Meet.

The next day, Colonel William P. (Pappy) Grieves, who was the Commander of the XVIII Airborne Corps Artillery, approached me with a proposition that absolutely stunned me! He said "Specialist Fortenberry, we are forming a special duty organization for Sport Parachuting to be called the STRAC Parachute Team (STRAC, being an acronym, for Strategic Army Corps). The members will be required to develop their parachuting skills by jumping as often as possible. They will then represent the United States Army in various Parachute meets and demonstrations throughout the world. If you are interested, we are offering you a position on the team."

Holy shit! Did I just hear what I thought I heard? Is he talking to me? I've only got 94 jumps! Somebody pinch me!

I must be dreaming! I stood at attention and shouted an elongated, "Yes Sir!"

The "We" he was talking about was himself and Brigadier General Joseph W. Stilwell Jr., Chief Of Staff for the XVIII Airborne Corps. and the son of General "Vinegar Joe" Stilwell of WWII Burma Campaign. "Cider Joe", as General Stilwell Jr. was known, was at first totally against Sky Diving as a military sanctioned sport. Colonel Grieves said "Just come out to the drop zone and see what these young soldiers are doing." The General did and the old sky diving "Bug" bit him just like it did all of us, from that time on, he was our biggest champion.

Col. Grieves also hit me with another big decision. "As you only have three months left on your current enlistment, you would be required to reenlist for three years." I asked "How long do I have to make up my mind Sir?" He said "About 30 seconds." It took me about three seconds to say yes!

Thanks to Ray Love, I have a copy of the original General Order assigning the *Team*, it reads:

> Extract SO 260 Hq XVIII Abn Corps & Ft Bragg, Ft Bragg NC, 8 Oct 59 Cont
> 44. FNE orgn indc this sta placed on SD W/ Post Sp Svc this sta as members of the STRAC Sport Prcht Team during pd 12 Oct 59 to approx 12 Jul 60 unless sooner rescinded. UCMR proper org. No tvl involved.
> SFC(E-6) HARRY E ARTER, RA13314337, 618th Engr Co
> SP4(E-4) HENRY L ARENDER, RA18541648, 82nd Admin Co 82nd Abn Div

MSGT(E-7) JOHN T HOLLIS, RA39745684, 77th SF Gp Abn
SGT(E-5) DANNY R BYARD, RA18403533, do
SP5(E-5) RICHARD T FORTENBERRY, RA28294032 do
SFC(E-6) RAYMOND L LOVE, RA16292417 do
SP4(E-4) LOY BRYDON, RA28296308, Hq Btry XVIII Abn Corp Arty

FOR THE COMMANDER:

> J. W. STILEWELL JR
> Brigadier General, GS
> Chief Of Staff

I'm definitely running with the big dogs now!

Chapter 5

I guess I should take the time to explain where I am now and what I'm doing. It will help later on when I start jumping around a bit telling where I've been and what I've done.

I initially retired in Herndon, Virginia, with my wife Linda and my twin daughters, Jennifer Keeley and Amanda Stacy. Since then, the girls graduated college where they attended ROTC and were commissioned as Officers in the U. S. Army. They also attended Flight School and were certified in the UH-60, Blackhawk, helicopters. Jennifer attended Jump School at Fort Benning and received her "blood wings" from me. We now live in Pigeon Forge, Tennessee.

Last January, Linda and I celebrated our 34th wedding anniversary; 34 wonderful, exciting and adventurous years (she is standing right behind me as I write).

I was a corporate pilot for Mobil Oil Corporation for the past 22+ years. Before that, I was the Chief Pilot for Imperial Aviation Services, Inc., out of West Palm Beach Florida who hired me after being discharged from the Army in June of 1968.

After my parachuting career, I went through the Army Warrant Officer Candidate Flight School program and went immediately to Vietnam where I flew Helicopter Gun-ships for a year.

That basically covers my life in a nut shell. I could quit now, but there is just so much to tell. So, I best get at it while I have time. They're dropping like flies out there, and Hell, I might be next. If I had known I was going to live this long, I would have taken better care of myself!

My friend Saul says, that "every time an old person dies, a library disappears."

Chapter 6

Colonel Bill Grieves was generous enough to administer the oath, and I was good for another three years in the Army, for better or for worse.

We moved into a section of the "Old Division" area. These were the barracks that the 82nd Airborne Division occupied during WWII.

They were built of wood and had the old coal burning furnaces which required a "Fire Watch" every night. This was a detail to stay in the furnace room all night and make sure it didn't go out or blow up. But it was *"The Team"* barracks and we were proud of it. We were still a military organization with all of the disciplines and maybe a few added ones.

The first Commanding Officer of the STRAC Team was Major Merrill Shepard. He wasn't very big in stature, but he was a good organizer, good parachutist and an excellent Leader. All the men liked him and worked well with him. I think one of his best traits was the fact that he knew all of the members of the *Team* were superior jumpers to him but never tried to hold us back. He encouraged us to excel, to experiment and try new ideas. Sometimes, if the idea seemed a little dangerous, he would make DDS (Double Damn Sure) that we thought it out thoroughly, designed it and tested it properly before using it in a live demonstration.

Sometimes, the only way to test it was to build it and go jump it. One such design was my "double cut-a-way."

I found an old seat pack parachute (CONDEMNED. NOT FOR PERSONNEL USE). Where had I seen that before? Anyway, I got the seat pack and two B-12 survival chutes and began to experiment with a design. When I finished, I had sewn two more sets of cape-wells to the harness which would accommodate two more parachutes. I cut the closing flaps off of one B-12 and sewed them onto the master harness and pack tray. On the left front risers of the seat pack and the top back pack, I sewed a reserve parachute ripcord handle, minus the cable. This provided me with something to hold on to after releasing the left cap-well and subsequently the whole left side of the parachute. Now, I had a seat pack parachute, two back pack parachutes and a reserve chest pack parachute. The concept was to open the seat pack, cut it away, open the first main parachute, cut it away and open the second main leaving the reserve for emergencies only, it kind of sounds like I had already 'built in' two emergencies.

We tested it as much as possible on the ground by pulling everything apart in sequence, re-packing them and pulling them apart again. I did this a number of times to check for snags, hang-ups and in general just smoothness of operation. The only thing left now, was to live test it. The complete rig weighed about 90 pounds and was extremely cumbersome. A couple of the team members had to help me into the aircraft.

The most dangerous part of the jump would be if I pulled the ripcords out of sequence. The seat pack ripcord, first to go, was located on the right main lift web just above my hip. The first main ripcord, second to go, was located on the left main lift web chest high and the second main ripcord, third to go, was located on the right main lift web chest high. The biggest problem would occur if I pulled the second main before the first. Then the pins holding the pack tray together would be out but the top main parachute would hold everything in. As soon as I pulled the top main parachute ripcord, both parachutes would try to deploy leaving me with either two mains deployed at once or a tangled mess. If I ever did this, I would have to decide whether to pull the top main and take the chance that both would deploy normally or leave them alone and deploy the reserve. I always thought that it would depend on the terrain, wide open fields, the reserve Over Long Island, and the mains. In the three years that I used this stunt, I never had to make that decision.

Back to the test jump.

We climbed to 7,000 feet for the test. It was a nice warm day with calm winds, so I wouldn't have to chase the cut-a-way chutes too far. I got out and began the free-fall. I was amazed that the rig was not so cumbersome in free-fall. At 4,500 feet, I pulled the seat pack ripcord. "Holy shit." I had never jumped a seat pack before. It was packed in what is called a quarter bag, I won't go into details, but suffice it to say, it opened in a hurry. Instead of the 4 or 5 G forces we normally felt, this thing must have given me 20 or 25 snap G's. Football players sometimes take up to 50 snap G's. Anyway, it was enough to make me see stars during day light and make my arms numb. I had to hang there for a few seconds to clear my head and get all my gyros synchronized. I reached up and undid both safety covers on the cap-wells.

Then I held onto the handle that I had sewn on the left riser and released it. Now I was holding the whole left half of the parachute in my left hand. It was like doing a one arm pull-up. I released the right cap-well and that side of the parachute collapsed up, giving the effect of a streamer. I held this for about 5 seconds then let go of the left riser and began free-fall again. I opened the top main at about 3,500 feet and repeated the whole event over again, opening the main, steerable, parachute at 2,000 feet leaving the reserve parachute for a "Non self-induced" emergency.

It went like clockwork, and when one of the Team Members asked "let me see your arms," there they were, three ripcords draped around my wrist. No case of beer tonight.

The jump served me for the remainder of my days with the *Team*, but as you can imagine, we had to prepare the audience for it in case someone had a bad "ticker." We would do this by telling them to not be alarmed, because whatever they saw was planned and normal. But you could always hear a collective gasp when the first parachute collapsed. I often wondered if people would think it was planned and normal if I streamered all the way in?

Our first official function as the STRAC Parachute Team was a competition held just outside of El Cajon, California, a place called Gillespie Field. It was not a memorable event except that on one of my jumps, the airplane ran out of gas. The pilot's name was Ron Freeze (maybe he doesn't want that printed, but the truth must be told), the aircraft was a Stinson Sedan and there were three jumpers, including myself. We were on final approach at 4,300 Feet for a 15 second delay accuracy jump. All of a sudden the engine sputtered and quit. The other two jumpers un-assed so fast that I heard them go more than saw them. I looked at

Ron who just had a silly grin on his face and asked "Do we have enough altitude to glide to the exit point and still be at 4,300 feet?" He said yes so I gave a couple of heading corrections, got out on the wing strut, said good luck to Ron, and jumped. It was my closest jump of the Meet; 7 feet 4 inches and they disqualified me! They (Bill Jolly was the Meet Director) said that it was an emergency jump. I tried to convince them that lack of prior planning on their part did not constitute an emergency on my part, but they wouldn't listen. The discussion got pretty heated until Danny Byard and Jim Garvey reminded me that it wasn't exactly the Championship of the entire universe, so back off. Incidentally, Ron made it down OK.

Our first official demonstration as a *Team* was conducted at Danville, Virginia, November 1, 1959.

We drove up from Ft. Bragg in our own cars, and paid for our own gas. When we arrived, the event officials were not aware that they were supposed to provide overnight accommodations, so they had to scurry around and find something. The "Something" was the basement of a roller skating rink. It had bunk beds that we had to make up. It was filthy, so they gave us brooms to clean it up, and all night long we lay there and listened to the skaters going around in circles. Not a most memorable start, but we weren't complaining. We were in "show business!"

Through the winter, we continued to hone our skills for parachute competitions and demonstrations. From November 1, 1959, to the middle of April, 1960, I made 160 jumps. That was a lot in those days. We were working up some fairly good demonstration routines, some of which are still being used by the *Team* today. Although they stopped performing my double cut-a-way, they still do the Baton Pass and The Diamond Track. I was beginning to excel in the competition category, along with Jim Arender. The *Team* as a whole was gaining popularity and attracting the attention of the higher brass, including the Pentagon. It could be a very good recruiting tool. We were also getting a reputation as innovators in the research and development department.

During the same time, at the Department Of Defense Joint Parachute Test Facility in El Centro, California, Captain Tony Lavere and Staff Sergeant Jim Howell were conducting tests on the Martin Baker "B" seat, a high speed, high altitude ejection system for military aircraft. They were doing gravity drops out of a C-130 Hercules at 20,000 feet.

Although Tony Lavere was the Chief Test Pilot for Lockheed and had done all of the preliminary testing of the F-104 Star Fighter, he was also a Captain in the Air Force Reserve, and had gone on active duty to participate in testing the "B" Seat.

I'm not sure how it all got put together, but I do know that Capt. Lavere was instrumental in getting us invited to the El Centro Test Site for some high altitude jumps.

We arrived in mid April, full of anticipation of the most exciting jumping we would ever do. The test facility was awesome. I had seen movies that had been made about the Parachute Test Facility. Movies like "Bailout at 43,000" where they were trying to keep people from spinning out of control and blacking out before opening their parachutes. A Hollywood theme, but none the less; exciting in those days.

The complete facility was geared for experiment and test, which rhymed with danger and intrigue, and we were hyped!

I was fascinated with Tony Lavere as soon as I met him. Tony was obviously short for Anthony, because he didn't have a hair on the top part of his head. He never swore and very seldom finished a sentence. He would say things like, "You know, this is really, I mean you guys are. I mean,. to have you here is . . . you know . . . I mean . . . this is really . . . I mean Wow . . . ." For what he had accomplished in his life, he was one of the most humble, unassuming people I had ever met. First off, his reputation and skill as a test pilot was unequaled. Then tag on his abilities as a test jumper! He and Jim Howell would have themselves strapped into the "B" Seat, loaded on a C-130, flown to 20,000 feet and dropped out of the back end. They would then ride this seat for 15,000 feet to see if it worked. First, long extension poles had to come out of the top of the seat to stabilize it. Then at a certain point, the seat had to separate from the body, which would continue to freefall. Then at a certain altitude the parachute would open automatically (you hope) and glide to the ground. All of this with no input from the jumper except in an emergency.

Our visit had nothing to do directly with the "B" Seat project but we were going to test the ability of the body to maneuver in freefall from high altitude. We had already met some skeptics who thought that in the thin air we would not be able stabilize and control ourselves. Our contention was that if the airplane could fly that high, then so could we. Because the jumps would be made from altitudes ranging from 15,000 feet to 30,000 feet, we would need supplemental oxygen. We would also wear automatic opening devices which were set to open the parachute at 1,500 feet in case we were incapacitated.

The supplemental oxygen was in way of a "bail out" bottle. A little green bottle about 2 inches in diameter and 6 inches long containing enough oxygen for between 8 to 11 minutes. The oxygen was breathed under pressure, meaning that it just came out in a steady stream, no more, no less. You relaxed and let it fill your lungs then exhaled, forcefully, out of the bottom of the mask. Basically, it is breathing backwards. Try doing this while falling about 130 mph and passing a stick (baton) back and forth between jumpers.

I should mention that by now we had picked up a few other parachutists on the *Team*. Three of which were Staff Sergeant Wilfred Joseph Anthony (Squeak) Charette III, Sergeant First Class Harold Lewis, and Pfc. James Pearson, who had enlisted in the Army to join the *Team*.

We got settled in and spent the rest of the day getting acquainted with the personnel that would be involved with the jumps. There were the C-130 pilots who would fly the jumps. They were the same ones who had been flying Captain Lavere and Jim Howell, so they were pretty well up to speed. One primary concern was that they had never flown the C-130 to 30,000 feet. They had stripped it down to make it as light as possible and were confident that it would make the altitude. We met the Flight Surgeon who would go along to observe any problems associated with the high altitudes such as hypoxia, the lack of oxygen in the blood system. Even though the outside air temperature would be about 60 degrees below zero, cold would not be a problem because the aircraft would maintain pressurization with the heaters going until we were about ten minutes out. At that time the pilot would rapidly decrease the cabin pressure until the aircraft cabin altitude was the same as the aircraft altitude. This would be a potentially dangerous time because your body would go from about 14,000 feet to 20,000 or 30,000 feet in a very short period of time, creating the same effect as a scuba diver coming up from a dive too fast. We could get the "bends," which was a situation where the nitrogen in the blood system tries to come out of solution. It is very painful and if left uncorrected could be crippling, or even life threatening.

We spent the next couple of days going over all of the equipment and being briefed on what we were going to do. We weren't out here to just have fun.

The parachutes would be our own. That little white lie was still ringing in my ears. "No sir, we wouldn't think of jumping these condemned parachutes!" The only difference was that they would be rigged with automatic openers set at 1,500 feet.

The helmets would be Navy flight helmets with visors that fit over the oxygen masks.

On the main lift web of the parachute harness, we fixed a "T" block that allowed us to have the oxygen mask, bailout bottle and ships oxygen all plugged in at the same time.

We would wear two flight suits, the outer one to be day-glo orange, so that the three radar cameras could lock on us and record our activities. There would also be an F-100 Super Saber Jet Fighter with a cameraman inside to help document the jumps.

Some of the events they wanted to record were; maximum and minimum trajectories leaving the aircraft; maximum and minimum rate of descents during the freefall; and how much of a sustained lateral track we could maintain across the ground. All of this would be filmed and tracked by the radar cameras, then mathematically worked out to a zero wind condition for the final results.

Oddly enough, our first jump was from a C-47, the military version of the DC-3. We went to 10,000 feet just to live check all of the equipment, including the automatic openers, which we set for 2,000 feet. Everything functioned normally, so we were "Go" for the high altitudes.

The first one would be from 20,000 feet. I was elected to do the "slow" fall, Harry Arter would do the "fast" fall, and Loy Brydon would do the "max track", which was to try and achieve maximum lateral displacement across the ground. This is accomplished by getting a slightly head down attitude, bending at the waist, rolling your shoulders forward and making yourself into an air foil like that of a non-symmetric airplane wing. It's roughly the same body position that a ski jumper gets. Loy was about our best tracker. You noticed I said "about." I always considered myself equal to the task! I forget who was selected for the other assignments.

It was April, 25th, 1960. Now I knew why they picked El Centro for a Parachute Test Facility, there wasn't a cloud in the sky. The visibility must have been 50 miles (this was in the days before the smog came out of L. A.). Absolutely no humidity and the winds were calm; just a gorgeous day for a new adventure. But then every day we were there was a carbon copy of this one.

We woke about 6:00 a.m., had breakfast, did the daily dozen, ran a mile and on the flight line about 8:30 a.m.

After going over all the equipment for the umpteenth time, we reset the automatic openers to 1,500 feet, discussed each event in detail and the mission overall. Our top priority was safety. Once we went on oxygen, communication would be hand signals only. The Flight Surgeon and the Flight Engineer would have the only communication with the pilots, who in turn would have the only contact with the ground. Because of the altitude we would be jumping from, it was decided to let radar "spot" us (tell us when we were over the Drop Zone). If, during de-pressurization, anyone started feeling symptoms of the bends, he would indicate it by pointing at the affected area with either one, two or three fingers. One finger being a mild discomfort, two being rather painful but able to continue and three fingers would be cause for re-pressurizing and scrubbing the jump.

We took off about 10:00 a.m. and started the climb to 20,000 feet. Until we de-pressurized, we would not be aware of what altitude we were because the altimeters on our instrument panels, (which consisted of a stop watch and altimeter attached to the top of our reserve chest parachute) would read what the aircraft cabin was pressurized at, usually, around 6,000 to 7,000 feet. The climb to altitude would take about 30 minutes. We would all go on ships oxygen at 15 minutes prior to de-pressurization. The aircraft would be de-pressurized at 5 minutes before the first pass. At this point, everything became critical. We watched each other for any signs of hypoxia, the bends or any other abnormalities that might occur. The Flight Surgeon was carrying a walk-around oxygen bottle so he could go from jumper to jumper and check on them. Because we were only dropping one man per pass and it would take about ten minutes for the aircraft to get turned around and lined up for another, we would be at altitude for a long time. At four minutes prior to each jump, the jumper would activate the bailout bottle by pulling a little green ball attached to a small cable that pierced the seal, allowing the oxygen to flow. Once he felt the pressure of the oxygen in his mask, he would give a "thumbs up" to the

Flight Surgeon, then unplug from ships oxygen and walk to the edge of the tail gate and wait for the "green light".

Everything was working as advertised. I was number three to go with the slow fall. I watched with wild anticipation as the first two jumpers went through the procedures, stood on the tail gate, and then disappeared. The aircraft began its circle.

The Jump Master looked at me and signaled "4 minutes." I pulled the little green "apple" as we called it, and my oxygen mask inflated. I gave a thumbs up and unplugged from ships oxygen. Now, I was a totally self sufficient high altitude projectile. I was determined to make this the slowest fall in history, so I unzipped all of the zippers on my flight suit so they would create as much drag as possible. The green light went on and I was gone. The prop blast hit me and I sailed away thinking, out of all of the billions of people on the face of the earth, the living, the dying, the loving, the hating, the shakers the makers, I was the only one, at that moment in history that was at 20,000 feet falling toward the earth, as 'slow' as I could.

In a normal freefall, you are fairly relaxed. There is no feeling of falling, just a feeling of speed as you lay on a cushion of air at terminal velocity, which is approximately 120 m.p.h. But this fall became tiring. Normally, you have an arch in your back like a swan dive. This keeps you stable, face to earth, and you just let your legs bend at the knees and relax. Today I was bowed up with a hump in my back, legs straight, arms extended to "grab" all of the air I could. This made me very unstable and I was fighting to keep from going out of control. Combine this with the fact that I had to breathe backwards and you can understand why it was getting pretty tiresome; all this from a guy that can't walk and chew gum at the same time.

The jump seemed to last forever, but it only took 1 minute and 40 seconds to go from 20,000 feet to 1,800 feet. I pulled the ripcord, opened and began the canopy descent. After all of the hoopla, planning, anticipation and the adrenaline rush of the actual fall, the canopy ride was resplendent!

After I got out of the harness, I watched as the aircraft came around for Loy Brydon's Max Track. The four-engine C-130 was so high that it was hard to find in the clear blue skies over El Centro. I finally picked it out and listened to the count down over the loud speakers. They would count down the seconds until Loy jumped and then count up until he opened, for instance, 5,4,3,2,1,0,1,2,3,4,5,6, etc. Some of the ground personnel had binoculars to observe the activity. Loy was supposed to fall for 100 seconds. We heard the count up start, and knew he was out. This was confirmed by the Aircraft Commander, but no one picked him up. Everyone continued to scan the skies, but no one could find him. The count went through 100 and continued. 101, 102, 103, 104, 105 . . . . We started getting a little nervous. If we didn't see a parachute pretty quick, something would definitely be wrong. Then someone yelled "there he is!" Loy was about two miles away on the horizon gently floating down. Later, the computers analyzed the radar trackings and came up with the figures. Loy had a horizontal speed of 68 m.p.h. for a vertical speed of 150 m.p.h. I had a slow rate of descent of 111 mph, and Harry Arter had a maximum rate of descent of 211 mph, exactly 100 mph difference. The analysts were amazed.

The only unfortunate incident of the day was on Harold Lewis' jump. When he landed, he got up and staggered around holding his head. We knew something was wrong because he really looked like he was in pain, and he was.

I know you all have been on airplanes or gone down a mountain road, and had trouble equalizing the pressure in the inner ear. This is usually associated with a head cold or because of a swollen Eustachian tube. You also know that to hold your nose and try to blow through it usually clears it. This is called a valsalva. With the oxygen mask on, Harold couldn't close off his nose and perform a valsalva. When we saw the blood coming from his ear, we knew that he had ruptured his ear drum. He later told us that he screamed the last 5,000 feet, trying to clear it. He was out for the rest of the trip.

The next day, we went to 25,000 feet. This would be a mass jump, all of us out at one time. The objective on this jump was to make a six-way baton pass. It had never been done before. We would exit the aircraft one after the other and by varying our rates of descent we would achieve the same relative altitude. By tracking, we could close on one another until contact was made and pass the baton. This was called "relative work." I think the record at the time was a three way pass. We had done this many times before from lower altitudes and expected the six-way to go fairly smooth, but the unexpected happened.

I was number three in the six man "stick" and got my pass off to Byard pretty quick. Then all of a sudden, Pearson, who was supposed to pass to Arender, was trying to pass back to me. I kept waving him off. The free-fall took 125 seconds. We all opened, landed, and looked around asking "did we make it?" Arender said "shit no. I never got it!" We had made the first five-way baton pass in history, but were not elated.

The problem had manifested itself from something we never considered. We all had on the same gold colored flight helmet, the same tinted visor over the same black oxygen mask and wore the same day-glo flight suit. In other words, we all looked exactly alike, and somehow Arender got missed. The lesson was learned, and on the next attempt, we would all wear different colored jump suits.

Later, someone asked the pilot of the chase plane if he had gotten any of it on film? He replied "Hell no! They were moving around so much up there that I got the hell out of the way before one of them ran over me!"

There was a three day lull in the jumping activity. By now the *Team* was getting a little notoriety so we were required to go on some of the local radio and television talk shows, but, the three days would not be without their adventure.

Tony Lavere came in one morning and informed us that the Air Force had changed an engine on one of their F-100F's, a Super Saber Jet Fighter with two seats, and he had to take it up on a test flight and "wring her out." He said "I've got one extra seat. You guys work it out."

We decided that the only fair way to do this was "duels to the death with bazookas in a telephone booth," but instead played "odd man out" with nickels. It came down to me and Jim Arender. We flipped our nickels and I said "I'm like you." We uncovered our coins and they were both heads. I had won! After Jim stopped crying, he sank to the lower depths of despair and offered me money, but nothing was going to keep me away from this ride.

Tony briefed me on the basic aircraft, the ejection seat and what the test flight would consist of: a series of engine tests and recording instrument readings. All pretty boring, but he promised to take me through the sound barrier, 'all pretty boring.' Yeah, maybe boring to him, but I was sitting on pins and needles.

Actually, I wasn't sitting on pins. A mechanic handed me a little cloth bag with some pins in it and said "tie it to the dash; you're sitting on a hot seat." He had just taken the safety pins out of the ejection seat. This was the days before zero altitude, and zero air speed ejection seats. That meant that if I pulled the ejection handle right now (which I had no intentions of doing) a great big bullet would blow me and the seat straight up, release me from the seat and let me hit the ground at 32 feet per second, per second. I just wondered if these things ever shorted out or anything!

Even the take-off was spectacular to me. When he hit the afterburners, it was like someone kicked us in the ass. I sank back in the seat and watched as the striped lines in the center of the runway went by faster and faster. In what seemed like a heartbeat, Tony lifted the nose and we were airborne. We switched our microphones to 'hot mike' so we didn't have to push a button to talk back and forth. There was a D Model, single seat, F-100 'chase plane' with us who pulled up into formation on our left wing. We climbed to about 25,000 feet and the chase plane loosened up. I could hear him and Tony conversing. Tony told me "Okay Dick, I'm going to do some maneuvers. If you start to get uncomfortable or air sick, just let me know and we'll stop." He also said I could make another fighter pilot sick, but that's not the point. I just want you to enjoy the ride. He put the aircraft at a ninety degree bank, pulled back on the 'joy stick' and the G forces began to mount. We had no 'G suits' so we were limited on how many we could pull. A 'G suit' will begin to inflate and tighten around your waist and legs, not allowing the blood to rush from the upper body to the lower extremities. This keeps you from blacking out too early. Tony continued to perform loops, aileron rolls, and snap rolls, all the time checking to see if I was OK. Finally, He said "Okay, let's put her through the sound barrier." I had seen a lot of movies about trying to break the sound barrier, so I was pretty excited and apprehensive. He said, "You will probably be a little disappointed, there's not much to it." He pushed the throttle lever "around the horn" to engage the afterburners. I watched as the Mach Meter began to climb. We approached 9.8, 9.9; I could see the shock wave moving back on the wing and then we were there, 1.0, 1.1, 1.2, 1.3. It was a little disappointing. I was waiting for some kind of noise or something but Tony said "Nope, they hear it on the ground but not us." This was really sucking up the fuel so we got ready to slow down. Tony said "Don't lock your harness, but kind of hang on to the dash." I said "What?" just as he pulled the afterburners out. It slammed me forward with such a force that I had trouble breathing or talking. Tony said "It feels like we stopped, doesn't it?" I croaked out a "Yes." He replied, "Look at the Mach Meter," we were still doing 1.2 Mach. Finally, the pressure began to ease off and we were subsonic again.

We were leisurely flying along discussing something when the 'shit hit the fan!' The pilot in the chase plane said "WATCH IT TONY, BANDITS AT 9 O'CLOCK HIGH." We had run across two Navy F-9's, or they had run across us, I never knew which, but the fight was on. I had no idea that they jerked those airplanes around like that in a 'Dog Fight.' One second we were right side up, the next, we were upside down. Then it was straight up followed by straight down. What happened to "Are you okay Dick?" "Are you uncomfortable Dick?" I thought he forgot I was even there except that every time we had a compressor stall (that's when the air going into the intake gets kind of piled up during a heavy 'G' load and then rushes through the engine all at once when you straighten out and it makes a "thudding" noise), Tony would yell, "DON'T EJECT." After about the third time he said this, I told him "I'm not getting out of here unless you say so and then we'll do it by the numbers."

The F-9's were no match for the Super Saber but sometime during all of this, two Navy F-111's butted in; with them, Tony had his hands full.

As fast as it started, it was over. Tony said "Are you all right Dick?" I thought 'Oh, yeah, now we're back to that,' but I just said "Wow!"

Before we left the area, we got one more crack at one of the Panthers. Tony came up on his blind spot and said over the hot mike, "rat-a-tat-tat-tat." He said "We'll pull up and let him know." Tony joined in formation on his right wing. There was a hood over the rear cockpit, obviously a student pilot on instruments. The instructor was in the front cockpit with his arms folded across his chest and he didn't see us. Tony said "Watch this," and proceeded to flip us upside down. We were now flying on our back in formation with a student pilot that couldn't see. Lovely! The instructor finally looked over and did a double take, gave us a thumbs down and Tony executed a "Split S" which is like doing the last half of a loop. From around 10,000 feet, Tony pulled about six and a half "G's". I don't know what the weight of my head is (some say I'm big headed), but my head was bent over to the left slightly so I could see past him. When he started pulling the high G forces, my head went down on my shoulder and I couldn't raise it. The ground was coming up at an alarming rate and I was getting "tunnel vision" from the blood rushing as fast as it could to my little toe. We leveled off at 800 feet. I told Tony "I'm glad you pulled out of that, I was getting a little woozy." He said "Don't worry about it, I was too." I thought, "Terrific!"

When we landed back at El Centro, all the guys were waiting to see how I did. I said "Piece of cake", but they all noticed how I was leaning on the wing of the aircraft to steady my legs, and maybe even keep from falling down. That afternoon, Captain Lavere and I would be in a free-fall together, making his first baton pass.

What a great day!

April 29th, 1960, was a repeat of all of the other sunny, bright, clear days that that part of the country is blessed with. Of course, in the summer time, you could swear you were four inches from hell because of the heat, but that's why we were there in April.

As we went through the routine of showering and shaving, the 'daily dozen' and breakfast, there was that feeling of excitement that I would often get just prior to a major parachuting event. Today, we were going to step off of the tail gate at 30,000 feet, to put that in another dimension, that's 5.6818181 miles high. We would free-fall 28,000 feet in 140 seconds and make the first six-way baton pass in history.

The air was electrified; everyone connected with the jump was witnessing some type of powerful emotion. To most of us, it was excited anticipation. To the pilots and flight engineer, it was another work day. To the ground personnel, partly because they had no control over the event, there was a mild apprehension. To the Flight Surgeon, it was a little bit more than mild. This was a little over his head and he was largely responsible for the overall safety of the mission.

Chuting up and equipment checks went without incident. The takeoff was normal and the climb pretty routine. There was the normal nervous yawns and the thousand yard stare, but everything was proceeding according to plan.

We went on ships oxygen early in order to oxygenate our blood cells. We were now breathing 100% pure, dry, oxygen. Somewhere prior to 25,000 feet, the pilot began de-pressurizing the cabin. By the time the cabin reached 25,000 feet, we were all feeling the effects, breathing was labored and any moving about was fatiguing.

We looked at Wil Charette and saw that he was in trouble. He had the "Bends." He kept pointing two fingers to all of his joints; knees, elbows, shoulders; the works. Damn! We didn't want to scrub the jump, but of course our first thoughts were to Wil's safety. By the time we got to 25,000 feet, Wil was laying on the floor, unable to stand, all the time pointing three fingers to all of his joints. The situation was getting critical. The Flight Surgeon was trying to get word to the pilots to close the tail gate and re-pressurize. We were trying to think of alternatives, Wil's safety and the continuation of the jump, with Wil's safety being paramount.

The solution hit all of us jumpers at the same time. In order to reverse the effects of the bends, we had to get Wil to a lower altitude, and as rapidly as possible.

So, keeping Charette's safety and well being in mind, we picked him up and threw his ass out of the airplane.

Somehow, I don't think this was the same solution that the Flight Surgeon had in mind! When I looked at him, the first words that came to mind were 'vapor lock', then 'conniption,' followed closely by 'apoplexy.' As my friend Saul would say, "He looked like a snail that had just learned the true meaning of escargot." I think the only reason that he didn't call the jump off was that we were all staring at him as if to say, "Try it and you're next."

Charette missed the 30,000 foot mark. He later said that as soon as he started the descent, he immediately began feeling better.

The flight engineer indicated four minutes out and we went on bail-out bottles. Everyone gave a 'thumbs up' to the Flight Surgeon, who had finally mellowed down to a mild hysteria and couldn't care less, then walked back to the edge of the tail gate.

It was spectacular! We could see for a hundred miles and could pick out the curvature of the Earth. I looked out and thought "I hope Charette's OK."

The green light came on and we all stepped out into space. I immediately felt the cold, but as I got busy with the baton pass, I forgot about it. It wouldn't have time to catch me before I was at a warmer level. I took my pass from Pearson, spun around, and there was Danny Byard right in my face, I gave him the baton. Not ten seconds had passed and we were halfway through. Even though we all had on different colored flight suits, I decided to track off a little ways so as not to confuse the issue.

We found out later that Loy Brydon and Jim Pearson decided to do the same thing and "tracked" into each other. They saw each other at the last moment and 'flared,' but still hit with such force that it almost knocked Brydon out. He said that he remembered thinking 'I hope the automatic opener works,' but because he was breathing 100% pure oxygen he shook it off.

There is a situation when you are falling over water where you can't estimate your height because there is nothing to relate it to, no buildings, trees or anything. The same holds true over the desert, so we really had to rely on our altimeters, and one another. For example, even if your altimeter says 5,000 feet, and you see parachutes start opening it's a good idea to follow suit! I often said that the death of me would be like a midget getting out of a Volkswagen.

It felt as if we had been falling forever, so I looked at my altimeter. Hell! We were still 15,000 feet. I didn't see any parachutes, so I continued the fall, did a couple of turns and loops and then just enjoyed the scenery.

Approaching 3,000 feet; be careful, scan the horizon, check the altimeter and stopwatch. 2,500 feet—there's one parachute. There's another. Altimeter check—2,000 feet. At 1,800 feet, I stopped the stopwatch and pulled the ripcord. There was that nice pull of gravity as the parachute opened. I looked up and saw that beautiful candy stripped canopy blossoming over my head with a large stencil on it stating, "CAUTION! CONDEMNED! NOT FOR PERSONEL USE!" Sure looked alright to me!

We all landed within twenty feet of each other and were shaking hands and slapping each other on the backs before we even got out of the parachute harnesses.

Loy had sprained his wrist in the collision with Pearson, but was OK, and there was Charette walking around looking none the worst from his ordeal.

We had fallen 28,200 feet in 140 seconds. That's 201.43 feet per second, or, at roughly, 137.33 miles per hour. What a trip.

For months to come we would get to rib Wil whenever he would come in and say, "Hi guys. What have you been up to?" We would retort with, "30,000, how 'bout you?" This lasted until Wil became the NCOIC (Non-Commissioned Officer in Charge) of the HALO Project. HALO was an acronym for High Altitude, Low Opening. It was a project to explore the possible military applications of freefall parachuting. Wil, along with Jim Garvey and a specially picked group would make a series of jumps from 43,500 feet wearing full combat gear; rifles, ammunition, radios . . ., the works. For this, they would also be awarded the Distinguished Flying Cross.

Wil tells of the first jump when they were told to "Go get the bail-out bottles filled with oxygen," They took the bottles to Womack Army Hospital and had them filled with therapeutic oxygen. What did they know? Well, therapeutic oxygen contains moisture. The air temperature when they jumped was approximately 60 degrees below zero, so as soon as they left the aircraft, the oxygen masks froze to their faces. All of them suffered various degrees of frost bite.

What the hell. "Live and learn!"

We arrived back at Fort Bragg with the news that we were no longer the STRAC Parachute Team, (special duty from other organizations). Because of the efforts of General Stilwell and Colonel Grieves, we had received our TO&E (Table of Organization and Equipment). We were now, officially, "The United States Army Parachute Team" assigned to the Continental Army Command, Fort Monroe, Virginia. We would continue to maintain our headquarters at Fort Bragg.

Chapter 7

The men's 1960 United States Parachute Team consisted of Jim Arender, Harry Arter, Danny Byard, Loy Brydon and I. Although we did not have a full women's team, Captain Bobby Gray and Sherry Buck, a civilian out of California, were chosen to compete for individual honors. Our Head of Delegation was Colonel William P. "Bill" Grieves. The Team Leader was Major Merrill Sheppard.

Bobby Gray was an extremely competent nurse out of Womack Army Hospital at Fort Bragg and a very good parachutist with a great attitude and personality.

Sherry was a free spirited young lady and although this would be her one and only World Championship, she was excited about the opportunity and was a constant morale booster for the whole team.

In the last week of July, we packed up all our gear and boarded a C-118 at Andrews Air Force Base. The C-118 was the military version of the Civilian DC-7, four engines, piston, and aircraft with the cruise speed of a turtle. The crew said that it took off at 200 knots, climbed at 200 knots, cruised at 200 knots, descended at 200 knots and landed at 200 knots. The flight to Rhein Mein Air Force base, Frankfurt, Germany would take over eighteen hours, but we were all too excited to care. Before I went into the service, I had never been west of the Pacific Ocean or East of Albany, Texas, so I was pretty hyped.

We had a couple of day's layover in Frankfurt in which to relax and recover from the airplane ride, so we took full advantage of it. In the evening, we would take the bus to the train station in Frankfurt, known as the Bonn Hoff. From there, we would take off in all different directions. I know not what choice others choose, but as for Loy and I, give us the Dolly Bar! We managed to entertain ourselves quite well there. (Loy, I don't know if you will ever read this or not, but I hate to tell you, the last time I went through there, I stopped by the Dolly Bar with my wife and brother-in-law and found out that it is now a Gay Bar). Is nothing sacred? Each morning we would meet back at the Bonn Hoff at 6:00 a. m. for Bratwurst and beer, and to catch the bus back to Rhein Mein. There, we would swap lies about the night and of our adventures. Only Loy and I know for sure. Arender showed up one morning with these god-awful bruises on his neck and when asked what they were from, he replied "riser burns." Well, we knew for a fact that Arender hadn't made a jump in over a week, so I guess that only Arender will ever know for sure.

August 1st, we loaded onto a Bulgarian airliner (I have been a Corporate pilot for the last 28 years and if I had known then what I know now, they would have had to drag me on board) and headed for Sofia, Bulgaria. Shortly after crossing into Bulgarian airspace, Harry Arter said "Hey, look out there!" I looked out of the left window and saw that we had picked up a Soviet Mig fighter escort. I took out my camera and clicked off a picture. When I did, the guy next to me, (whose mother had obviously told him at an early age that we capitalist brought on all of theworld woes), gave me a real dirty look. So I gave him one of those real dirty 'capitalist' looks that said 'go suck an egg!'

U.S. Intelligence briefed us before leaving the States, that all of our rooms would probably be "bugged" and that we would have a 'tail' on us wherever we went. That just made it more intriguing to us.

We were introduced to an Air Force Colonel who was the Air Attaché' for the U. S. Embassy. I can't recall his name, but he had his head shaved and looked a lot like "Kojack," so we'll just call him Kojack. Colonel Kojack had a beautiful Doberman Pincher and liked to walk the streets with it. People would really get out of his way. He confirmed that all of our rooms were probably bugged and might even have cameras in them, so 'be careful.'

The next day, we went sightseeing and shopping with Colonel Kojack as our guide. At one point, he stopped at a store and was looking in the window. I thought he was admiring some rugs or something. He said, "See the guy across the street," describing what he was wearing; I started to turn around when he grabbed my arm and said "Don't turn around dipstick; use the window as a mirror!" Well, that made my jaw muscles tighten up a little because this James Bond shit was a little new to me but I just acknowledged that I saw him. Kojack said, "That's our tail." For the next thirty minutes or so, we played games with our newly acquired Commie friend. For instance, Kojack had us all go into a restaurant. He would tie his Doberman outside and follow us in. After having a snack and chatting for a while, Kojack left out the back door, circled around so as to come down the street behind our tails back. He would purposely bump into him as he went to retrieve his dog. It was fun to watch the expression on this hot shot spy's face when he knew he had just been had, again!

My favorite was to walk down the street and check the second hand on my watch as I passed some landmark, like a telephone booth and then time how long it took him to pass the same landmark. For instance, if it took 14 seconds, then we would walk around a corner and stop; wait 12 seconds and then walk back around the same corner and run right smack into him. He would try as hard as he could to not act surprised, but he never carried it off. He knew we were playing with him. And we knew he knew we knew.

August 3rd, we got on our assigned, and probably bugged, bus and drove to Mussachevo Airport where the parachute meet would be held. The psyche jobs started as soon as you got off the bus. Loy had been here before and knew most of the better competitors, but this was all new to me. Everyone was sizing each other up. For the veterans, it was 'there's so-and-so'. 'Yes, he was good in Tivat', I wonder how good he will be this year?" "Aaahh there's a new face; I wonder what his talent is, etc., etc." For me, it was "Holy shit! There's Klima and Zednich Kaplan from Czechoslovakia. Over there is Tachinko, the World Style Champion. Man, if I can just place in the top ten, I'll be happy."

In Tivat, Yugoslavia, the U. S. Team picked up the nickname, the "farmers," because on their accuracy jumps, they kept landing in the surrounding fields. We had come a long way in our training and were bound and determined to wipe out the nickname.

Sport Parachuting was considered a very precarious sport in Eastern Europe in 1960; so on the way to the airport the sides of the road were filled with banners, flags, signs and even pictures of their national team members. It was if they were gladiators or bull fighters. I think that in Eastern Europe there had been a large number of fatalities in the sport. Looking back on it, I can understand why.

Entering the meet, I had 357 jumps; in my short career, I would accumulate 1,500 jumps. I would also be privileged to meet and compete against one of my lifelong friends, Nick Velacu from Romania. I knew that Nick had 3,000 jumps when he entered this competition. Years later, after Nick had defected to the United States, we were in my home in New Fairfield, Ct., discussing our varied pasts and he asked me how many total jumps I had. After I told him he said, "Hmmm. I had 1,500 jumps before we started wearing reserve parachutes." I said, "Holy shit."

On the 5th of August, we made two practice jumps. This, again, is a psyche job. You know that every competitor is watching and judging your performance, because you are doing the same to them. So, you don't want to show them your whole hand. Our accuracy was still pretty good. We couldn't help from showing off a little. I was a rookie at these mind games, so I landed two and a half meters from the center. That would be my second to the best jump during the meet and I wasted it.

The following day, we made three of the four jumps that would decide the team accuracy event. One team member would spot for the whole team (guide the airplane to the exit point by giving hand signals to the pilot). At an altitude of 6,600 feet, we would exit the aircraft one after the other and fall for thirty seconds before opening. You had a five second window in which to show a pilot chute. If you opened before twenty-five seconds, points were deducted. If you opened at thirty-one seconds, your jump didn't count; it was considered a safety violation for opening too low.

In each event, we would make four jumps of which the best three would be counted. On this day, my scores were 11 meters and 50 centimeters, 7 meters even and 3 meters 30 centimeters.

It was always very difficult to sleep at night because of the anticipation of the next day's activities. We might as well have had a good night's rest because the next day we miss-spotted and landed outside the 100-meter circle. But when it was all over, we were fourth place in the team accuracy event. The nickname "Farmers" was never mentioned again.

On the 11th, they held the style event. This always separated the "flash in the pans" from the serious contenders for the world title. By that, I mean that there were always those who were great at accuracy but fell way short in style competition. Conversely, there were those who were excellent in style but found it difficult to hit Bulgaria from 2,000 feet.

These competitors would most likely win a medal in the event they excelled in but would not be in contention for the "overall" title. In the style event, you would receive one of three scenarios to accomplish in a thirty second free-fall from 6,600 feet. You had no idea which one until you exited the aircraft. There was a large, white, arrow on the ground, which you would line the aircraft up on by using hand signals to the pilot. On each side of the arrow, there were shudder panels, which they would flash for five seconds after you departed the airplane. If a left panel was flashed, you would execute a left 360-degree turn, right 360-degree turn, back loop, left 360 degree turn, right 360 degree turn and another back loop. If a right panel was flashed, everything started to the right, i.e. right turn, left turn, back loop, right turn, left turn, back loop. If it were both panels, you alternated the turns beginning to the right, i.e. right turn, left turn, back loop, left turn, right turn, back loop. Sound complicated? Wait until you hear about the scoring.

Scattered around the arrow were five judges with stopwatches and binoculars. They would time the speed in which you accomplished the maneuvers and judge the accuracy of your "heads" after each turn and loop. The highest and lowest times were thrown out and the other three averaged for the speed. How they decided on accuracy in those days I'll never know. I think it was based on an S.W.A.G. (Scientific, Wild Assed Guess).

Anyway, when you left the aircraft, you had 200 points. You would either add or subtract from that by the following: for every second under 20 seconds that you accomplished the complete series, you received 5 bonus points. for every second over 20 seconds you lost 10 points; if you under shot a turn by one degree, it was considered an incomplete maneuver and you lost all 200 points. If you over shot by up to 90 degrees, it was self penalizing because you had to do a 270 degree turn to complete the next maneuver on the proper heading. If you overshot by 91 to 180 degrees, you lost 50 points. If you over shot by more than 180 degrees, you were considered "out of control" and lost all points. If you "buffeted" on a loop, you lost 50 points and if you were off heading on the last loop, the watches continued to run until you corrected it. Cute huh?

When it all washed out, James Arender was the United States first Gold Medalist in parachuting history.

The Soviet Union's Tachinko was walking around shaking his head trying to figure out who this 150 pound rookie from Tulsa, Oklahoma was.

I had placed high enough in both events to have a decent shot at the overall title. We would see what the "Sky Gods" held in store.

The final accuracy event was a thirty second delayed fall from 6,600 feet. It was August 13th, 1960, and the entire event was to be completed that day. That meant four jumps for each competitor; a busy day to say the least. Little did I know!

The one problem that we encountered on almost every accuracy jump was the difference in the rates of descent between our nylon parachutes verses Eastern European silk parachutes. The air seemed to slip right through the nylon resulting in a much higher rate of descent, and in some cases, a conflict of airspace over the target.

The distance from the center of the target on my first jump was 2 meters and 42 centimeters; the target being a 7 centimeter disc in the middle of a large, white X panel. It seemed that the safest place for the judge to stand was on the disc being as no one in the history of World Competition had ever hit it. On that jump, I felt that I could have hit it because my feet were aimed right in the middle of the judge's back, but at the last minute I yelled for him to move. In doing so, I lost my concentration and had to make a last minute adjustment. But, still, 2.42 meters was about as good as it got in those days. I was hovering somewhere in the top five in the overall scoring and the heat was on.

My next jump made history and a record that can never be broken. It's mine for eternity.

I brought the AN-2 around for a long final to let me gather myself. The only other parachutist in the air was a Bulgarian who was almost on the ground. There would be no conflict. The sky was mine. Two or three small corrections and I was over the exit point. I started the stopwatch as I left the aircraft and looked at my position over the ground. Sometimes, what looks like a good spot from inside the aircraft has a different perspective once you are out and falling, but today that wasn't the case. It looked perfect. There was nothing to do now but enjoy the fall and make DDS (double damn sure) that I opened in the prescribed 30 seconds. After opening, I made a few turns to test the winds and make sure they hadn't shifted on me. Everything looked good. The most critical part of an accuracy jump was the last 200 or 300 feet. Don't be off the wind line. Don't get anxious and turn in too early, yet don't hang out too long and undershoot the target. For every accuracy jump, there is a "golden" point where you know that you judged everything just right. When I turned toward the target, I felt it. This is good! There was only one problem; the damn judge was standing on the frigging target again. I thought 'to hell with him.' I was going to kick him right in the back of the head. At the last second, he turned and saw me bearing down him. He jumped off of the disc and I hit right where he had been standing! It was the first dead center landing ever made in a World Parachuting Championship! A part of history that can never be changed!

I had no way of knowing that my next jump would be my last one in this World Meet. It was the third jump in the last event and would have to be scored.

I mentioned earlier about the difference in the rates of descent between the silk and nylon parachutes. Well, I was about to find out that one Russian and one American wouldn't fit on a 7 centimeter disc at the same time. I had the pilot turn towards the exit point with what appeared to be plenty of room between the jumper ahead and myself. I watched him exit and open. I could tell by the color and design of the parachute that it was a Russian. I still had a long way to run on the final approach so there seemed to be plenty of room between us. Another small correction to the pilot and we were over the exit point. I started my stopwatch and got out. Around 3,000 feet, I began to concentrate on my timing, when I saw 28 seconds on the watch, I pulled. The opening was good. I checked the canopy. Everything that was supposed to be there was there. I always liked that part! I grabbed the guidelines and made a couple of turns to make sure the parachute was maneuvering okay. It was, and I saw that my opening point was perfect for a good shot at the target. I also noticed that the Russian was a little closer than I would like him to be. Did I open low? Did he open high? Whatever the reason, this didn't look like it was going to work. I couldn't think of any rules, regulations or right-of-way etiquette governing this situation, but I did know that this was World Class competition and no one, especially a Russian, was going to run me off the target. At about 100 feet off the ground, we were dead (bad choice of word) level and rubbing canopies. At the last minute, the Russian must have thought well, that idiot isn't going to move so I better. He turned off of the target. I still had a shot at it, but all of this pushing and shoving had really screwed up my approach. I was too high and would have to make a 180 degree turn at the last minute. When I did, I ended up traveling over the target backwards at a very high rate of speed. I should have done a school style PLF (parachute landing fall) but in order to land as close to the target as possible, I threw my feet out in front of me and hit heel first at about 15 miles per hour. I instinctively put my arms behind me to help break the fall. When I stopped rolling and sat up, I was completely wrapped up in my suspension lines. I was in no pain, but had this uneasy feeling that something was out of whack. It was! I couldn't close my fist or even flex the fingers of my right hand. I looked farther back on my arm and saw that my elbow was dislocated about 2 inches from where it was supposed to be. Out, frigging, standing. One of the scorers was the first one to reach me and collapse my canopy. That kept me from dragging and causing more damage. To his credit and the credit of all athletes everywhere, the next person to come to my aid was the Russian whom I had run off of the target.

Colonel Bill wasn't far behind. He held onto my arm while they untangled me from the suspension lines and assisted me to the (for lack of a better work) ambulance. In just a few minutes, I found myself in a dilapidated old building that was supposed to be a medical facility. I still wasn't feeling any pain. Everything was just sort of numb. Before they could reset my elbow, they wanted to take x-rays of the area to make sure nothing was broken. It didn't take long to take the pictures, but they had to run them into Sofia to have them developed. That took the better part of an hour during which Colonel Bill stayed right by my side. He was a lot more worried and nervous than I was. At one point, he asked if I wanted a cigarette and I said yes. He lit it for me and continued to stand there and smoke it himself.

When the doctors finally returned, they asked to talk to Colonel Bill privately. That made me a little nervous! He came back in a few minutes and said "Hang on buddy, this may hurt." He held onto my shoulder while two big burly bastards started trying to separate me in the room. One was pulling on my upper arm, and the other on my forearm. It didn't really hurt; I just felt this tremendous release of pressure when it snapped back in place. I could, now, flex my arm and fingers and make a fist. I said, "Aaah, that feels better." I felt that I could go right out and make my last jump of the event, but the medical staff said "no dice" or the Bulgarian version of that. They put a half cast on the bottom of my arm from the wrist to the shoulder then wrapped it up with gauze. I was finished as far as this meet was concerned, but Colonel Bill had been keeping up with the scores and told me at present, I was in first place for the overall title. There were only three competitors who could beat me; a Russian, a Romanian and the Czechoslovakian, Kaplan.

Because of the order of competition it took about three hours agonizing over those jumps. The Russian and the Czech both landed far enough out to leave me in first place. I was feeling pretty confident because the Romanian was not a very good accuracy jumper. He made his landing. The judges measured it. Holy shit. I was the World Champion.

Everyone was pounding me on the back and congratulating me, including some of the iron block countries. My teammates were going bonkers. I was in a state of shock and disbelief. My first World Competition and I had won it.

During all of the commotion, someone said "Hold it, what's this?" Colonel Grieves started in a dead run toward the judges to find out what was going on. The last competitor had landed. Why was a jump plane taking off and who was on it?

The judges said that the Czech jumper, Kaplan, had protested that smoke had drifted across the target and obscured his vision. It was an out and out lie. Everyone on the drop zone watched that jump and knew the smoke that had been started to indicate the wind direction had been placed downwind of his approach. It was a communist ploy.

Colonel Bill argued that it was not a decision for the judges to make, but that of the International Jury. He protested, strongly, that the AN-2 land, and that evidence be gathered to present to the jury so they could decide if a re-jump was in order.

They stated that they had no communication with the aircraft. Another lie.

By now, we, and some of the other Western countries were beginning to worry. How do you fight a conspiracy in which all of the conspiring parties have no sense of moral dignity, pride or shame? A win at all cost attitude.

We knew that whatever the outcome of Kaplan's jump, would be the outcome of the Championship. I couldn't believe that Kaplan would be in on the sham. You might ask then, why couldn't he just miss the target on purpose? It is not the nature of an athlete, and especially one of Kaplan's talents, to perform poorly. I knew he would do his best.

Colonel Bill continued to argue with the judges while the rest of us waited and watched. It seemed forever for the aircraft to get to altitude. He finally started his jump run. The line was good. He passed across the target and continued up wind. Someone said, "He's out." A perfect exit point. I watched as he played the wind to set up his final approach down wind. He hung out just the right amount and began his final approach to the target at about 300 feet. When he made that final turn, I knew he had it; he beat me by 4 centimeters.

I can't express my feeling of frustration. I had one more jump to go but couldn't make it because of my injury. A Swiss Doctor that was there offered to give me an injection that would give me full use of my arm but couldn't guarantee that I wouldn't damage my elbow further. I said I would take it, but Colonel Bill said no. He said, "I'm not going to let you destroy your arm for this one meet. There will be another time."

The United States committee protested to the F.A.I. Jury and the debate went on for eight hours. There were four Western countries and seven Eastern countries on the Jury. Guess what the vote was? You got it. Seven to four against me.

The awards banquet that night wasn't much fun, but I was as gracious as I could be. I even congratulated Kaplan. He didn't look very happy or jubilant either.

One of the Russian jumpers kept toasting me as the World Champion all night. I appreciated his gesture, but it didn't help much.

The only humorous thing that happened that night was that one of the Russian jumpers fell head over heels in heat for Sherry Buck. He literally chased her around the building from room to room. Every time she ran by us, she would yell, "Stop him." We would say, "Okay, next time around, we'll catch him." Then, when he would pass, he would confirm that he had our approval by giving us a thumb up signal and asking "Okay?" We would give him a thumbs up and yell "Okay!" I never did find out whether he caught her or not.

Oh well, wait until '62.

Chapter 8

On the trip back to the United States, the *Team* had a short break in Frankfurt in which to wind down. My short break was at the Air Force Hospital in Rein Mein; no return trip to the Dolly Bar for me. Loy said that he would be happy to explain the situation to any of my acquaintances and properly console them if necessary. Thanks Loy.

After checking into the hospital, the doctors took off the half cast and gave a collective groan. The cast had been placed on my arm before it had a chance to swell. When it did swell, it cut off the circulation to the back of my arm which was now a very pale white with a long yellowish purple line down the two sides of my arm. Their reactions made me a little nervous, but they said that there didn't seem to be any permanent damage. The size of my arm was amazing. The doctors put a full cast on it and sent me to my room.

I didn't realize how tired I was until a nurse asked if there was anything she could get for me. I asked for a cup of coffee. When she gave it to me, I sat on the edge of the bed and relaxed a bit. The next thing I heard was a crash and the sound of something breaking. I don't even remember dropping it. I think I fell asleep momentarily. I apologized but she said "not necessary, just get some sleep." I slept for over eighteen hours.

I woke to a pleasant surprise. Someone was gently shaking me and saying "Wake up, you Gold Bricker." It was Jane Garvey, Jim's wife. Jim had been reassigned to the 10th Special Forces Group in Badholtz Germany, and she was on her way to join him. It sure was nice to talk to a sympathetic person and it gave me the opportunity to tell all about my woes in Bulgaria.

After arriving back in the States, it would be September 15th before I could make my next jump. The swelling went down in my arm to the point that I could rattle it around inside the cast. I thought when the cast came off, the arm would be as good as new, but I only had about 5 degrees of movement in my elbow. It took weeks of therapy to get most of the flexibility back. I still don't have full range of motion to this day.

The United States and the Army was pretty pleased with our performance. Jim Arender had brought back America's first Gold Medal for the style event and I had brought back the first Silver Medal for highest overall points. The *Team* was just out of the trophies with a fourth place finish but our heads were held high. For the Army Team, it was back to the grind of the demonstration circuit and start thinking about the next U.S. Nationals.

From the 15th of September to the 18th of October we would put on demonstrations at the Oklahoma State Fair, then Clarion, Pennsylvania, and for numerous events at Fort Bragg.

The next interesting event was a trip to Rio de Janeiro. We were invited by the Brazilian Special Forces to come down and train them in body stabilization techniques. While we were there, we could also planned on performing some demos. We (Captain Jim Perry, Sergeant Jim Arender, Sergeant Danny Byard and myself) were met at the Alfonsos airport in Rio by BrazilianS.F. Captain Hamilton, pronounced (Ham-eel'-ton) who arranged for our stay at their Special Forces base. We were also informed that we had arrived right in the middle of a military Coup in progress. It seemed that one General with twenty tanks and a few 'balls' was trying to oust another General with fifteen tanks and a "whole lot of 'balls.' It appeared to be a local grudge thing and the Special Forces was staying out of it for now. On the way to the Base, which was about ten miles out of Rio, we were stopped and challenged by two or three road blocks manned by a Sergeant and a few wide eyed privates carrying great big rifles, all pointed at us. I didn't know how everyone else was handling this but as for me it made me more than just a little nervous. Capt. Hamilton said something to them in Portuguese and they backed off to let us through.

When we got to the Special Forces Base, we were taken directly to the Commanding General who welcomed us and stated how much he appreciated our acceptance of his invitation to help train them. After that, we met the paratroopers that had been handpicked to receive the training. We could tell in a flash that these were a special breed of cat. They all spoke at least three languages, wore paratrooper wings and didn't have an ounce of fat on them. We had a lot to cover so we got started right away.

These guys were already free-fall qualified so what we had to do was to tweak them up on technique. There would be some "firsts" for me during this time in that I had never jumped out of a H-13 helicopter, a C-82 "Flying Box-car" or a Beechcraft D-18.

I had been experimenting filming jumpers with an 8 millimeter movie camera for some time now. The camera was mounted on the side of my helmet on a little bracket I had rigged up and I used a wire coat hanger to make a sighting frame. It was attached to my helmet on each side and stuck out in front, forming a square that I visualized as a movie screen. It was roughly bore-sighted but somehow I got some pretty good pictures out of it.

One of the things I almost documented was one of the students going "all the way in"; a phrase meaning, never opening his parachute. We were doing a 20 second delay from about 6,000 feet which would give us a little extra room for me to film his opening. Although we had altimeters on our instrument panels mounted on our reserve parachutes, our primary timing devise would be the stopwatch located next to it. We both started our watches and I exited a second after him. The fall was going good and the filming was going good right up to the point where he didn't pull his rip-cord at the designated 20 seconds. I kept falling with him and waiting. I had reverted to my altimeter now and was watching the altitude get lower and lower. I kept saying to myself, "Pull, pull, and pull." He was about 100 feet lower than me and at 1,500 feet; I told myself "I'm out of this scene." I pulled! It seemed like slow motion but even after I opened, he kept falling and falling. I thought "holy shit", he's going in and I'm filming it. Finally, I saw the white flash of his pilot chute and wondered if he had enough altitude to open, I couldn't tell from my angle. After what seemed like an eternity the main parachute opened. Later, he said that the first time he looked at his altimeter; it was reading about 500 feet, that's when he pulled. After getting his ass chewed royally by Capt. Hamilton, I asked him what happened. It was standard operating procedure (SOP) for all of them to start their watches after practice in order to let them run down and relieve the pressure on the main spring, thus extending the life of the watch. Well, he had forgotten to rewind the watch so when he pushed the stem to start it, it ran for 10 seconds and stopped, nearly shortening the life of the user. He kept glancing down at it looking for 20 seconds and it kept indicating 10. When he could see the individual leaves of the palm trees, it dawned on him that something was awry. Running their watches down quickly became non-standard operating procedure.

The U.S. Army Team had requested to go through the Brazilian S.F. jump school which they were happy to oblige. We spent a day going through all of their obstacle courses and then made a "troop" drop using regular military T-10 parachutes. We made the jump out of the C-82. Shortly after I opened I felt a thump on my parachute. I looked up to see that one of the Brazilians had landed on top of my chute and that the air from his parachute had been stolen causing it to collapse. It was hanging down the side of mine and the jumper was stranded on top of my parachute. Now, this wasn't going to bother me, but when I landed, he was going to have a nice little fall of about 20 feet. Well, this guy hadn't just fallen off of a papaya truck, so he calmly gathered up the parachute in his arms, gave out a Geronimo yell and half walked, half slid off my parachute and threw his to the wind. To my extreme relief, and I'm sure his, it opened.

Being on the Army Parachute Team carried a social obligation that we all welcomed and in most cases enjoyed. The social obligation on this trip was to go to the American Embassy and meet the Ambassador, Henry Cabot Lodge. He welcomed us to the Embassy and to Brazil in general. The Ambassador was a very nice, cordial man with a fine sense of humor, which we would put to the test later.

During our visit to the Embassy we introduced ourselves to the Marine Guard. This was the Armed Forces Unit that traditionally and very seriously, had the duty of guarding the U.S. Embassies all over the world. Some may consider this assignment a piece of cake, but if you will remember back to the capture of the Iranian Embassy, at least one Marine was wounded defending it. It's no walk in the park by any means, but can have its fun side.

The Brazilian Embassy Marine Guard was housed in an apartment building ten stories up over looking Epanima Beach, just south of Rio. Not a shabby barrack by any means. They invited us up for a party (they only party on days that end in "y"), and we, not daring to commit a blunder by shirking our social obligations, accepted, and what a great party it was.

The Guard had invited a number of Embassy employees over, of which some were of the gentler persuasion which brightened up the evening. The Marines had devised this great idea for defraying the cost of a party by having this great big clear vase in the living room in which everyone would throw their 'extra change.' paper only. This would accumulate over a period of time to finance the next party. We gave generously.

As the party developed and the "barley pop" was consumed, situations began to develop as they often do. Arender and I had always had this competitive thing going between us and tonight wasn't any different. The Marine House was only about five feet away from the building next door and ten stories up. Jim dared me to jump across to the next building. Everyone said "no way," I said "Way." Rules were made that you could make one hop, then jump. I made the firstjump and Jim followed. We were safely on the roof of the other building. Now it was Jim's turn. He jumped and I followed.

Nowhere in these writings have I ever claimed being smart, and this is one of the dumber things I've done in my life. Not only was I endangering my life, I was making everyone at the party nervous and uncomfortable, but Jim and I kept jumping back and forth, waiting for someone to miss.

Finally, the NCOIC, (Non Commissioned Officer In Charge), said "okay, that's enough fun for you two, knock it off". Hey, definitely enough fun for me. I wasn't enjoying it but I would be damned before I would let Arender get one up on me.

During the party, we met the personal secretary for the Ambassador and asked if she could do us a favor. She said "Yes, as long as it doesn't involve visas." So, we asked if she could steal the Ambassadors' umbrella. She was confident that she could but asked "why?" We said "trust us," and to our amazement, she did.

Two days later, Danny and Jim tied a strap around the umbrella so it couldn't accidentally open. I put on the helmet camera and away we went. We took the D-18 to 7,200 feet and jumped. Danny went first with the umbrella, Jim second and me third. When I was in position and filming, Danny passed it to Jim. We had the film developed, took one frame showing the pass and gave it to the local newspaper. It must have been a slow news day because the next day's headlines read AMBASSADORS BUMBERCHUTE PASSED IN MID-AIR by members of the United States Army Parachute Team. We had a small brass plaque made up and attached to the umbrella commemorating the event and presented it to Ambassador Lodge. He said that he had been looking for the umbrella for three days and had no idea where it was until he saw the newspaper. He thought it was fabulous and promised to keep it forever.

One of the things I always enjoyed about traveling with the *Team* was being introduced to the many varied cultures and customs, one such custom in Brazil really got my attention. Captain Hamilton and some of the other Officers and men of the Special Forces gave a party for us to meet their families and present a slide show of one of their field exercises. They had flown up the Amazon well into the jungle and jumped. It took them three weeks to walk out and they documented it all on film. There were tribal people who had never seen an airplane much less men descending from the sky. They were immediately honored as Gods and shown sacred rituals that had never been seen or filmed before. It was fascinating.

After the slide show, we ate, drank and danced; it was just like any social function we would have had in the States. Husbands danced with their wives and we talked with the wives and children. But then something strange happened. On what seemed like some invisible cue, the wives and children began to leave until there were only us guys left. Then these beautiful women began to show up. It was the husband's mistresses! I thought 'holy shit!' Although the husbands were totally devoted to their families it was a socially accepted practice for them to have mistresses and the wives left to allow time for them. We thought 'Hey, let's take this custom home with us,' but we knew it would never fly.

November 6, 1960 was a beautiful warm day (you have to remember that south of the equator, November is summer), and one that we were looking forward to with great anticipation. We were scheduled to put on a demonstration water jump at Copa-Cabana Beach. The jump would be out of the WWII C-82 "Flying Boxcar" from an altitude of 12,500 feet. For a water jump we had to wear extra equipment like a 'Mae West' inflatable flotation device named after the bosomy movie star of the same name. We would also wear a smoke bracket which held (two) red smoke grenades which would enable the audience to see us during the fall. Water jump demos had their own particular headaches. Number one was keeping things dry. We would carry a plastic bag which we used to put our reserve parachute and instrument panel in after opening. We also had to take off the smoke bracket and attach it to the parachute harness. The most critical thing was not to inflate the Mae West until after entering the water and clearing the harness. If it were to accidentally inflate under the harness, it could crush you.

We boarded the C-82 and took off; the ride was gorgeous. We climbed to 2,000 feet and made a pass over the raft that would serve as our target and safety craft and dropped the wind drift indicator, a 22 foot piece of crape paper attached to one and a half ounce weight. We could see the large statue of Christ on the mountain overlooking the city and Sugar Loaf Mountain jutting out in the Atlantic Ocean. There was also, a large crowed gathering on the beach. The Life Guard Association was on station with life boats and everything seemed in place so we headed out over the jungle to climb for altitude. Captain Hamilton and three of his men would be making their first water jump. On a water jump, you had to pretty much rely on your instruments because there were very few items to relate size to like buildings etc.

We made the first pass and then let Captain Hamilton and his men go. We watched their fall and then the opening of their parachutes. They all landed relatively close to the raft and we came around for our jump run. Captain Perry went first followed by myself, Arender, and Byard. Captain Perry and Arender made a baton pass while Danny and I did the diamond track. We tracked 180 degrees away from each other for 20 seconds then turned toward each other and tracked back, crossing side by side at a closing rate of over 100 miles per hour. After opening, it really got busy. Off with the reserve, put it in the bag, tie it off and attach to the harness. Off with the smoke bracket and attach it to the harness, all the while trying to steer the parachute as close to the raft as possible. The practiced procedure for a water landing was to unsnap the chest and leg straps and sit in the saddle like a swing. Because it is so hard to judge your height above water, you wait until your feet touch and then slide out of the saddle and swim away from the parachute so as not to get tangled in it. Well, Jim Arender, who elected to jump barefooted, was never one to pay much attention to rules, practiced procedures or suggestions, misjudged his height and came out of his harness about 75 feet from the water and hit flat footed. Needless to say that he hobbled around for the next few days. I landed as close as possible to the raft without landing in it. Most of my pals said it was because of my fear of sharks and they were probably right.

The Guarda Vida (Life Guards) picked us up and said they could drop us off at the guard house or the beach. Which would we prefer? There were about 15,000 people on the beach ofwhich over half were women of which over 90% were gorgeous. You guess where we had them drop us.

A couple of days later we, reluctantly, bid farewell to Rio de Janeiro with many fond memories and a gift from the Special Forces in the form of a cigarette lighter with Brazilian paratrooper wings on it.

A few days after returning back to Fort Bragg, we made a demonstration on Sicily D. Z. After landing, I couldn't find my cigarette lighter. I figured I had lost it forever, but the next day two men from the Army C.I.D. (Criminal

Investigation department) walked in and asked me if I was on the demo the previous day. I said "Yes" He then turned to his partner and said "See, I told you he wouldn't be hard to find." I asked what was going on and they informed me that my cigarette lighter had fallen out of my pocked and landed in the bleachers next to a Lieutenant Colonel. Of course, if it had hit him, it would have killed him. He 'put' the C.I.D. on me.

I told them that in a way, I was glad that it happened. No one was hurt and now I know better than to carry it in my outer garment. They said that because of the rank of the individual and his request, they had to show some follow-up action. I said I understood, and they left. I figured that was the end of it.

The next day, General Stilwell walked in. Any one of the Parachute Team would stick his head in fire for General Stilwell; we thought so much of him. He addressed us by our first names and allowed us to call him General Joe. This day I said "Hi, General Joe." He replied "Good morning Sergeant." I thought 'oh shit!' He continued. "I understand you had a mishap yesterday sergeant." I said "Yes, Sir." He said "That's most regrettable Sergeant. And the most regrettable thing about it is, (he let that hang in the air for a second), it didn't hit that son-of-a-bitch!" I found out from the General's Aide, Captain Chapman, that General Joe had called the Colonel in and went up one side of him and down the other. He said "That's my *Team* Colonel! If you have anything to say to any one of the *Team* members, you go through me first! Is that clear Colonel?" I'm glad I never had the purpose of running into that particular Colonel again.

Chapter 9

As I open Parachuting Log Book number 4, beginning February 11, 1961, I am struck by the fact that there is only one autograph and is entered on the very front page. In all of my other log books there are humorous signatures with, mostly, well wishes. Then, again, there may well be some hidden sarcasm or meanings in some of them that I'm not aware of. I will get to some of those later.

This particular signature is very meaningful to me. The hand writing is bold and eloquent. It depicts a person who has been there and done that; a person who can walk the walk and talk the talk. It simply reads:

> To Dick Fortenberry-
> A fine jumper and friend- always full of surprises!
> Very best-and thanks-
> J. W. Stilwell
> B/Gen USA
> C-345

The "Always full of surprises" was a reference to the time I asked the General, during the awards banquet for the 1961 National Championship, if he was a 'turtle'. The turtle club dates back to World War II when the enemy had compromised most of the challenge and response password codes. An American unit came up with the brilliant idea of devising a challenge and response that made absolutely no sense and confused the enemy. The challenge was "Are you a turtle?" The response was "You bet your sweet ass I am," the tradition continued after the war but with a new twist. First, you had to answer three out of four questions. If you are ever in the presence of a turtle member, he will be glad to administer the test. After becoming a "Turtle" if you are ever asked by a fellow member "Are you a turtle?" and you do not respond with "you bet your sweet ass I am" because of embarrassment or any other reason, you forfeit a beverage of this choice. This night, the General's response, in front of about two hundred guest was "I owe you a drink, and I'll talk to you later." This drew a roar from most of the crowd, and a bunch of bewildered looks from the rest.

General Joe always loved flying. He had asked that the Army send him to flight school, but they never did; so any time he had reason to fly in an OH-1 Bird Dog or L-20 Beaver he would have the pilot teach him a bit about flying. One day he was on an inspection tour in the field. He flew out in a Bird Dog with a young 1st Lieutenant. On the way, the General asked the Lieutenant if he would be ready to solo if he were a student. The Lieutenant said "Sure". After the inspection they returned to the aircraft where the General told the Lieutenant that he had forgotten to inform his aide, Captain Chapman, of his return and would the Lieutenant be kind enough to go call him? "Yes Sir," replied the Lieutenant! When the Lieutenant was far enough away, the next thing he heard was his airplane roaring down the runway with the General at the controls. The General made two touch and go landings and a full stop that would have qualified him as a solo student pilot if he were in flight school, which he was not. The General never mentioned it again and the Lieutenant certainly did not, but he never got more than a couple of yards away from his airplane again.

General Stilwell spent as much time as he could possibly spare from his busy schedule on the drop zone with the *Team* making as many jumps as he could. We always had to coordinate with range and D.Z. control to schedule our activities. The 82nd Airborne Division and all military exercises had priority on use of the drop zones, but it could usually be worked out very easily. Now, when the general came out to jump, he normally dressed in cut-off Levi's, a sweat shirt with the sleeves cut out and jump boots. With his gray hair and general (no pun intended) appearance, he looked like a crusty old Sergeant. The only thing that he had around to show his rank was a red baseball cap with a beaded star on it, which he normally left in his jeep.

I witnessed times when an officer would come out to the D.Z. and say something like "Excuse me Sergeant, but we have a Division drop scheduled for 1,300 hours; I don't see why we can't coordinate our activities to cause as little disruption with yours as possible. How about I give you a call about fifteen minutes before the drop, then you clear the Drop Zone and we'll complete our activities and be out of here. I'll give you an all clear signal, at which the General would say something like 'sounds great, thanks.'"

Then there were other times when a Captain or Major would come out and say something like "Listen, we have a military drop coming in a while and we have priority over your sport activity. You're going to have to clear the Drop Zone until further notice!" At which point the General would tell one of the guys, "Get my hat!" As soon as they said "Yes Sir!" the officer would start suspecting something was afoul. General Stilwell would put his hat on with that big beaded star blaring at the officer and reply, "Would you like to rephrase that Major?" the next thing you heard was "Aaahh, sputter, aahhh, ugh, Sir, I didn't eh, sputter!"; now this was a mild reaction by the General. If anyone confronted one of the *Team* members directly, (in a derogatory manner), the General would rain all over him. Of course, sometimes we paid for it when the general wasn't around.

Looking through log book #4, beginning on February 11, 1961 I noticed that a few interesting things happened on the way to the National Championships. The *Team* had picked up some new members including Bill Edge, (my old platoon sergeant in jump school), Ron Brown, Bobby Letbetter, Al Solis and Coy O. McDonald among others. We had also divided the *Team* into three groups—The Demonstration Team, The Competition Team and The Research and Development Team. This didn't mean that you would only participate in one event. You could contribute to any or all three teams depending on your individual talents. For example, everyone had the ability to perform on the Demo Team because that was our core business. Brydon, on the other hand, had an aptitude for developing new steerable designs and was also a very accomplished competitive parachutist and one of the better accuracy jumpers on the *Team*. My specialty was competition, so I was placed primarily on the Comp Team with secondary roles on the other two teams.

Another change that would affect the future of the *Team* more than any of us realized, especially Captain Perry, was giving the *Team* a "Show Name."

Everyone on the *Team* felt that we should have a "Show Name" like that of the U.S. Air Force's Flight Demonstration Team, the "Thunderbirds", or the Navy's "Blue Angles". Captain Perry was adamant about keeping it just plainly, "The United States Army Parachute Team." We all agreed that it would always be that, but we needed a flashy, and at the same time, traditional and meaningful name for air shows, etc. Captain Perry wouldn't budge! Danny Byard and I bugged him to the point where I was afraid he was going to put us in leg irons and shackles, and throw away the key. Finally, just to keep from driving him insane, he said "I don't want any part of it, but get every body together and see what you come up with." That was all we needed.

Danny and I gathered every *Team* member we could find and went to one of the barracks to change the *Teams* destiny. The ones that I recall who participated were Danny Byard, Joe Norman, Bill Edge, Jim Arender, Loy Brydon, Jerry Bourquin, Jim Pearson, Ray Duffy, Bobby McDonnell, Harry Arter, Ray Love and myself. There were a few more I can't recall. Anyway, Danny said "what should we call ourselves"—and it started. Ask a simple question from this group and you would not get a simple or straight answer! How about 'Shit from the Sky'? Naw, that's too crude—how 'bout 'Feces from the Blue'? Danny and I decided to let it go until they got it out of their systems, otherwise we would never get anything done. "How about we kick your ass inside out and whatever it looks like is what we'll name it." I vote on the' Pink Pelicans.' Someone else suggested "The Fuzzy Fairies." Danny, who always had the ability to calm things down finally said "all right guys, let's get serious". Someone replied "we were serious!" I said "Why don't we make a list of colors on one side of the blackboard and a list of names on the other side and start matching until we come up with something. It started again—'Chartreuse, aqua marine, titty—pink, artichoke green, etc.; pelicans, parrots, buzzards, aardvarks.' It continued for a while until they ran out of silly colors and names and began to get into the spirit.

A long list of colors and names were put up on the black board and we began to cross match. I happened to catch the cross match of 'Yellow Knights' and said "wait a minute, think about this—the official Army colors are black and gold. The West Point football team is known as the *Black Knights* of the Hudson. If they're the *Black Knights*, why don't we be the *Golden Knights*? Whether Captain Perry liked it or not, it stuck. It was that easy, and from that time on, (although we were officially the United States Army Parachute Demonstration Team) we were always billed as the *GOLDEN KNIGHTS*.

February 22, 1961, The *Golden Knights* boarded two C-130 Hercules Aircraft, along with a lot of military equipment and personnel, and headed for Howard Army Airfield, Panama Canal Zone. We were to conduct a demonstration for some high ranking Generals and local dignitaries. My flight was uneventful, but the other guys had an engine failure and had to divert into a tiny little island named San Andres. In the world Atlas it is listed as a colony; it doesn't say whose so I would assume it was British. They were a day late arriving at the Canal Zone, but had some great stories to tell.

The engine didn't just fail; it partially exploded and caught fire. The crew was able to extinguish the fire but was concerned about continuing the flight, so the decision was made to land at San Andres. The only runway on the island was made of coral, was very short in length and had no runway lights. Somehow the crew got the word to the local inhabitants that they would have to land so everyone who had a car or flashlight showed up at the runway. They all shined their lights on the runway to illuminate it. This worked very well; the only problem was that when the pilot made his approach, everyone was standing in the middle of the runway to see what was going on. He had to buzz them to get them off the middle of the runway and then make another approach.

There was only one other non-native on the whole island and the islanders treated the *Team* like monarchs. They stayed in private homes until repairs were finished then bid a fond farewell to their newly acquired friends and continued their journey.

The rest of us spent the time waiting for our comrades by getting the lay of the land, learning the local customs and checking out the indigenous personnel. The terrain was mountainous and very close to the airport which could cause problems on our opening altitudes. The weather was tropical—hot, humid and rainy. It would rain in spurts, but when it did, it came down in buckets. As my friend Saul would say, "It sounded like a cow pissing on a flat rock."

When the rest of the *Team* arrived, we got right down to briefings on what events were taking place, along with weather briefings and meeting the pilots that would fly the Sikorsky H-34 helicopter that would be our jump platform. The senior Pilot was a crusty Warrant Officer named Julian "Scratch" Kanach. Years later, I would have the opportunity to fly with him on off-shore oil rigs in the Gulf of Mexico.

Basically, the entire event (tanks, troops, artillery—that sort of thing) was to be a show of power for the local inhabitants; we (*Golden Knights*) were to be the main entertainment.

We finished the briefings, changed into civilian clothing and headed for town. Since a few of us had been in Panama twenty-four hours longer than the rest, we felt like old timers and obligated to introduce the rest of the guys to the local culture. It was pretty difficult. There were bars, beers, booze and girls, but we played the roll of entertainers and by 11 o'clock everyone was pretty well blitzed. Joe Norman and I took a cab back to the base. When we arrived at the main gate, the driver said that was as far as he could go and demanded about a dollar more than the normal fare. Well, Joe was not one to be taken, and a heated discussion broke out. Pretty soon the MP (military policeman) at the gate came over to see what the fuss was. He confirmed that we had been over charged by a dollar and that the fare included transportation all the way to the barracks. The driver was not going to argue with the MP and begrudgingly took us to the barracks. After we got out, Joe paid him the exact fare and the drive started to drive off when Joe yelled "wait!" With an elaborate flair, Joe tipped him a dollar. I thought the driver was going to kill him. He threw the dollar back at Joe and began a tirade in Spanish. From what little we could understand, I think there were references to Joe's ancestry, his mother and all of his future children and grandchildren. Joe bowed and said "Gracias," then we got the hell out of there before he decided to run over us!

The next day we were above 9,000 feet before my head stopped throbbing.

We were headed for 12,500 feet for the demo. I kept wondering why, with my fear of sharks did Kanach have to climb downwind of the target area and way out over the gulf. I spent the whole time calculating whether or not I could track to land if the engine quit and we had to bail out; at the time, I knew nothing about auto-rotations. I thought that if the engine quit the rotor blades stopped and the whole mass took on the aerodynamic characteristics of a jagged rock. After I eventually went to helicopter school, I would build a healthy respect for the H-34.

It was a clear day and we got 12,600 feet for the jump. It was a little windy but not a problem. The only drawback was that our opening point was over about a 500 foot jungle hill, which meant that we should, and I emphasize should, open 500 feet higher on our altimeters. Danny Byard and I did the baton pass, which would be presented to the ranking civilian or officer. I opened at 1,800 feet, as indicated on my altimeter, and thought 'hmmm' those trees look awfully big.

The landing area was a concrete aircraft parking ramp in front of the bleachers. We had to make sure we landed into the wind to keep the impact down. Everything went well and we impressed everyone by making 'standing' landings about 20 yards in front of the spectators.

The next day's jump was equally as impressive even though we could only get 11,800 feet because of the clouds. 'Those trees are getting bigger and bigger, and, why does this bastard have to keep climbing out over the water.'

Same demo, different day, different story!

We woke up to heavy rain and high winds; the weather forecast didn't seem much brighter. The cloud ceiling would probably be enough for us to do the 'high' show (between 6,000 and 8,000 feet) but the winds were forecast to increase. We decided to take off and make the decision in the air.

It was never a dictatorial decision whether we jumped or not. The situation was always relayed to each jumper and a consensus taken, at which time we all decided what to do and the decision had to be unanimous.

When it came time to *"put up or shut up"* we were told that the winds were steady at 15 knots with gusts to 20 and 25 knots. We knew that there were some very high ranking officials who had not seen the previous days' demonstrations and we did want to razzle-dazzle them. On a normal, sandy drop zone, this would not be a problem, but that concrete ramp was going to be awfully hard.

When decision time came, it was with a mighty grin and hearty "Hi-Ho Silver" that every one would give the thumbs up sign. All "Scratch" did was shake his head in disbelief. To top it off, because of the high winds, the exit point was farther out over the water; which did not please me at all.

We could only get 8,000 feet, which would give us about a 40 second delay before opening at 2,000 feet; plenty of time to perform a respectful demonstration.

Because of the deteriorating weather, we decided to do a mass drop; everyone on one pass. Even during the free-fall in excess of 120 miles per hour, I could tell that we were drifting back toward the target area. Danny and I missed the baton pass but who's to tell. After opening, I made some turns with the canopy to test the wind. We were right on the wind line but there was precious little room to maneuver. As we got lower, I began to realize that we were in the throws of the gustiest winds of the day. What started out as a razzle-dazzle performance was rapidly turning into an 'Oh Shit' exercise in survival! There would be no impressive "standing" landings on this demo. In fact, I began to review the PLF (parachute landing fall) procedures that we were taught in jump school. This landing had the potential of a very high pain threshold.

I managed to steer clear of the spectators, all protruding obstacles on the ramp, and to get turned into the wind but still landed traveling backward at about twenty miles per hour. My school-learned PLF turned out to be three points of contact; feet, ass and head, in that order and about that fast.

In order get up after a parachute landing in windy conditions, you have to be able to do one of three things. The school solution is: as you are dragging along the ground, pull on a riser and at the same time throw your feet over your shoulder allowing the parachute to pull you to a standing position, and then run around the parachute, thus collapsing it. The next method is to continue pulling the raisers and suspension lines until you collapse the chute. The third method is to pull down the safety cover over the cape-well and release one side of the parachute.

Well, first off, I can't run twenty miles an hour. Second off, trying to pull the suspension lines in against the forces of a 25 knot wind while dragging across a concrete apron is damn near impossible and thirdly, the original design on the cape-well safety covers was to keep anyone not roughly resembling King Kong from releasing them.

Somehow, I got up and collapsed my parachute. At the same time, I could see Joe Norman dragging toward me. I released my harness and got out of it, figuring I had a one shot chance at Joe's canopy. If I missed he would probably end up in Ecuador or some other place farther south. I was in luck, or rather he was. I got hold of the skirt of the canopy and hung on; the parachute collapsed. When Joe got up, I started laughing. He said "What the hell's so funny?" I said 'look at your boots and pack-tray." The heels of his leather jump boots were worn almost all of the way through to his skin where he had been trying to 'dig in.' his pack-tray was worn through to the medal ribs which were the only things that saved the skin on his back.

Some of the other guys didn't fare as well. Ron Brown sprained his ankle and had to take a short jaunt to the hospital for treatment. Wil Charette landed on a hangar and fell off before he started his dragging trip south. He had bumps and bruises but otherwise was OK. All in all, we were pretty lucky. Those of us who could still walk reasonably well went by the helicopter where 'Scratch' Kanach and the other pilot were both shaking their heads and muttering something about 'dumb shits who jump out of perfectly functional aircraft!'

That night we decided that we were entitled to celebrate "Panama Survival Day" and headed into town. The night started innocently enough but somehow we ended up in a bar that was "OFF LIMITS" to military personnel. Don't ask me how, but we just had a knack for finding these places.

The night was going reasonably smooth. We were enjoying ourselves and causing no problems. The locals had accepted us as friendly "Gringos" and we were having a great time, when in walks the MP's; some of the *Team* escaped out of doors and windows, the rest of us hid as best we could. The MP's were not looking for us in particular, but for soldiers in general. They had no trouble finding us at all. In fact, we were puzzled as to how they walked right to us until we noticed our team mate, Al Solis, who was of Spanish decent, calmly sitting at the bar pointing us out to the MP's!!! They thought he was a local and never bothered him and he thought it was hilarious watching us squirm. "Hey senor MP, there's one over there." Pay backs were going to be hell!

Some of the escapees didn't fair much better.

Bill Edge and Bobby McDonnell walked by a police car when Bill decided to do some re-decorating. Not knowing that a policeman was watching, he ripped the red light off of the car. The next thing they heard was "Hey senor!" Bill turned around and was looking right smack into the muzzle of a 'cocked' 45 caliber pistol. This could have been career threatening to say the least. Bill would later say, "You have no idea how big one of those barrels is until you're looking into one."

The Saint that watches over fools, drunks, idiots and skydivers was working overtime that night. Bill didn't get his brains re-arranged by a bullet and we all just ended up in jail or what they called a jail. I wouldn't have liked to have spent any more time in there than absolutely necessary.

Much to his chagrin, Captain Perry was notified of our situation. He let us sweat it out for a while then came down and pleaded our case. It took some talking but he got us released in his custody.

There was one last memorable moment for that evening; Wil Charette got re-nicknamed 'Stinky' for a while. For some reason or another, he couldn't find his bunk so he just threw a mattress on the floor and went to sleep. As drunks often do in the wee hours of the morning, Ron Brown had to take a whiz. He stood up and because of his sprained ankle, or whatever reason, decided to just whiz where he was standing, which happened to be right over the top of Charette.

On March 1, 1961, a beat-up, bedraggled, but much wiser United States Army Parachute Demonstration Team bid a mixed emotion farewell to Howard Army Airfield, Panama Canal Zone.

The next few months were relative quiet. We spent most of the time back at Fort Bragg practicing routines for air shows and in my case; turns, loops and accuracy for the next competition.

I also continued to experiment with aerial photography using hand held cameras and helmet mounted cameras.

On April 20, 1961, we had the honor of putting on a demonstration at the Main Post Parade field for Cardinal Spellman. He was nice enough to bless a St. Jude medal and give one to each of us. I wasn't Catholic, but what the heck, it couldn't hurt; sure wish we had them in Panama.

In mid May, we went to Tyndall Air Force Base, just south of Panama City, Florida, to perform some high altitude demonstrations. There would be two jumps from 21,000 feet; unlike the test work in El Centro, these jumps would be for the general public and military dignitaries.

The day before the demo, Coy McDonald and I damn near drowned in the Gulf of Mexico. We didn't have bathing suits so we went swimming in our flight suits. We were trying to do some body surfing and before we realized it, the waves weren't carrying us in, but the current was carrying us out. Neither one of us had any idea what a riptide was, so we elected to try the shortest route to the beach—straight ahead. I was a very good swimmer and was once a life guard in high school, but I was making very little headway. I could measure it by looking at the pier down the beach, and I wasn't going any place. I figured my flight suit was creating too much drag so I decided to take it off and hold it under one arm. I did this for two reasons; one, I had nothing on but my white jockey shorts, and two; my St. Jude medal was in the pocket. But as hard as I swam I couldn't make any headway. It was getting critical now. I was beginning to tire. I saw that Coy had made it to the beach and was yelling encouragement to me. I let the flight suit go! The rip tide was so bad that Coy could only wade out up to his knees. At one point, I yelled to him that I didn't think I could make it. I remember his exact words, "Then you're going to die!" it wasn't a joke and there was no sarcasm in his voice. It was just a very accurate, chilling, perception. It gave me that extra ounce of determination to get close enough to grab his hand.

I half staggered and half crawled up onto the beach totally spent. I have never in my life, before or after this, been that exhausted. I was about one breath away from giving up and drowning. I lay on the beach for what seemed like hours, gasping. I didn't care who saw me in my shorts. Our hotel was across the street and somehow I made it to my room and laid down on the bed still panting for breath. The salt water on my lips was making me nauseous, so I showered and collapsed on the bed where I slept for about 18 hours. I later talked with Bill Edge, who was a beach life guard before entering the service, and he said "Dick, I've seen better swimmers than you go under in a rip tide." He also told me that rip tides were usually very narrow and if I ever found myself in that situation again, just swim parallel to the beach until you are out of it. Then it's easy to swim to shore. Why do I always find these things out after the fact.

The next day we climbed aboard the C-130 that would carry us to 21,000 feet for the demonstration. Again, we had the same supplemental oxygen setup as we did in El Centro during the test jumps.

One of our ex-enlisted members, Sergeant Roy Martin, had gone to OCS (Officers Candidate School) and was now a 2nd Lieutenant. He was the Team Executive Officer and was running the show today.

One of the big differences in today's jump, compared with the high altitude jumps in El Centro, was that we would be spotting ourselves or selecting the exit point instead of having it done by radar.

The take-off was normal and the climb out routine. It was a clear day and the view out over the emerald green water of the Gulf was fantastic. The drill would be the same as before; stay on ship's oxygen until we de-pressurized, then at the four minute warning we would go on bail-out bottles. As we began to de-pressurize, I looked down for my altimeter to see how fast the cabin was climbing. It wasn't there! I thought "Holy Shit, where's my instrument panel" then I remembered that I had re-packed my reserve parachute the day before and had forgotten to put the instrument panel back on. It was 21,000 feet below me in my parachute bag.

These high altitude jumps didn't come along every day. In fact, I would venture to say that there are parachutists today with thousands of jumps that have never been above 14,500 feet. Well, there was no way I was going to miss out on this jump. I had all kinds of references to judge my opening altitude. I could open when the other guys opened, I could open when people looked like ants. I could open when busses looked like cars or when "high rise's" looked like "outhouses". Or, I could open when I heard voices, but that's cutting it a little close! Anyway, I definitely kept my reserve parachute hidden from Lt. Martin!

The pilot gave us a green light indicating that we were approximately four minutes from the target. I pulled the little "green apple" lanyard on the bail-out bottle and felt my oxygen mask inflate with 100% pure oxygen. After unplugging from the ship's oxygen, I was independent of the aircraft. Loy Brydon and I would do the diamond track and from that altitude we would fall for 105 seconds. That would be 50 seconds out and 55 seconds back. We would get about a mile apart then turn and head back toward each other with a closure speed of over 130 miles an hour.

We checked our smoke brackets and smoke grenades then stepped up to the tail gate. What a beautiful sight. The Gulf of Mexico spread out on one side of the aircraft, and the state of Florida on the other with 21,000 feet of space underneath us. We pulled the lanyards on the smoke grenades and stepped out of the aircraft.

My direction of track was way out over the water. I was going like crazy and getting a long way out over the Gulf. I sure hoped that there wasn't an unknown wind pushing me out to sea like that damn riptide did. At 50 seconds (which I had to time on my stupid wrist watch) I turned 180 degrees and looked for Loy. I couldn't see him and the shore line was a long way off. I continued to track back to the opening point. I picked up Loy and started to adjust my fall so we would cross side by side (on each others right) and as close as possible. We crossed about 20 yards apart at the exact same altitude, waited for our altimeters to read 2,000 feet, or in my case, until the people looked like ants, and pulled. The spot was good so we both did standing landings in front of the bleachers to a big round of applause. We looked at each other and nodded. Damn nice jump. It seemed like we fell forever but it was only 1 minute and 45 seconds; or, 19,000 feet!

After our social obligations and meeting the dignitaries, we climbed on the bus which would take us back to the hotel. I told Lt. Martin about my instrument panel. He said "Yes, I noticed, but my bail-out bottle didn't work so I didn't figure I would say anything to you." I asked 'what did you do for breathing?" He said "I just took a deep breath of ship's oxygen and jumped." Hey, whatever works? I would put that phrase to the test the next day!

Jump number 504, May 20, 1961; another pretty day in Florida, and the opportunity to jump again from 21,000 feet. We went through the routine of 'chuting up (double checking our equipment), and yes, I had my instrument panel. We climbed aboard the C-130 and took off. We got to 21,500 feet and the pilot began to de-pressurize the aircraft. With that done, the flight engineer lowered the tail gate and we began a long approach to the drop zone. I was spotting and had radio communication with the pilot. The plan was to make just one pass. Everyone would jump and do what ever they wanted, kind of a "Joy Jump."

The first test came when the pilot turned on the green light indicating four minutes from drop. We all went on our bail-out bottles and unplugged from ship's oxygen. The next thing I heard over my headset was the pilot saying "Hey guys, I kind of miscalculated on that timing, we're probably seven or eight minutes out. You better get off of the bail-out bottles." I thought to myself "Get off of the bail-out bottle? What are you talking about, you idiot!" what I said was "These things don't have an on/off switch, once they're activated (which they were) they run from eight to eleven minutes, so I suggest you do whatever it takes to get this thing over the drop zone!" He said "OK" and the next thing I heard were the engines rev up. I have no idea how fast we were going when we got over the exit point. I do know that when I jumped there was kind of a vacuum right behind the aircraft. I looked up and saw everybody jumping, but there was no wind. Then it hit! I thought "Holy shit!" it about ripped my arms off. We had to be traveling in excess of 200 knots indicated airspeed. I finally got slowed down to a comfortable speed. The next test came when my oxygen bottle quit. I was at 18,000 feet and all of a sudden it felt like I had a plastic bag over my head; I couldn't breathe! I had to lift the bottom of my mask to take a breath, and there's damn little oxygen at that altitude. In fact, the atmospheric pressure is half of what it is at sea level. It seemed like it took forever for me to get my oxygen mask released on one side, but falling at over 120 miles an hour, I was finally at an altitude where breathing was easier. I looked to see where I was in relation to the opening point. Everything was OK. I continued the fall until 2,000 feet and saw parachutes starting to blossom around me, then I pulled.

After landing everyone was talking about how fast we were going when we exited. Danny Byard told me that he was right on top of me when I started fumbling with my oxygen mask. He had no idea what I was doing. He said when he saw my arms go in, he thought I was about to pull my rep-cord. It scared the hell out of him because he would have gone right through my parachute.

Well, thank God that day's activity was done. It was definitely Miller Time!

We returned to Ft. Bragg where in the next eight days I made 20 jumps, mostly relative work with General Stilwell, Danny Byard, Keith Jorgensen, Bobby Letbetter and Joe Norman. We then departed for a series of demonstrations—June 11th, Suffolk Virginia, June 13th, Fort Riley
Kansas, June 16th and 17th—Larson Air Force, Washington State. After that, we returned to Bragg to prepare for the 1961 United States National Parachuting Championships, which was being hosted by FT. Bragg.

Chapter 10

For the first time since parachuting became a sport, television decided to cover the National Championship. The ABC network sent a small crew of cameramen, a producer, and announcer Bud Palmer to Fort Bragg, none of them knowing what to expect. I was introduced to Bud Palmer who had heard of some of the aerial photography I had been doing and wanted to see some of it. After viewing it he asked if I would be willing to film some stuff before and after the Championship. I said "sure." They gave me a huge 35 millimeter camera that contained two reels of film. I made a makeshift bracket to attach it to my helmet, and with a wire coat hanger, made a square frame that stuck out about 5 inches in front of my face. It roughly resembled a TV screen and gave me something to sight with; crude by any stretch of the imagination, but it served the purpose. Some thirty years later, Bobby McDonnell found a copy of the film, had it made into a video and sent me a copy. It really wasn't that bad. The sponsors were Vitalis hair formula and Schlitz Beer. The man in the hair commercial was baseball player "Gentleman" Jim Gentile. The guy in the beer advertisement was some twit trying to put an end table together and had to get drunk before he could do it!

Jim Arender had been discharged from the Army and was competing as a civilian. He was the reigning World Style Champion, so naturally a lot of the filming would center on him. I did a number of aerial shots of Jim and other people which would be edited in later, along with a weird sound track. Bud conducted interviews with many of the jumpers, some spectators and a great interview with Colonel Bill Grieves. I emphasize this interview because, in one brief phrase, Colonel Bill changed the image and the perception of sport parachuting to the entire world forever. Bud Palmer asked, "Do you consider this a safe sport?" To which Colonel Bill replied, "There is less time lost to bodily injury in this sport than any other body contact sport including basketball. In fact I have a 16 year old daughter jumping and if I didn't consider it safe, I wouldn't let her do it." In those two sentences, and on national television, Colonel Grieves took Sport Parachuting out of the realm of the black leather jacketed daredevil, and made it respectable. Considering Bud Palmer's lack of knowledge of the Sport, and not knowing what to expect when he got here, I think he did a terrific job, and intensely contributed in the evaluation. I know he fit right in with the *Team*

Okay, now to the downside of the meet; after repeated requests from Colonel Bill and General Joe, nobody in the Pentagon would step out on a limb and allow the civilians to jump out of military aircraft, so we had to segregate the jumpers into military and civilian groups. Although it wouldn't effect the overall outcome of the meet, it took away some of the 'togetherness' and the 'camaraderie'. It made it feel as if civilians and military were competing against each other. That wasn't the case. We were all competing against the skill of anyone who had a parachute on his or her back.

We were still using 1.1 ounce rip stop nylon survival parachutes with that old familiar stamp on it (<u>CONDEMED</u>: not for personnel use), but we had gone from the 'blank gore' to the 'double blank gore' to the 'double "L"' and then to Brydon's brain storm, the 'Conquistador'. It seemed like the more material he cut out of the parachute the slower it came down and the more maneuverable it became. The 'Conquistador' looked like a giant "U" cut out of the back with one more panel cut out on each side of the bottom of the "U", which aided in the steer ability. Compared to today's standards, it was a dinosaur, but in 1961, it was the "cutting edge"; even if it did have <u>CONDEMED</u> stamped on it.

The meet was grand! It had been advertised locally so there were a lot of spectators. All of the parachutists were eager to mingle with onlookers and explain their equipment and brag about their home towns and parachute clubs. The spectators ate it up. Captain Perry also kept up a running commentary on what was taking place; who was jumping and a short background on each of the participants. He was very good at connecting with the audience.

There were a lot more civilian participants that year and the event was also being covered by Carol Carson of "*Skydiver Magazine*." More women were showing up in the competitions and, although they were doing the same events, there was a separate category and set of requirements established for them. It was based on the same limitations set forth in the World Championship. Basically, it meant they competed against women only and were limited as to what wind velocity they could jump in.

When I think of that year of female participants, the person that comes to mind is a very nice, unassuming young lady named Roxanne Rogers. She even looked like a "Roxanne Rogers." Blond hair, blue eyes, knockout figure and a personality that said "Hi, I'm Roxanne Rogers and I'm very pleased to meet you!" She looked like anything but a sky diver, but she was out there, facing the high winds and jumping out of airplanes like the rest of us. She was one of those "Beautiful People" that wasn't impressed with that fact. I've often wondered what happened to her and hoped that it was all nice things! "Hi Roxanne!"

The Nationals lasted two weeks and were filled, as always, with joys, frustrations, fellowship, winners and losers; although I personally don't think that anyone ever lost in those competitions. Everyone gained something, whether it was a new friend, better respect of the competition, more knowledge or just a better overview of your own self esteem.

Jim Arender, the style champion of the world, won the style event. I was second place following by two tenths of a second and Leroy K. Smith, of the *Golden Knights*, was third.

For the overall championship, the *Golden Knights* swept the field; 2nd place went to Gerald Bourquin, 3rd place was Coy McDonald and the National Champion was yours truly, Dick Fortenberry. I couldn't help but have a flash back to that young teenager sitting in the Fox theater in Banning California and think, "I'm not only running with the big dogs, now I AM the big dog! Or the Biggest Dog in the United States anyway". I would learn, later, what an awesome responsibility that can be.

We spent until July 29th training for the International Invitational Parachute Meet that was to be held in La Ferte-Gaucher, France—a quaint little town about 30 miles East of Paris on the Morin River.

We had no civilian members on the *Team* and no female members. The *"Golden Knights"* had swept the U. S. Nationals and the United States had yet to field a full women's team, plus, this meet was not considered a big event on an international scale. There were only four countries competing, The United States, France, Russia and Bulgaria.

The U.S. Delegation consisted of Colonel Bill Grieves, Head of Delegation; Captain Jim Perry, Team Leader and Judge; Sergeant Don Kidd, Public Relations and competitors Danny Byard, Jerry Bourquin, Jim Pearson, Loy Brydon and myself.

The trip over was much more affable than the previous one. We were in a four engine turbo-prop Lockheed Electra which was much faster than the DC-6 and a hell of a lot more comfortable. After arriving in Paris, we boarded a bus for the pleasant little ride to La Ferte-Gaucher.

The drop zone, Slash Airport, was a small grass field surrounded by small farms and villages where the pilots could take off and land in any direction they wanted. This meant that they never had a cross wind, which was very convenient. We were also introduced to a new jump platform, the De Haviland dragon. It was a small, twin engine bi-wing tail dragger, with fixed landing gear and fixed pitch propellers. The whole airplane was fabric covered making it very light. The plane was flown by a single pilot located in the center of the nose, which gave him an excellent view. As for the parachutist, spotting was a nightmare. The jump door was located just behind the left, bottom wing. In order for the jumper to guide the aircraft over the exit point, he or she would have to lie on the floor, stick their head out of the door and look under the wing. Still, I thought it was a gorgeous airplane. The designer was, obviously, an artist at heart. One of those people who thought that it was as easy to build a pretty airplane as it was to build an ugly one.

Speaking of pretty, the Bulgarian Team had two girls that besides being very good parachutists were knock out hard bodies by any standards. But what got our attention was when they got ready to pack their parachutes after each jump. With the heat being what it was we all took off our jump suits and packed in various stages of dress like T-shirts and shorts or cut-offs. They stripped down to bras and panties and 'holy shit', they were the see-through type. They were little skimpy, flowery things that left nothing to the imagination. I thought 'Man, if this is another Communist ploy, bring it on.'

The meet started out as all others did. First there were the psyche games and the "sizing up." This didn't take long because all of the team members were the same ones that had competed in Sophia. The first day each team member was granted two practice jumps. This let us shake out our equipment and check the other team's equipment for new innovations. There were none. It also let us get familiar with the "Dragon", the drop zone and it's surrounding area.

We were quartered in old military type barracks that were constantly cold and drafty but the food was hot, hearty, good and plentiful. To our surprise, there was always wine and beer on the table, even during the noon meal. The French thought nothing of having wine with their meal and then making a parachute jump. We Americans abstained until the evening where we made up for lost time!

When the competition started, the U.S. Team was hot. We jumped right out to an early points lead and continued to improve on it. We were in competition from the 11th to the 19th of August and never once fell out of first place. This so rattled the other teams that it became a three against one competition. The atmosphere seemed like 'Somebody get them! Somebody stop the Americans. "Anybody!"

The Russians got so far behind that it was a little embarrassing. There were a number of occasions where a coach ran out to the target, grabbed a jumper by his parachute harness, yanking him to his feet, berating him. It was very unprofessional and so Russian. On one occasion, the competitor was so frustrated that he shoved the coach, who fell on his ass. And, of course we didn't help matters by applauding. In the years to come we never saw that parachutist in another meet, but we never forgot him.

The meet went extremely well for us except in one instance. During the last event, style, Jim Pearson came in complaining about a buffet on the completion of his last loop. He said "the judges couldn't have missed it, I stood almost straight up. It's got to be a point reduction". We all sympathized with him and tried to give him encouragement. At the time, I was standing in first place overall, with a fairly comfortable lead. Later that afternoon, Captain Perry came and floored me with "Dick, the judges penalized you seventeen and a half points for your buffet". I said "I didn't have a buffet". He said "Yes you did, we all saw it". I said "I never buffeted. You obviously got me mixed up with someone else or got us out of sequence during your judging". I didn't want to point the finger at Jim, I was hoping that he would stand up to it, but he didn't. Captain Perry said "We all saw it, you buffeted". I said "You're all full of shit, I didn't buffet". Captain Perry gave me that Company Commander look and said "All of us"? I said "Every damned one of you!" It was getting pretty well out of hand and I was going to come out the loser either way, so Colonel Grieves stepped in and defused it. I got the penalty and went from first place to fifth. I never could figure Captain Perry's stand on the matter. It didn't advance our cause at all. I think he was just pissed at me and being hard headed.

But, when it was all over, the U.S. won 1st Place Individual Style, 1st Place Individual Accuracy, 1st Place Team Accuracy and 1st Place Team Overall. We got the parachuting worlds attention and hopefully set the stage for the next World Championship which was to be held in the United States in a little town named Orange, Massachusetts.

Chapter 11

The trip back from La Ferte Gaucher was uneventful until we started our descent into Andrews Air Force Base. We were all sitting there FD&H (Fat Dumb and Happy) when all of a sudden the aircraft gave two violent lurches in opposite directions. On the last one, we ended up almost in a 90 degree bank. Anyone standing up was thrown all over the place. We had cabin attendants scattered all over the aircraft. I had a fresh cup of piping hot coffee in my hand and it became obvious that I was going to spill it some place; so, I just dumped it in Jerry Bourquins lap. He wasn't any to happy about it but I felt better! We later found out that we almost had a mid-air collision with a C-133 that was on climb out.

The *Team* popularity was growing and the demonstration schedule was demanding. On the first of September, 1961, we hit the road again with two separate schedules. The easiest one was a one day demonstration for the Civil Air Patrol day at Wilmington, North Carolina, then return to Fort Bragg until the Inner Service Parachute Meet in Fort Campbell, Ky., beginning on October the 6th. I was assigned this demonstration and was looking forward to a few days at home. The other, and more demanding schedule was to attend the National Aviation Association (NAA) Convention in New York City and spend a little over a week jumping into the Roosevelt Raceway on Long Island. From there, the *Team* would go to the Oklahoma State Fair in Oklahoma City until the 30th, when they would proceed to Fort Campbell and meet up with the rest of the Competition Team for the Inner Service Meet.

Fate has a strange way of dealing its cards and you never know what kind of hand you have until fate decides to show you.

The day before the team members slated to go to New York left, Jim Pearson, who had recently graduated from Officers Candidate School and was now a 2nd Lieutenant and Executive Officer of the *Team*, called me in to announce a change of schedule. The NAA had just voted me as the 1961 recipient of the Helms Foundation Award for Sport Parachuting Athlete of the year and I would have to go to the Convention to receive it. Although I was extremely happy about the award, I wasn't looking forward to the long trip. But, anyway, at the last minute, I traded trips with Joe Norman.

The Roosevelt Raceway on Long Island was a quarter mile track designed for trotting horses surrounded by interstate highways, parking lots full of cars, telephone wires and back yard Bar-B-Q sets, a tough place to locate from 14,500 feet much less land on. The predominant winds were fast and gusty and required that the final approach be made over the bleachers, which were about five stories high. We were still using the Conquistador or TU parachutes, so the entire approach and landing would be tricky to say the least. If you missed, you either got run over by a truck or cooked either by high voltage wires or someone's Bar-B-Q. We would make one jump every other day for a total of five jumps. The Army had loaned us an

AC-1 Caribou, which was a twin engine STOL aircraft with two side doors or a tail gate style ramp to jump from; this was a luxury for us. The aircraft was roomy and could climb to altitude rather quickly.

My first jump was a baton pass with Danny Byard. It went smooth, but the remarks in my log book says 'crabbed all the way' or if you are a sailor, it would be like 'tacking,' but we made the raceway.

The next jump was a little more eventful. Ralph Palmer hung out a little too long for his final approach and when it became obvious that he could not clear the bleachers; he elected to land in the parking lot. Now, mind you, there are attendants and cars moving and parking all over the place. Ralph picked the best spot he could under the circumstances and crashed. He hit the pavement hard and slid up under a parked car right in front of an astonished parking attendant. In obvious pain with his newly acquired broken leg, Ralph looked up at the attendant, whose jaw was hanging down somewhere around his navel, and asked "Is this spot taken?" He drew quite a crowd, and wouldn't you know it, one of them helped him by picking up his reserve parachute by that convenient, shiny, handle.

The next evening was the conventions awards ceremony and I really didn't know what to expect. I was briefed that when my name was called, to proceed to the podium, receive the award and leave. Simple enough.

When it came time, they announced "And to present the Helms Foundation Award for Sport Parachuting Athlete of the year, Mrs. Jackie Cochran". Holy shit, it was the famous aviatrix who held more awards and trophies than any other woman in aviation. She was born Jacqueline Cochran in Pensacola, Florida in 1910. An orphan, she left her foster home at an early age, and by 1935 had her pilot's license and a cosmetics firm. She was the first woman to fly in the Bendix Trophy Transcontinental Race (1934), to win it (1938, the year I was born), to fly a bomber across the Atlantic Ocean (1941), and to receive the Distinguished Service Medal (1945, as head of the WASP, Women's Air force Service Pilots of World War II). She was the first woman to break the sound barrier (1953), to take off and land on an aircraft carrier (1960), to attain a speed of 842 mph (1961) and to serve as president of the F.A.I., Federation Aeronautique Internationale (she was elected in 1959).

As a pilot Jackie received more than 200 awards and trophies. Her autobiography, *The Stars at Noon*, was published in 1954, and here she was, presenting me an award that faded by comparison. Mrs. Cochran presented me the trophy, shook my hand and in a conspiratorial voice, told me, "This is one award I don't think I ever wanted." and then laughed that hearty laugh of hers. What a thrill!

Our next jump was a little out of the ordinary. The Roosevelt Raceway is located on the final approach course for a number of airports in the New York area including JFK and La Guardia. On our jump runs, the Caribou pilots would get approval from New York Center to make our jump run. Today, Jerry Bourquin and I were going to do the "Diamond Track". I was spotting, and as we started our final approach on the jump run, I noticed a jet airliner approaching underneath us on our same course. We were at 14,500 feet and the airliner appeared to be about 5,000 feet below us. I kept waiting for our pilots to turn on the red light to scrub the jump run, but it stayed green. Jerry and I looked at each other and shrugged our shoulders. I continued toguide the Caribou to the exit point and the airliner continued on its course to whatever airport. When we reached the exit point, I looked at Jerry and he just grinned. I nodded my head and away we went. When we got out, it was obvious that we would be directly beside it when we reached the same level. I began my track to the right and Jerry began his to the left. We passed about 200 or 300 yards on each side of the aircraft, turned, tracked and crossed underneath it. We made a perfect red diamond around the airliner. I can't imagine what anyone would have thought, especially the pilots, if they were looking out and saw us. Nothing was ever said about it, so we just filed it under 'another weird experience.'

Our last jump was made on September 18th and would be a mass, formation jump. We all got out at the same time, formed into a formation and held that until about 4,000 feet where we all turned and started tracking in every direction, creating a "bomb burst" effect. When we opened, it was obvious that we were a little short, or close to the raceway. Unfortunately, Danny Byard, who weighted less than any of us, had tracked back toward the raceway and it was going to be dicey whether he made it or not. The rest of us landed and watched as Danny continued to hold into the wind and drift toward a high wooden fence that bordered the raceway. The crowed began to murmur as the struggle between parachute and wind began to loose against the gap between them and the fence. There was a collective groan as Danny's feet hit the fence and he disappeared backwards behind it. A silence fell over the entire stadium and just hung there. Then, an arm appeared over the fence, followed by a leg and then the grinning face of Danny peered over the fence. The crowed let out a tremendous roar. It seemed to be the most exciting thing that had happened to them all week!

We spent that afternoon as we did at most demonstrations, signing autographs, mingling with the crowed and answering questions. I always enjoyed this time. The people were always very interested in our activities and asked good questions. "How fast do you fall?" "How hard is the opening shock?" "How does the parachute work?" "How hard is the landing?" "Are you scared?" etc. We always tried to give them straight answers and to impress on them how safe Sport Parachuting was. I always let them know how small the malfunction rate was on the parachutes, how few injuries we received and dispel any image they might have of us being hell-bent-for-leather daredevils.

We stayed on Long Island for the remainder of the NAA Convention then departed for the State Fair in Oklahoma City and the most devastating news that I would ever receive during my five year tour with the *Golden Knights!*

We all looked forward to this demonstration. State Fairs were a lot of fun. The crowds were always happy and it was usually a family affair which meant lots of excited kids, they were my favorite audience. Plus, speaking of excited kids, the *Team* usually got a lot of free rides! The demonstration would consist of the normal routine for an 'open arena,' meaning that the surrounding area had lots of open spaces such as farms and meadows. We would perform the Baton Pass, the Max Track and the formation with bomb burst. We decided against the cut-a-way, it wasn't quite that open.

On the 21st, we went to the fair grounds to look over the surrounding area, pick out alternate landing areas (just in case), and pick out the high risk (stay away from) areas and to just hang out.

The fairgrounds were already packed when we arrived. All activities like this had a Public Relations Coordinator whose job it was to maximize the publicity impact on the event. The PR man introduced us to a fascinating and very flamboyant guy named Joe E. Chitwood. He was a stunt driver with a flair for dramatics, but he gave the audience their money's worth. He was the first man to drive a car on two wheels like a bicycle (I wonder how many cars you destroy practicing that?). He had a group of stunt drivers that did everything from the bicycle bit, jumping from ramp to ramp while another car drives under you, and lots of crashes. Like anyone else, Mr. Chitwood had to do some practicing and the PR guy said "Anybody want to ride along?" I forget who exactly took him up on it, but a couple of the *Team* members rode with him. I said "I'll pass!"

We also met a group of go-cart racers who let us drive their go-carts. These weren't your everyday, run-of-the-mill go-carts. These babies had two and sometimes three chain-saw engines. They said that one of them had been clocked at 120 mph. They sure were fun to drive! The first time I drove one, the owner told me to take it easy around the first lap in order for the engines to warm up. I did just that, hand choking the engines to keep them running smooth. When they seemed to be running good on their own, I 'floored' it. The acceleration was so rapid that it scared the hell out of me. My head snapped back and my hands almost came off of the steering wheel. This was, obviously, no toy. After we started to get the hang of it, we had some pretty heated races. I was feeling like Sterling Moss (boy that dates me); when a ten year old kid put me in my place by going around the outside of me on a curve. He passed me like I was sitting still. 'Brat!'

Well, we were just having a hell of a time when word got to us that Captain Perry wanted all of us to report back to the hotel for a briefing. Our first reaction was what the hell could he want? We are having such a great time and we have all of the information that we need for the demonstration, but we all headed for the hotel. When we arrived, everyone was a little apprehensive and was asking, "Anybody know what this is all about?" No one did or could even make a good guess, but when Captain Perry walked in, we knew it was bad by the look on his face. He got right to the point. "Gentlemen, I have some very bad news. At 1330 hours, Eastern Standard Time, the rest of the *Team* in Wilmington was involved in a plane crash. I don't know to what extent the damages are at this point, but I have been informed that Bob Turner (our *Team* photographer) was killed." A stunned silence followed. I had to sit down. I was remembering that at the last minute, I had changed places with Joe Norman. Captain Perry continued. "There were other fatalities, but we don't know if they were *team* members or not." The *Team* was scheduled to jump an H-21 helicopter, but at the last minute, the 'Thunderbirds' offered their C-123 cargo aircraft. Besides the *Team*, there were some civilian photographers and a crew of three on board. They apparently crashed on take-off." Everyone was sitting now. Captain Perry said "The other reason that I called you here is that we have a decision to make. I will ask for and respect youropinion on this. Do we go home and try to comfort the *Team*, or do we stay here and fulfill our obligation to the people of Oklahoma?"

We asked Captain Perry numerous questions, for which he had very few answers. He said that if we elected to stay, he would keep us completely informed of the details as he received them. We discussed it thoroughly and decided that at this stage, the *Team* was receiving the best medical attention possible and that there wasn't much else we could do. We also felt that if the situation were reversed, we would want the *Team* to continue. Captain Perry said "OK then, we stay and perform. But I'll leave the option open that if you decide at any point it would be better to return to Fort Bragg, we'll leave."

It would be three days before we made our first demonstration. They were spent sitting around the hotel lobby or in our rooms mulling over the situation. I think it was one of the first times I really started thinking about my mortality. I remember that Danny and I talked about it a lot. Were we prepared to die? What did that mean exactly? I know that I didn't want to die. There were too many things that I hadn't done or accomplished yet. But I don't think I was afraid to die as long as it wasn't a useless or stupid death like a car accident. If I was, I don't think I would be in this particular profession. But I did know that I wasn't prepared to die right now.

What does prepared mean? I think it means different things to different people. To some, it is a religious preparation. 'Have I led a good life, and am I prepared to meet my maker?' To some it is 'Have I lived my life fully?' To others it may be 'I'm too young to die!'

I think it has had different meanings to me as the years passed and the situations changed. I probably went through all of the reasons mentioned above, but it has finally come down to a couple of things. First, I hope that nobody that I've met through the years is going to be glad that I'm dead. And second, I don't want my family to be inconvenienced. I want to have, through the years, prepared them mentally and provided them financially for my departure. Sure, I want them to mourn me briefly, that will just prove that they loved me. But then I want them to, as my friend Saul would say "Deal with it," and get on with your lives.

Personally, I don't think anyone's ever completely prepared for death. It's like if you have a very close loved one, father, mother, etc., that has a long terminal illness. You know they are going to die, and in most cases, approximately when, but when death comes it is still a shock. I think the closest I ever was to being prepared for old man death, was in Vietnam. One time, I took a round through the door jam, just six inches from my head.

I've already instructed Linda on what I want on my tombstone, and if she doesn't do it, I'll come back to haunt her. 'IT'S BEEN A LONG STRANGE JOURNEY. NOW WHAT?'

The next day, we received most of the particulars of the crash and the cause was debatable. The pilots had decided to demonstrate a 'maximum performance' take-off. In doing so, the aircraft would be right on the verge of a stall throughout the initial take-off and climb stage. This was an approved maneuver, and in military operations, was done routinely. On this particular day, it stalled. Which means the wings lost all lift and the aircraft just fell out of the sky. They estimated that it hit the ground at approximately 80 mph forward and 80 mph down. The wing caved in on the aircraft and caught on fire.

One horrifying aspect of the incident was that it was televised, and as soon as it hit the ground, the cameras zoomed right in on it. All of the *Team* member's wives and children in Fayetteville and Fort Bragg were watching!

As the details came in, we found out that Sgt. Turner was the only *Team* member killed but that the co-pilot and flight engineer were killed on impact. Two civilian photographers would later die at the Fort Sam Houston Burn Center, in San Antonio, Texas.

Jim Pearson and Joe Norman were the least hurt. A silent 'thank you' went up to my God. Jim was unconscious outside of the aircraft with just bumps and bruises, but damn near suffocated in the foam that was used to put out the fire. Joe Norman had been standing in the door on take-off when he felt the airplane shudder. He later said that he just turned and sat down with his back toward the wall of the wheel-well, and the lights went out! All he had was a cracked pelvis and a terrible case of stomach gas.

The rest of the *Team* didn't fair so well. 1st Sgt. John Hollis suffered a broken back in which his tail bone went into the floor of the aircraft. He would spend many months in a full body cast; Wil Charette had a broken pelvis, jaw and a mangled right hand which required pins to hold it together. Bobby Letbetter had a broken jaw and a hole the size of a half dollar in the front of his skull. He also had to have a tracheotomy (a hole cut into the throat and wind pipe in order to breathe). Both he and Wil had their jaws wired shut and a tooth extracted through which they could receive liquid nourishment through a straw.

The worst and most critically injured, was Bobby McDonnell. He had been pinned under the wing with burning hydraulic fluid spraying all over him. As soon as he was stable enough, he was medically evacuated to Fort Sam in extremely critical condition with third degree burns over half of his body. His left hand was burned so badly that he eventually lost most of the fingers on it. He lost the two middle fingers on his right hand. The tops of his ears were burned off along with part of his nose and the hair on the top of his head. Both elbows were burned right down to the bone. The doctors gave him less than a 50/50 chance of surviving, and if he did he would go through years of plastic surgeries and operations.

Bob Turner had been decapitated by a loose tool box that sailed the length of the aircraft and hit him.

The fact that anyone survived was attributed to an Air Force helicopter crew that had a Kaman 'Husky' on static display. The 'Husky' had twin, opposing, rotor-blades offset at an angle and counter-rotating to counterbalance the effects of torque. It was specifically designed to fight aircraft fires by hovering over the top of the crash site and blowing the smoke and fire away from the wreckage.

When the Thunderbird C-123 crashed, the 'Husky' crew immediately jumped into the helicopter and hovered over the crash providing fresh air to the rescue teams and blowing the flames away from the survivors pinned in the crash. I hope they got some kind of medal for their quick response, because they certainly deserved it.

Years later, while researching information for these writings, I called Bobby in Glen Cove New York and asked him when the crash occurred. He said, "At approximately 1:31 P.M. on the afternoon of September 21, 1961." Because none of the *Team* members ever remembered the crash, I asked, "How did you know the exact time?" He said, "That's when my watch stopped!"

We made our first Demonstration at the State Fair on the 25th.

As we normally took off from an airport located some distance from the jump site, we very seldom had any idea of the size of the spectators until we landed. Today was no exception.

It was a relatively clear day with good visibility, so we would do the 'high' demo from 14,500 feet. Danny and I would perform the 'baton pass' while the other *Team* members did the 'diamond track' and 'formation with bomb burst'.

Danny and I got out first and made contact. We held onto the baton and began our spin to give the red smoke coming from the smoke grenades a 'barber pole' effect. At 3,000 feet, we separated. At 2,000 feet we pulled the rip-cords and opened. After opening, it always got very quiet hanging there in the harness, and you could hear a few sounds from the ground. That day I heard a roar like I had never heard before. I looked down from about 1,800 feet and saw a mass of humanity. It seemed like every person at the fair was at the landing site to watch our demonstration. After the last jumper landed, the crowd descended upon us. They began to shake our hands, pat us on the backs, thanking us and telling us how great we were. I couldn't figure it out for a minute, and then found out that it had been announced over the P.A. system about the crash and our decision to remain and complete the demonstrations. The crowd was very appreciative and sympathetic. For the next five days, we would draw very large crowds. The demonstrations were routine except on one jump I lost my watch, but later I found it wedged between my instrument panel and reserve parachute. Danny lost his wallet only to have it returned in the mail some weeks later with everything intact including the money. A farmer found it in his field; things like that renewed your faith in the human race!

The guys back at Bragg were taken off of the critical list and upgraded to serious. Bobby was still very much on the critical list but still alive. Each day he continued to live made his chances of survival better.

We were scheduled to go to Fort Campbell, Kentucky for an inner service competition before returning home, but we were determined to get back to Bragg and try to help our comrades. But it was them who asked us to go to Campbell and 'kick butt.' So we did. And we 'kicked butt!'

It was at Fort Campbell that I first met Brigadier General William C. Westmoreland, who would have a small hand in my career later on. I also met someone whom I would always have a very high regard for; Father Walldey, simply referred to as 'Padre' by the *Team* members. Father Walldey was an Army Catholic Chaplain, and the first time I ever laid eyes on him was on Yomoto Drop Zone at Fort Campbell.

Yomoto was a grassy, rock hard, Drop Zone with the one tree (that I mentioned earlier) right in the middle of it. On one jump I landed particularly hard and after gathering my parachute up in my arms and starting to walk off of the D.Z., I heard a loud 'THUD' immediately followed by 'son-of-a-bitch!' Someone had just had one of those hard landings that rattle your teeth. I turned around and saw a Captain picking himself up and brushing himself off. I thought nothing of it and started to turn around when I noticed the silver cross on his collar. I thought holy shit, it's a chaplain! That was 'Padre'.

In later years, 'Padre' would ascend to the rank of Full Colonel and become the Chief Chaplain in the United States Army.

One story went, (and I don't doubt it for a second), that Father Walldey was sent to Camp Lajuene Marine Corps Base in North Carolina to give a talk to their Chaplains. No one had ever seen him before and had no idea what he looked like. They sent a First Lieutenant, Assistant Chaplain to the airport to meet him, and all he could do was wait for an Army Colonel with a cross on his collar to get off the airplane. When the Lieutenant saw him coming down the aircraft stairs, he said "Excuse me, are you Father Walledy." at which Father Walledy replied, "You're fuckin' right I am!" That was 'Padre!

145

For us, the Parachute Meet was an enormous success. We won every first place trophy there.

When we arrived back a Bragg, we went straight from Pope Air Force Base to Womack Army Hospital. We got out of the bus and walked into the administrations room with all of our trophies and asked, "What floor are the *Golden Knights* on?" A Sergeant told us but added, "You can't go up there in flight suits with those things in your hands." Somebody said, "Watch us!" As we started for the elevators, I saw the Sergeant reach for a telephone, but the only person who came up was a nurse to see if we needed anything.

We walked in and said, "Hey guys, look what we brought you". No one tried to hold anything back. Hugs and tears for everybody. Even the nurse left crying. After hugging everyone I could without hurting them I walked over to Sgt. Hollis and said, "Hi 'Top," he was in a full body cast and couldn't move any thing but his arms and hands. Big tears came in his eyes and he said, "Dick, I don't think I've ever felt lower." I said, "I know 'Top." He continued, "It just hurts so bad seeing these guys all mangled up like this."

I reminded him, "We know. None of us do, but you don't look like a bed of roses yourself." He said, "I can handle that, but it just hurts so much to see them in pain."

I believe on that day the *Team* consummated a bond that lives to this day and will continue forever!

Dick Fortenberry Orange Mass VI World Championship

Dick Fortenberry Early Aerial Photography 1960

**Sophia Bulgaria V World Championship 1960 (left to right)
Dick Fortenberry, Zednik Kaplan and a Russian**

**Returning from Bulgaria Dick Fortenberry with cast
Joe Crane and James Arender**

Portoroz (left to right) Phil Van DerWeg, Loy Brydon, Coy McDonald, Jerry Bourquin, Dick Fortenberry & Deke Sonnicsin

WaterJump Portoroz Yugoslavia that cost
Dick Fortenberry 50 points

Team Briefing

**Orange Massachusetts (left to right) Dick, Borquin,
Arender, Brydon**

Dick Fortenberry 1964 Team Training

1964 U.S. Parachute Team

Men's Team: L to R: Loy Brydon, Coy McDonald, Dick Fortenberry, Jerry Bourquin, Bill Berg, Ron Sewell.
Women's Team: L to R: Gladys Inman, Anne Batterson, Eve Taylor, Carol Penrod, Maxine Hartman.

1964 US World Parachute Team

**Col Bill Grieves being Briefed on Dirt
Diving by General Joe**

Chapter 12

The real healing process started after our reunion. You could tell by the rise in their morale, their humor and the amount of pranks they began to play. Some of these stories became legendary and would be told over and over through the years at various reunions.

It was as if, somehow, we could either assimilate part of their pain, or they absorbed our energy, and it lingered on after we parted. They followed every event that we performed in and we in turn brought every trophy to the hospital. The hospital gave us free rein to visit almost any time. The only exceptions were meal times and during the rounds.

August 31st found us back at Tyndall Air Force Base for some high altitude demonstrations. We were to make three demos from 22,500 feet, 21,000 feet and 27,000 feet respectively. We were all hyped about it because it was only the second time that we had ever gone above 25,000 feet.

Again, we would be spotting ourselves, as opposed to radar telling us when to get out. We would still go through the procedure of dropping a wind drift indicator at 2,000 feet in order to obtain an opening point. But then we had to get the upstairs winds, in layers, to decide where the exit point would be. The winds at those altitudes could be in excess of 100 mph if the jet stream was in the area. And it was.

The first jump was on October 31ˢᵗ and the weather was fabulous. Light surface winds and the visibility was "severe clear", meaning, you could see forever. Summer was over and the temperature was in the mid 70's. It would be just one pass at 22,500 feet. Because of the velocity of the winds at the higher altitudes, the exit point would be well out over the water (approximately a mile). We would perform the formation jump with a bomb burst at the bottom. The free-fall would last 1 minute and 55 seconds, and would appear as one smoke until about 3,500 feet, when we would separate. At that point, the one smoke would split into five, headed in five different directions (the bomb burst). Also, by falling in formation, (we could touch each other if we wanted to), the formation leader could keep track of our position relative to the opening point and adjust accordingly. I was to be number two in the formation, which would place me right off the leader's right foot. Simple enough. We had practiced and performed this many times. But, as my friend Saul would say, "Never stand flat footed!"

Because the outside air temperature at 25,000 feet would be well below zero degrees Fahrenheit, the pilots kept the aircraft well heated until time to lower the 'tail-gate'. As I recall, SFC Bill Edge was the formation leader. When he gave the signal to go, we followed him one at a time off of the ramp. My body heat was pretty high and as soon as I hit the sub-zero temperatures, my goggles fogged over.

I need to explain a couple of things here. One, I very seldom wore goggles, but at high altitudes and these temperatures, you needed them to keep the tears in your eyes from freezing. Second, the goggles I had on were of the World War II aviator type. They were glass with felt trimming with no air holes. Furthermore I had the band around my head, under the helmet, so they were pretty well fixed.

So, as soon as I got out of the aircraft, I was blind. I couldn't see my nose, much less the rest of the formation. I couldn't take them off because the band was under the helmet and besides, I didn't want my eyes to freeze. I reached up and lifted them off of my face to get air underneath and clear them. I did, but my eyes began to get cold so I put them back on. As soon as I did, they fogged up! Well, I figured 'What the hell, I'll just fall blind for a few thousand feet, or until it gets warmer and rip them off.' Now, that's a weird sensation, and a little scary! For the first time in my life I found myself falling at about 200 mph thinking about something totally unrelated to the task at hand. I wonder if anybody is going to the club tonight. What uniform should I wear for tomorrow's demonstration? Wait a minute, get back to what you are doing here! What does the temperature feel like? How long have I been falling? The rest of the *Team* and the spectators must have thought, 'Where is that yahoo going?' A nice formation with one lone smoke drifting off on his own.

I tried to rip off my goggles, but they were designed to stand the stress of combat and refused to break. I couldn't get them down around my neck because of the oxygen mask. First, I would have to release the mask. The oxygen masks were old vintage and didn't have the quick release hardware available today. I had to push in a release button on the male fitting with my thumb, and with my index finger pull the female fitting over the top of the latch. Not a problem standing on the ground, but falling blind at some

150 mph while breathing backwards adds a new dimension. Anyway, I got the mask released and pulled the goggles down over my chin. First, I glanced at my altimeter, then at my position across the ground. I was at about 10,000 feet and pretty close to where I should be, but I couldn't see the rest of the *Team*. I felt like the proverbial ostrich that walked up to all of the other ostriches with their heads buried in the sand and said "Hey, where did everybody go?"

I figured out later, that the reason I couldn't see the *Team* was by falling in formation they created more drag than me falling alone, and they were above me when it came time to open. We all landed in front of the spectators and after the obligatory question and answer period with the spectators, we packed up and left the drop zone. On the way out, Bill Edge walked up and said "What was that all about?" I gave him one of those 'Groucho Marx looks and said "There's some weird shit out there man. I mean, weird!" Well, for a man that loved to read Greek Mythology, he wasn't about to pursue that. He gave me a look like I had just dropped in from another planet, shook his head and walked off.

The next days jump from 21,000 feet was uneventful. A perfect 1 minute and 48 second formation fall with bomb burst. I had gotten myself a set of goggles with air holes in the sides. No one can accuse me of being a slow learner.

On our last day at Tyndall, we jumped from 27,000 feet, just 3,000 short of our record. We were trying to get higher, but the outside air temperature (52 degrees below zero) was too warm for the C-130 to climb that high. My log book records Five-way baton pass between Bill Edge (D-23), Danny Byard (D-11), Coy McDonald (D-70), Jerry Bourquin (D-22) and myself,(D-38). The fall was 2 minutes and 10 seconds. Again, it was another 'shitty day in paradise,' surface temperature 75 degrees, clear skies and CAVU (ceiling and visibility unlimited).

On the final jump run, we went on bail-out bottles unplugged from ships oxygen and waited for Bill to give the "Go" signal. When he pulled his lanyard on his smoke grenades, one blew the igniter completely out of the grenade and the full length of the aircraft. Luckily, no one was behind it, but it also blew Bill of the tail-gate. We all followed.

The high altitude winds had died out some and after making the five-way pass, we formed up and began tracking toward land. At a horizontal ground speed of over 50 mph, it was pretty impressive. We performed the bomb burst opened and all made standing landings right in front of the spectator's bleachers.

With this mission over we were anxious to return to Bragg and see how the guys in the hospital were doing.

Well, what they were doing was driving everybody crazy—hospital staff and patients.

Wil Charette was constipated for the first week or so after the crash and had to have an enema, at least once a day. The doctors and nurses began to refer to it as 'Charette's prayer meeting' because after closing the curtains all you could hear was Charette saying "God . . . God . . . God! Oh God . . . God . . . God . . . !" One day the nurse had the curtain pulled and said "I can't seem to find the hole." At which Joe Norman said "Why don't you just sprinkle talcum powder over his ass and wait 'til he farts?" This brought the ward down! After this dilemma was over and Wil could handle his own toilet necessities, they gave him a wheel chair to go to and from the latrine. But not Wil! He began to wheel it up and down the halls visiting with people, so they took it away from him and replaced it with crutches. Now mind you, he still had a cracked pelvis, so he used the crutches to go up and down the hall and socialize. So they took his crutches away from him. So, he just walked up and down the halls. So . . . . They took his pajamas away from him.

Wil also had a half cast on his shattered hand which could be taken off when the doctor wanted to examine it. One day the injured *Team* members took the cast off of his bad hand and put it on his good hand. When the doctor came around with some interns, he took the cast off and said "Flex your fingers", at which Wil did. The doctor said "Squeeze my hand", at which Wil really gave him a grip. While replacing the cast, the doctor gave the interns a briefing about how amazing it was that "this man was in a crash not three weeks ago and the mending process is remarkable!" After he left, the *Team* took the cast off and put it back onto the injured hand.

Another Charette story was, one day during an examination of his hand, he asked the doctor in a somewhat melancholy tone, "Doc, do you think I will be able to play the guitar when the cast comes off?" At which the doctor replied, "I don't see why not. The hand is mending very well." Wil perked up and said "That's great, because I couldn't play one when you put it on!"

One day, while a close friend of the *Team*, Sergeant Claude Webber and I were visiting Bobby Letbetter, the nurse left for a while. I took the opportunity to light up a cigarette at which Bobby said "Hey, give me a drag. I haven't had a cigarette in two weeks." I handed him mine and he took a deep drag, inhaled and blew out. Nothing happened. He took another, deeper drag and blew out. Claude and I were having laughing fits in the corner. Bobby walked over to the mirror, took another drag, inhaled and blew out. The smoke was coming out of the hole in his throat where the tracheotomy had been performed.

We were still there when the dietitian came in with Bobby's dinner meal. Now, mind you, Bobby had a broken jaw with his teeth wired shut and one of them extracted in order for him to put a straw in the hole and take liquids. The dietitian got the rooms mixed up and left Bobby a steak, mashed potatoes, a vegetable, and bread and butter. When she realized her mistake and returned for the tray, all the mashed potatoes were gone. Bobby had stuffed them in between his cheek and gums and sucked them all between his teeth.

By the middle of November, Joe Norman was well enough to leave the hospital on 'Profile', which meant that he was not allowed to do anything heavy and was not on jump status until re-examined by a doctor. He and I decided to catch a military 'hop' and go to Fort Sam Houston to see Bobby McDonnell. When we arrived, the doctors gave us a briefing on how the Hospital operated and what to expect when we saw Bobby. Because of the nature of the injuries and the susceptibility to infection, we had to keep sterile and wear masks any time we were in the room with Bobby. The Hospital also had an all day visitation policy accept during meal times, they said it was a big morale factor. They even had us visit some patients who didn't receive many visitors. One was a black guy who was in a truck wreck and had both arms burned badly. They looked like over-done hot dogs. There was also a young girl accompanied by her father, who was burned when a T-33 Jet Trainer crashed in their yard killing her mother.

No matter how much they try to prepare you for a burn center, you are mortified when you see your first burn patient! Just the visual impact is horrifying, but the amount of physical and mental suffering is frightful.

When I first saw Bobby, I had to mentally brace myself to keep from appearing too startled; it was difficult. He looked terrible with all of the bandages, plus, they had already started some of the plastic surgery where they would shave some of the skin off of the areas that weren't burned and let it hang there until they used it on some of the burns. Bobby's left hand was just a big round scab, and they had already amputated the two middle fingers from his right hand. But, he was still Bobby! The first thing out of his mouth was "Hi Guys want to play cards?" Later on, we made him do just that and hold his own cards.

We stayed with Bobby for a few days' playing cards, clowning around and just talking. We told him how good the rest of the *Team* was doing and that they all sent their love and best wishes. During that period, I asked one of the doctors why the other two civilians that were in the crash and sent to Fort Sam died and Bobby didn't? Bobby was burned much worse than they were. The doctor simply said "Because he wouldn't allow it!" I asked what he meant by that and he said "He just refused to die." I nodded my head. That was Bobby.

One day, Joe and I decided to play a joke on Bobby after his lunch break. They always made us leave during that period. When we returned, we grasped each others shoulder, put our hats way over our heads and came inside stepping like a couple of vaudevillians coming on stage going "Ra ta ta ta ta ta, Ra ta ta ta ta ta, Ra ta ta ta ta ta". We looked over at Bobby who was sound asleep and then at the rest of the ward who was looking at us like we had just stepped out of a Nut House! Oh Well.

We finally had to catch a hop back to Bragg. We said a teary eyed farewell to the bravest man on earth and promised to stay in touch and make double damn sure the rest of the *Team* wrote him. We all did, but it would be a long time before we saw Bobby again.

Jump number 681, dated November 29, 1962, states Brrrrrrrrrrrrrrr! in the remarks column. I can remember it like it was yesterday. The temperature was something like 32 degrees on the ground. Danny Byard and I were going to take an L-20 'Beaver' to 10,000 feet and do a baton pass. These were the days before 'jump doors' that could be opened and closed in flight to keep the aircraft and jumpers warm. This door would be open all the way to altitude, and guess what 'dipstick' left his gloves on the ground? It would take about thirty minutes to get to altitude with the air temperature dropping 3 degrees per thousand feet. By the time we got there, the OAT would be 2 degrees above zero. Now, when they talk about wind chill factor, the wind was about 120 mph. I don't know. You figure it

I kept my hands under my armpits during the climb to keep them as warm as possible, but when jump time came, I could just barely feel my fingers. I was to be the anchor man. Jump first and carry the baton, so I got the baton in my left hand and 'took off'. Danny was right behind me.

When he got to me, he grabbed the baton, but I couldn't let go, my fingers wouldn't move. Danny kept pulling and finally yanked the baton free. The fall was 45 seconds at those terribly cold temperatures and when it came time to pull the rip-cord, I couldn't clasp my fingers around the handle. I couldn't even feel the handle! I finally got my thumb hooked in the 'D' ring and pulled. I got the rip-cord out but couldn't hold on to the 'D' ring. You would think that everyone on the ground would have better things to do, but, no! "Fortenberry lost his rip-cord!" That night, I bought a case of beer and was happy to still be around to drink one of them! Danny asked me later "How dumb can you get?" and I said, "I don't know, I'm like Duffy, I'm still young."

Not much went on for the remainder of 1961. We stayed at Bragg and continued to train and research new ideas. One event was kind of interesting. A few of us spent a whole year in free-fall, literally. We took off just before midnight on December 31st 1961 for a 60 second delay free-fall and had the pilots time it to be over the drop zone at 20 seconds before midnight. So, we jumped on December 31, 1961 and opened on January 1, 1962.

1962 was an interesting year for all of us and me in particular. As I open up log book number six, I notice some interesting autographs. The Navy formed a Parachute Demonstration Team called "The Chuting Stars". It didn't last long because the Navy couldn't justify the cost of two demonstration teams, "The Chuting Stars" and "The Blue Angles." Guess who won that one big time? But I did meet some characters; Frank Moncrief (who went on to be one of the members of the first Seal Teams), and Ed Kruse. There are other signatures i.e., 'Thanks for making me a has-been at 22,' Jim Arender. I'll explain that later. Another was "He who does not pull cord must come to a sudden stop—'n everything', Carol Carson ('62 Nationals). P.S. I'm leaving Jose with you. Be good to him, huh." I have no idea what that meant. I asked Wil Charette to autograph my log book and got this; Sgt. Wilfred Joseph Anthony Charette Jr. III, United States Army Parachute Team, Post Office Box 126, Fort Bragg, North Carolina. Federation Aeronautique Internationale License Number C and D ninety, issued by the Parachute Club of America, a non profit affiliate of the

National Aeronautic Association. It took up one and a half pages!

During the later part of January 1962, we embarked on the first of two massive attempts breaking as many world parachuting accuracy records as possible. Most of which were held by Communist Countries, and most of those by the Soviet Union. We began this assault in El Centro, California at the Parachute testing facility. My first jump was signed off in my log book by Wil Charette. He had been released from the Womack Army Hospital on 'Profile'. Off jump status! Court Martial offense! All that—! He would end up helping set numerous World Records and one dubious record; that of most number of jumps made while on Profile. Joe Norman and John Hollis were also released. But only Joe was off 'Profile'. John wouldn't jump during the attempts but would do most of the organizing and officiating.

The other *Team* Members participating were: Danny Byard, Bill Edge, Harold Lewis, Capt. Jim Perry, Jerry Bourquin, Coy O. McDonald, Billy Lockward, Loy Brydon, Ray Duffy, Phil Vander Weg, Gene Paul Thacker and Sherman Williford.

The record attempts were a combination of; Number of jumpers, beginning at three and graduating up to nine. Height of the jump, 1,800 ft., 3,500 ft., 4,500 ft., and 7,200 ft., and amount of delayed fall before opening the parachute, beginning at 0 delay and graduating to 15 seconds, 20 seconds and 30 seconds. For example, we would start with a three man team (it didn't have to be the same three men on every attempt) and jump from every altitude with "0" delay. Then we would do the same thing with 4 men, then, 5 etc. We would then start over and do the same progression with delayed falls from the prescribed altitudes. Realizing that we could not break every record on just one attempt, you can begin to visualize how many jumps would have to be made to accomplish our mission! Once we had attained our goal on daytime records, we had to turn around and do it all over at night! From January 20th through March 21st, I made 105 jumps and setting 25 World Records of which 3 were "zeroed out," meaning every jumper made a dead center landing. Those three can never be broken!

When we began, one of the most difficult problems we faced was getting "stacked", or separated for the landing. The more the jumpers and the lower the altitude, the more difficult this became. The worst case scenario possible would be nine jumpers getting out at 2,000 feet with zero delay (all opening at the same altitude) and all trying to hit the same 7 centimeter disc at the same time. That would be like trying to land nine Fighters on the same Aircraft Carrier at the same time. Or as my friend Saul would say, "Like nine dogs trying to piss on the same fire hydrant and staying dry."

Well, you get the picture. So, we had to work out some method of "stacking" ourselves. The first we employed was logic. The heaviest jumpers would go first and the lightest last. This wasn't enough so we used physics, the bottom of the stack had to come down faster. The only way to do this was to decrease the lift on the parachute. We had a very "clever" way of doing this. We simply started climbing a riser. Or more precisely, pulling one side of the parachute down to the point that it became so lopsided it collapsed. The rules said that we had to jump and open at prescribed times and altitudes, it said nothing about staying open. The first three or four jumpers, depending on how many were in the stick, would use this method of loosing altitude. The first four usually consisted of Brydon, Duffy, me and Harold Lewis, in that order.

Parachutes are designed to open and are very good at doing what they are designed to do. They are not, however, designed to be closed after opening, and they sometimes rebel against it. They had a habit of not re-opening exactly when you wanted them to, or, trying to invert (open inside out). Or in the worst case, start to invert, then pick up one or two suspension lines on its way back to open, pulling them up on top of the parachute creating a "Mae West."(so named because it took up the appearance of a giant bra). This was dangerous because it increased your rate of descent and had the possibility of sawing your parachute in half.

On all of the record attempts that I participated on, I ended up "spotting" the aircraft for the opening point. During the day, it was no big deal. We just used the normal wind drift indicator. But night created a new challenge. No one could see it. So, we invented a new wind drift indicator. It consisted of a small parachute with an electric powered lantern under it. We would drop it over the target at whatever altitude we were going to open and the ground crew would follow it. Where it landed, they would park a jeep with a rotating beacon on it. We would go an equal distance up wind and jump. Simple? "Not!"

Our other problem was seeing each other at night. We bought these little, battery powered, flashing red beacons with suction cups on them to attach to the top of our helmets. The suction cups were not sufficient to secure the beacons, so we had to tape them to our helmets with duct tape. Now, as long as you were off to the side of another jumper you could see him, but if you were directly under or over him, the canopy blocked out the beacon. On really dark nights, this was a real problem and more than once there were near misses and a few collisions. Openings were also a concern. On a delayed fall, we tried to stay close enough to each other during the fall to see the beacons and stay separated during openings. Do all that and keep an eye on your stop watch and altimeter and you can see how busy it could get.

Sometime during this first attempt at record breaking, it was decided that we could concentrate better and have much more flexibility and freedom if we moved to the Army test site at Yuma, Arizona. This really worked out well. The Drop Zone was so far out in the desert that we were out of everyone's way and left alone to really intensify our efforts.

During this period, we concentrated mainly on the daylight records.

Besides the jumping, a couple of other events took place that needs mentioning.

One night, I was coming in from a time on the town. I was on the last bus from Yuma, 'is that a song or something?' Normally, when arriving at the Base, the bus was just waved through by the MP's, but tonight, they stopped the bus and started checking identification cards. When they got to me, I asked who they were looking for and the MP replied "Sam Spade." I thought, 'You gotta be kidding?' The only Sam Spade I knew of was a shady private detective in a crime novel, but they continued their search. The next day I found out the story.

Some of the team members went into town to have a few beers and unwind at a bar called "The Snake Pit". The name of the bar ought to tell you something right there! There was also an Army Lt. Colonel who frequented the place. Somehow, he got cross ways with Sergeant Coy McDonald, and Coy knocked him on his ass. The Colonel said "Do you know who I am?" Coy said "no, who?" "I'm Colonel So-and-So. What's your name soldier?" At which Coy replied "Sam Spade." Hence the gate searches.

Another notable event was Sergeant Charette getting hurt. Now, mind you, Wil was still on Profile from his injuries in the plane crash at Wilmington. He had a dislocated vertebra in his back and had to be evacuated to the Naval Hospital in San Diego, California. If Wil was to keep from receiving a Court Martial, we would have to keep this completely 'under wraps'. The vertebras are numbered L1, L2, L3, etc. One day, we got a letter from Wil, and he said that after the x-ray's, the doctor's came in and said that "L5 don't jive with L4 no more." Somehow, they took care of the problem and within a couple of weeks Wil was back jumping with us; hospital pajamas and all. This was definitely going to have to be hidden from the Flight Surgeon at Fort Bragg!

We took every precaution. Even Captain Perry was assisting in the 'cover up', but as fate would have it, Wil got caught!

As I mentioned, being way out in the desert gave us anonymity until we began to break a lot of records. All of a sudden the deserts of Arizona weren't so remote. I have no idea of which record number broke the media's back but all of a sudden we were hot news. Either that or it was a 'slow news day'. Whichever! Anyway, we had taken a lot of pictures during the record breaking attempts. One of which was Wil Charette just leaving the aircraft in a 'spread eagle' position with this big, silly grin on his face. In the picture, he has a front tooth missing and San Diego Naval Hospital pajamas sticking out from the ankles of his jump suit. Out of all of the hundreds of pictures we took out there, guess which one the news media picked to plaster all over the world? It was on the Sport pages of the *L. A. Examiner, New York Times, Washington Post,* and guess what—the front page of the *Fayetteville Observer* at Fort Bragg, N.C.

When we got home, Wil went to the Flight Surgeon for a Physical to see if he was well enough to get off 'Profile'. After the examination, the doctor was filling out the medical forms and asked, "Did you do any parachuting while on profile Sergeant?" Wil knew right then that he better not lie to him and said "Yes Sir." The doctor said "I know. I saw your picture on the front page of the *Observer*. How many jumps did you make out there Sergeant?" Wil looked at him and said in a barely audible voice, "A hundred and five, sir." The Flight Surgeon just flipped his pencil in the air and said, "You guys amaze me!" He took Wil off profile and not another word was ever said about it.

I gave that picture to Wil at his retirement ceremony in Langley, Va. after serving 35 years with the CIA.

We left Yuma at the end of March. We had not accomplished everything that we had set out to do. We broke most of the daytime records but the nighttime records remained. It had just taken more time than we expected, and time ran out. We had other obligations and commitments to fulfill, but we made a vow to come back and finish the task.

One night, we had been working on low altitude attempts and decided about 10:00 o'clock to try a 7,000 foot, (nine men) without delay, attempt. This would result in us hanging in the harness from 10 to 12 minutes. Sometimes our leg straps would cut off blood circulation enough for our legs to go to sleep. That was always a weird sensation and potentially dangerous on landing.

I came over the target and dropped the parachute with the lantern and we began to circle and watch. I saw the jeep driving in the direction that the parachute was drifting. After a while the jeep stopped, the driver turned off his head lights and turned on the rotating beacon. The distance from the jeep to the target looked reasonable, and a radio call was received by the pilot that the ground crew was ready for the jump. I lined the aircraft up on the jeep and target, flew an equal distance up wind (maybe a mile) and said, "Let's Go." We got out and opened immediately. The first thing after opening was to turn toward the target and test the winds to see what the drift was and then set up the 'stack.' Tonight we turned toward the target and "holy shit," we were drifting away from it! I looked at our position over the desert and its relationship to the target and the jeep. Everything matched, but we were drifting away from the target at an alarming speed. Sound really carries at night and the next thing I heard were the encouraging voices of my fellow jumpers yelling things like "Fortenberry, you dumb son-of-a-bitch. What did you do?" "Fortenberry, you dip-shit, where are we?" I remember hearing the distinctive voice of Coy McDonald (never one to mince words). "Fortenberry, You rotten son-of-a-bitch, if I hit a cactus, I'm going to carry it back and shove it up your ass!" And, as an after thought, he yelled "sideways." Bill Edge's voice now, "If I land on one your ass better not be there when I get back." Well, I was too busy trying to analyze what had happened to worry about these obviously, idle threats. I continued to try and run to the target but was still drifting in the opposite direction, but, it seemed, not at the same rate. We were a little below 4,000 feet when the wind shear hit us. All of a sudden, we just shot toward the target. "Shit!" Now we were all turned into the wind and holding, but it was obvious that we would overshoot the target. Sure was quiet up there now. Everyone's concentration was on trying not to overshoot the target! Well, we didn't set a record on that attempt, but I didn't get a cactus shoved up my ass either!

Chapter 13

Upon arrival back at Fort Bragg, we immediately began training for the National Championship that was to be held at Olathe, Kansas, beginning at the end of May. The remark's section of my log books next 20 jumps read; L00 BL L00 BL Accuracy; LOO BL ROO BL Accuracy; ROO BL LOO BL Accuracy, etc. This was my code for style practice. It meant; Left 360 degree turn, right 360 degree turn, back loop, left 360 degree turn, right 360 degree turn, back loop, then, if I was in position, I would work on hitting the target.

There were three sets of turn Series that could be accomplished after leaving the aircraft at 7,000 feet. They consisted of alternating 360 degree turns beginning to the left with a back loop in the middle and at the end. That was if a left panel was flashed on the ground. If a right panel was flashed, all series of turns would begin to the right. If a double panel was flashed, the first series of turns began to the left followed by a back loop and the second series of turns began to the right followed by a back loop. You never knew what you were going to do until you left the aircraft, and then the panel only flashed for 5 seconds.

As I scan through my log book for information, my eye catches an up-side-down entry. Jump #800 on 8 April,

1962 is signed off my Claude Webber, parachuting license number D-92. Lots more about Claude later!

We were all working hard and focusing on the Nationals, but we also had obligations to the public. One of which was to do a demonstration at the NASCAR race in Bristol, Tennessee.

We arrived in Bristol on May 23rd, 1962. Two things were going on at Bristol in May of '62. One, naturally, was the race. The other was that the number one song on the top ten hit parade was "The Bristol Stomp." We were invited to a party that night and I thought the dancing was going to bring the house down, literally, doing "The Bristol Stomp."

The race track at Bristol is a 'short track' event and is about a half mile around. It is also located in a bowl surrounded by hills. I am a NASCAR enthusiast, and was recently watching the race. I noticed that, today, there would be absolutely no place on the race track to land, because of all the trucks and support equipment. In 1962, there was a small patch of green grass in front of the bleachers at the finish line on which to land. It didn't make a very big target, but if you missed, the surrounding area had plenty of alternates.

I recall that it was a pretty day with light winds, so we could put on the 'high' show. I was on the formation fall with 'bomb burst'. We got out at 14,500 feet and put on a really good show. Nice tight formation and a well-executed bomb burst at the bottom. I opened at about 2,000 feet and we began to maneuver and arrange a 'stack' in order to arrive at the target one at a time. During the parachute descent, you begin to look for signs of the wind direction. These signs were normally in the way of smoke stacks, ripples on water or flags. In the case of a racing event, there were always lots of flags and Bristol was no exception, except. The race track had flags all the way around it, 360 degrees, and every one of them was blowing to the inside of the race track! It was like something was sucking the wind and us right into the track. We hit hard. Nobody made a standing landing, but no one broke anything either. I didn't like those kinds of jumps just prior to the Nationals. You might break something. Fate was about to teach me that lesson!

We went back to Bragg to continue our training for the Nationals, but I wouldn't get another chance to train prior to Olathe.

Somebody, I don't even remember who, had a Cushman motor scooter that we all decided to get out and play with one day. We were on a dirt surface and I recall that I was driving with Wil Charette on the back. I had done a lot of motorcycle riding, even some racing and could handle one pretty well. I mistakenly thought that I could handle a motor scooter as well. I decided to do a 'donut' with it, which is easy on a motorcycle because you have plenty of power to spin the rear wheel. Well, I tried it with the scooter, which promptly dug in its back wheel and flipped Charette and me over the side. Wil was all right, but when I got up I immediately knew something was wrong. There was no pain, but I just couldn't move my shoulder very well. X-rays confirmed that the collar bone was broken. It wasn't a bad break because it was still lined up, but it would keep me down at least until the Nationals started, which was just twenty-six days away. 'Holy shit!'

The doctor put what is referred to as a figure 'eight strap' around my shoulders to hold them back and motionless so the bone could mend. For those of you who have ever had one on, you know how irritating and uncomfortable it is. It's impossible to find a comfortable position to sleep in, and your back is constantly itching. It's miserable! The most agonizing part was not being able to train. I had held an inner contemplation that, just maybe, I could be the first person to win the Nationals two years in a row. But that desire seemed to be down the tubes now. Even if I could hold my own in Accuracy, Style would be my undoing. Like any other sport, retaining any proficiency in the style series took constant practice in order to keep the muscle memories up to date. All I could do between now and the time the Nationals started was watch the *Team* practice and assist by keeping scores and critiquing the guys on their style form, etc. It was the longest twenty-six days I had ever spent in my life, up to this point.

Time went by like one of those slow motion dreams you have. Or, maybe I'm the only one who ever has those. It's a dream where you are trying to run to something or away from something as fast as you can. Everything else in the dream is at normal speed, but everything you do is in slow motion. You know that it's a dream, but it seems so real and you can't wake up.

Time went by like poring molasses out of a jar on a cold day, but finally, we were in Kansas and things were getting intense.

The first day was spent greeting your old friends and catching each other up to date on the year's activities. It was also spent like every other meet, sizing up the competition. As the sport grew, so did the number of competitors. There were always the tried and proven rivals, but there were a lot of new faces too. And each and every one of those faces had high hopes and lofty goals; that was to be Number One or at least make the top ten. The top ten men and top ten women would go on to training camp as the United States Parachute Team. Of those, five men and five women would be chosen to represent the United States. The spare person would remain as a *Team* alternate. Right now, it was all up in the air and the mind games were already beginning.

In my mind, I didn't hold much chance of winning the overall competition, but I sure wanted to make the training team list. As I said before, you do whatever it takes! I figured that if I could place in the top 4 or 5 in each Accuracy event and then place high in Style, I might make it. I didn't know it yet, but I would go on to pull off one of the classic coup's of parachuting history. Of course, there wasn't that much parachuting history in those days! It would be against Jim Arender, the World Style Champion.

Each competitor was given two practice jumps prior to the meet starting. You could use these jumps any way you wanted. Most of the guys elected to do style jumps in order to get their proficiency up to peak form. This year, I was the exception.

In the past, I was the only parachutist who ever gave Arender any real competition in style. I had placed 2nd to him in style in the last Nationals, and during training, I was always a split second average behind him. I was counting on Jim not trying to beat himself, but rather beat whoever it took to be first, and, as I say, that was usually me.

I knew that Jim would be watching in anticipation, and timing me on my practice jump, so I played my ace.

Now mind you, I haven't had a practice jump in twenty-six days, and I could really use a good Style series to tweak up my proficiency. But I thought I needed to screw with Jim's mind more!

I got into the aircraft and we climbed to 7,000 feet and began the jump run. When I was over the exit point, I got out and entered my tuck, which was to make yourself as small as possible in order to build up air speed. When it came time to begin the series, I did half of one, and I did it real slow; like that dream I was talking about. For the rest of the jump, I just fell until opening time. At that point, I stood straight up for the opening. I did this partly for effect and partly to ease the pressure off of my collar bone during the opening shock.

When I got on the ground, Jim casually came over and asked "How did it go?" I got a very pained and exasperated look on my face and said, "I'll tell you Jim, it really hurt. I don't know if I can finish the meet much less the Style event. You know, I had to stand straight up on the opening to keep the pain out of my shoulder!" Jim tried to equal my pained expression and said "Gees, that's too bad Dick!" I didn't say anything else, but thought "Heh, Heh, Heh!" The next part of the plan was the luck of the draw, virtually. Jump positions for all events were decided by drawing numbers out of a hat. It would be imperative that Jim make a Style jump before me if my psych job was going to work. We drew for slots. Jim drew a few positions ahead of me. The die was cast. "Let the games begin!"

Prior to going to Yuma for record attempts, we had been issued brand new parachutes manufactured by Pioneer Parachute Company. Gone was my old companion, the stencil stating "CONDEMNED, NOT FOR PERSONNEL USE!" The new parachutes were made of 1.6 ounce rip-stop nylon, but the steerable modifications were the same old "Conquistador" that Loy had designed. The new, heavy, material let the parachutist descend much slower. Not as many of those "slam, bam, thank you maam" landings.

It would remain the most popular design until the "Para-Commander" hit the scene on June 24, 1964.

One of the new faces on the parachuting scene was a guy by the name of Clyde Jacks. I had never heard of him until arriving at Olathe, and had no reason to be concerned with his ability. Normally, if someone had really shown something during the year, you would hear about it either through one of the parachuting magazines or through the 'grapevine.' I should have heard something about him as his license number was D-42, only four higher than mine. Clyde was also an accomplished aerobatic pilot with his own Pitts Special By-plane.

The first round of jumps was Accuracy. We were jumping a brand new Cessna built airplane that year called a Cessna 206. It was very roomy and had a rear window but was still very breezy because no one had yet designed a "jump door." The surface winds were high and the direction on the ground was indicated by the smoke of a tire kept burning at the edge of the target area. My first jump was 3.5 meters and I was conscious of protecting my shoulder. That jump was signed off by Frank Carpenter, D-111, another one of those 'nice people'. The 3.5 meters was respectable, but would not win a National Championship.

The month layoff from that stupid motor scooter trick was taking its toll. I was just glad that the first event was Accuracy. It would give my shoulder another couple of days to mend, if I didn't break it again first.

The winds picked up the next day, which I thought might be in my favor because it was windy a lot at Bragg and we never stopped training. But, that wasn't the case, seems like everyone else was as serious as me about this meet; especially this guy Clyde Jacks. My next two jumps were 7 meters 20 centimeters and 1 meter 93 centimeters. Very respectable average, but the guy with two first names was ahead of me by a few points. Who was this unassuming guy from Texas? The next day, I had a 1 meter and 38 centimeters jump. Now this is World Class accuracy.

Clyde had 1.35. 'Holy shit, Is this guy teasing me or what?' My Style feud with Arender was taking 2nd place to this accuracy dual with an unknown quantity, and my shot at being the first guy to win the Nationals twice in a row was rapidly being threatened by a surprisingly good parachutist. I hate surprises! The tension was rising but it would have to wait because the next event would be the Style, which also should prove interesting.

As I mentioned, Arender had drawn a jump slot ahead of me and I was anxious to see if my 'mind game' was working. Of course this could backfire and work against me if Jim knew that I was 'sand bagging!'

It was May 30th, 1962, and we would soon find out. Jim's plane was in the air and I was standing by with a stopwatch in one hand, and binoculars in the other.

The anxiety mounted as his airplane turned on final approach for the jump run. He would be at 7,200 feet lining up on the arrow by giving the pilot hand signals. The more lined up you were with the arrow, the less chance the judges had of making a mistake and misjudging your headings.

"HE'S OUT," somebody yelled. I watched as he compressed himself into a position that would create as little air resistance as possible allowing him to have as much airspeed as he could when starting his first maneuver. As soon as he flinched, I started the stopwatch. He was as smooth as silk and every maneuver was perfect, but I could sense that he wasn't pushing the limits. When he came out of his last loop, I stopped the watch. He had done the required six maneuvers in just over 11 seconds. That was respectable, but he was capable of doing a faster series; so far, so good on the "mind games."

It would be a couple of hours before my jump and I had to spend it getting myself mentally prepared. Once I got over the first Style jump, and if it was good, the rhythm would start and the pace would be set.

I hadn't made a real Style jump in the last month because of the shoulder injury so I spent the time doing two things; both mental. The first was to relax by picturing things like golden, waving wheat fields, blue skies with puffy clouds and cool waterfalls. The other was to close my eyes and picture the jump from every aspect. Mentally put myself through every Style sequence. Try to push the limits, in my mind, without making a mistake.

My lift was called. Times up. Got to work. Ready or not, here I come!

Clyde Jacks was on the same lift. We chatted and wished each other luck, silently hoping the other would fall on his face. Nothing personal!

As we climbed for altitude, I continued to mentally prepare myself; a little less on the golden wheat field and blue skies' side, and a lot more on the psycho cybernetics side.

Clyde jumped first and I automatically hit my stopwatch to time his series. He was in the mid eleven's which meant that he was still a serious contender for the overall title. The aircraft did a slow 180 degree turn. There were usually as many as four airplanes at a time in the jump pattern. We came around in sequence and started my jump run. When the pilot lined up, he was on a perfect line to the arrow (good omen). I never had to give him a correction. As we got closer to the exit point the adrenaline rush started. I asked the pilot to throttle back and put my left footon to the airplane step, leaned out and put both hands on the wing strut. To me, it was always important to get a good start. I pushed off and started my stopwatch, knowing that the five official stopwatches and umpteen unofficial stopwatches as well, were poised to start timing my series as soon as I made my first move. I compressed myself into as little of a drag surface as possible and looked at the arrow. A left panel was flashed; another good omen. For some reason, my left turn series was usually faster than the other two options. I didn't mechanically time myself to begin my turns; I just let the wind tell me. Terminal velocity occurs about 12 seconds into the fall. I listened to the wind speed increase and pictured the complete series in my mind. Left turn, right turn, back loop, left turn, right turn, and back loop. The wind speed stabilized and I shot into my first turn. From there on, it was mostly muscle memory, but each maneuver felt good. I came out of the last loop instinctively glancing at my watch. Under 25 seconds so I was in the ball park. I gave it to 28 seconds and pulled the rip-cord. Turns felt good. Loops felt good. Shoulder felt good. Body felt good. Mind felt good. "It doesn't get much better than this!"

After landing, I was told that my official time was 10.9 seconds. There were all kinds of unofficial times, depending on who you were or weren't friends with. I knew I was capable of faster times, but under the circumstances, I was ecstatic! The psyche job had paid off and the pace was set.

Jim walked up and said something like "You sandbagging son-of-a-bitch!" There was a grin on his face as he said it, as if to acknowledge my felonious nature. I now had a very fragile edge over him that he just couldn't quite recover from in time. On my next three jumps, I turned in an 11.0, an 11.5, (which I threw out) and a 10.6, my all time best. I was the new National Style Champion. It was the one and only time I ever beat Jim Arender in Style, and he never let me forget it. Nor I him! It was also my 24th birthday, June 4th, 1962. What a nice present to myself!

But, that was just a battle. The war was still raging, and there were a lot of big name competitors still in the running for the overall title. Among those were; Bill Berge, Ron Sewell, Hank Simbro, Phil Vander Weg, Loy Brydon, Gerry Borquin, Joe Norman, Coy McDonald, Gene Paul Thacker, Bob Buckner, Frank Carpenter, Jim Arender, Lynn Pyland, and this guy with two first names! Clyde Jacks was still my main competition and was ahead of me in aggregate score. I just couldn't shake him off, and it was having quite an adverse effect on me. He didn't even appear too concerned. He just seemed to be openly having fun. Talk about psyche games!

And as if choreographed by some dramatic movie director, it all came down to the last day and the last jump.

We had two jumps left on the final accuracy event. Clyde was ahead of me by just a few points and Bill Berg was behind by fewer points. It was getting brutal on my nerves, and to make things worse, I had to lead off on our first jump of the day.

Don't get me wrong, the three of us, by no stretch of the imagination, had the first three positions wired. All it would take, would be two bad jumps by us and some hot shot kid from Podunk, Indiana (that's kind of like Banning California) could find himself as the new National Champion. And, there was still a lot of competing going on behind us for the other top ten positions, of which the six members of the United States Team would be chosen.

The three of us were scheduled to jump about mid-morning, so we sat around watching the other parachutists. We would observe their opening points and watch their canopy work to try and get as accurate an indication of the wind line as possible.

The winds seemed a little spurious today and I was worried. No one seemed to be on the same line. They were all searching, including those jumpers whose Accuracy ability I highly respected. Most were landing short of the target, which could mean about anything. The surface smoke generator was still indicating a constant direction and speed, but most of the guys were misreading the winds at altitude. This could be anywhere from 2,000 feet to 50 feet off the ground. And just go ask someone. You couldn't believe anything these ding bats said. I proved that in the style event.

Well, time was up—my turn in the proverbial bag.

I chuted up, climbed aboard the Cessna 206 and began the long ascent to altitude. Bill and Clyde were in an aircraft behind me. At least they wouldn't get a chance to watch my canopy work, as good or as bad as it might be. All the way up, I continued trying to read the other jumpers' efforts, but it was virtually impossible because you can't tell where they are over the ground.

We got to altitude and interred the "daisy chain." This was the circle that all of the other aircraft used to stay in sequence, and to keep from running into each other. As the pilot turned on a long final approach to the target, I looked at the smoking tire. It was still indicating a wind out of the Southeast at about 5 to 7 mph. And Jumpers were still landing short, except those few who landed so far off the target that it was obvious they didn't have a clue as to what they were doing. But, they were having fun and gaining valuable experience for the future.

To be honest, I didn't have much of a clue as to what I was going to do. I was going to have to play this 'close to the vest'. The wind panel that had been laid out earlier, showing where the wind drift indicator had landed, was still there. I lined the pilot up on it and flew the same distance past the target allowing for trajectory and got out. I opened at 2,000 feet and began to feel for the wind. There was none. It seemed to be absolutely calm. Okay, but on the surface it was 5 to 7. Where did it start? Unlike the parachutes today, with the seven gore TU, if you ever got past the target you would never get back. So like everyone else, I hung out waiting for the wind to start. 1500 feet, . . . 1000 feet, . . . where was it? 800 ft . . . 700 ft . . . 400 ft . . . ! "Damn, where is it!" 300 ft . . . "Damn it, I'm hanging out too long!" I turned in to run for the target, but too late. 200 ft and still no wind, 150 feet and the canopy gave a little tug like the giant sail that it is. There's the wind, but too late. Like everyone else, I was going to be short. Not as short, but short nonetheless. I came in straight down wind doing about 15 mph, stretched my body horizontal and landed (a controlled crash) as close as possible, 7 meters and 93 centimeters. That just might lose it for me. Shit!

But, I would get another chance. In the remarks section of my log book for that jump, #836, it simply states, "Undershot, Clyde missed and so did Berg." One way or another, it would all be over on the next jump. Clyde Jacks and I were assigned the same airplane for the last jump, along with one other guy.

Before going up, I took one last look at the canopy work of a couple of jumpers. The wind direction and velocity on the ground had not changed all day. Jumpers were getting on target a little better and there seemed to be a definite wind line to follow from the opening altitude. It would only take about 15 to 20 minutes to get to our jump altitude of 5,200 feet and in the 'daisy chain'. The order of jump was still in my favor. The guy with us would go first, Clyde second and I would be last.

As we climbed for altitude, I continued to watch the parachute's land. Even though I couldn't see their wind line, I could tell if there were any drastic changes in the wind. At about 4,000 feet, I began to notice that more and more canopies were landing short of the target, some as far as 10 to 25 meters. By the time we began our final approach for our first jumper, canopies were landing as short as 30 and 40 meters. I glanced at Clyde and could see the concern on his face.

As our airplane lined up for the final jump run, the guy ahead of us gave the pilot a few corrections, flew straight ahead for a few seconds, signaled to cut the engine and got out. Clyde and I were in the door immediately to see where he got out. It was the normal point dictated by what the winds were doing when we left the ground, the same place that I had planned on.

I watched his canopy to see if he was holding, running, crabbing or what. You could usually tell by which way the modification holes in his parachute were facing. He was running, meaning facing and driving toward the target. He never changed direction and landed about 50 meters short of the target. "Holy Shit!" There was a wind shear or inversion! The winds at altitude were in the opposite direction of the winds on the ground. Two more parachutes from airplanes behind us landed in the same place.

Clyde looked at me as if to ask "What do you think?" I looked at him as if to say, "This is for all the marbles. You're on your own pal!" He lined up on the same flight path as everyone else, gave a few corrections, asked for a cut and jumped. I was in the door like a shot! He turned toward the target, never changed direction and landed in the same place the previous guy did. They probably could have shaken hands.

I said to myself "OK Fortenberry, as your friend Saul would say; don't believe what you hear or feel, believe what you see." I yelled to the pilot, "Turn around and make the jump run in the opposite direction!" He said, "That will be against traffic." I yelled, "I don't give a shit if it is. This is my jump run. Tell them to either follow me or get the hell out of my way!" He made a couple of transmissions on the radio, and then made the turn.

My plan was to get out over the target and track to a point about 100 meters down wind or Northwest of the target, then play it by the seat of my pants. Whatever happened, I didn't want to get to far away from the target.

I asked for a 'cut' and jumped. I picked the spot I wanted to open over and tracked for it. I got there, flared and watched my stopwatch. When it hit 18 seconds, I pulled. It opened with that familiar tug and I unconsciously checked for any rips or tears, grabbed the guideline toggles and faced into the wind. I could tell that I was just barely holding my own over the ground. I had guessed right, but I had to test the velocity. I turned to face the target and took off like a shot. I turned back into the wind. The wind line seemed to be constant. It was 180 degrees from that on the ground. The trick was to try and guess where the wind shear took effect.

I decided to maneuver so as to be about 50 meters southeast of the target at about 300 feet. This was going to be dicey, and I dared not get too far off the wind line. The trick was to be in a position to start the final approach at about 100 feet high and not have to make any drastic turns from there to the target. But where in the hell was the wind shear? If you have ever watched a sailing Regatta at the start then imagine this; I was turning, jibbing, tacking, twisting . . . ., whatever it to took be in a position to cross the start line at the exact time the starting cannon went off. My heart sank as I finally turned into the wind shear and watched the target go under my feet as I drifted backwards past it. It appeared that I was going to do what everyone else had done and land short.

I continued to hold my heading, facing the target, and watching my hopes drift away when, just barely perceptive, I felt a change in the wind. It was just a slight tug in the lag straps and saddle, but it was there. My heart sprang to my throat. My backward motion had stopped. I hung there at about 300 feet, then just as advertised, the wind increased and I started toward the target. I couldn't have been in a better position if I had planned it, which I had! I pulled both guideline toggles down to slow my forward movement and held that until it appeared that I would land about 5 meters short, then let the brakes out slowly. I stretched out and hit the ground at full speed, obliterating the target. My final mark was 1 meter and 86 centimeters. In the remark's section of my log book, it states "I needed this one." I was now, the only person who had ever won back to back National Championships.

At the awards ceremony, I received trophies for 1st place Overall, 1st place Style, and 2nd place in the last accuracy event. I also received a trophy from the Chamber of Commerce called "The Heart of America Traveling Trophy." I never did know what that was, but it was a nice gesture from the people of Olathe.

A classic statement came out of this awards banquet. One that no matter how many times we relive those moments during reunions, it's always brought up. As I received the 1st place trophy for Style, Jim Arender yelled from the audience, "I'm a 21 year old has-been!" At which, from the back of the crowd, Joe Norman yelled, "That's better than being a 33 year old never-was!" It brought the house down!

I felt pretty bad for Clyde Jacks. After such a super effort, he missed the top ten and a chance to tryout for the U. S. Team. I figured, "Oh well, he's young and there will be another time." That was not to be. About three or four months later, we learned that Clyde was killed in a plane crash while performing aerobatics in his Pitts Special Bi-Plane.

Chapter 14

Well, I told you about my first wife. Now it's time to tell you about my second, Linda Luella Marquis Firth Fortenberry.

When people ask me to describe Linda, I can only tell them that "she is the last of the Great Broads!" Most everyone's response, and especially the women, is "What did you call her?" I'm always ready to repeat myself. "My wife Linda is the last of the great broads, and I say that with the highest regard!"

There used to be some really great broads in the world but somewhere along the line, most women turned into whining, complaining, protesting, grumbling, fretting, and griping, bewailing, fussing, moaning, objecting bitches! You want to be man's equal and in the process, you end up trying to castrate us! You can never be like us. You can be co-equal, similar, equivalent even better, but you can never be like us. Why would you even want to, any more than I would want to be like you? The Great Broads never set out on a crusade to be man's equal, they were born that way!!

Look what you have going for you. You're pretty as hell and, (sorry guys) on the average, smarter than we are, either that or you apply yourselves more. You have a higher threshold of pain, you can grow another human being in your body, (wow, that's a biggy), and you live longer than we do. What the hell do you want? If it's a matter of equal wages for the same job, or equal opportunity for your qualifications, I'll be right out there on the picket lines with you with the biggest sign! But I still reserve the right to give up my seat to a lady and open doors. Chivalry is not belittling and it sure as hell isn't dead!

Here is a short list of some of my favorite Great Broads; Cleopatra, Joan of Arc, Ann Bolyn, Golda Meir, Margaret Thatcher, Bess Truman, Eleanor Roosevelt, Mae West (my all time favorite), Rita Hayworth, Carmen Miranda, (my third grade math teacher), Lauren Bacall, Anne Batterson, Joanita Maria Elena Hergert Lindberg Craft Mullins Taormina, and her man in cell block number 5, (That's a story in its self) and Second to the last of the Great Broads, Katherine Hepburn. So, when I say my wife is the last of the Great Broads, don't try and dispute it or you may have a fight on your hands!

I used to fly DC-3's with a pilot who was maybe a year younger than me, named Robert Firth. Bob was, and still is, an excellent pilot, and close friend. He has a great wit and a wonderful sense of humor, smart as a whip and maybe, too much ambition. We lived in Fort Lauderdale, Florida and flew for the Atlantic Undersea Test and Evaluation Center on Andros Island in the Bahamas. Bob had flown for Air America in Vietnam because, as he put it, "Greed overcame better judgment." He used to fill out his personal flight log with dollar signs instead of flight hours. When he filled up his log book, he quit and came home. I used to envy Bob because he was single, looked a little like Burt Reynolds and lived on a 30 foot sail boat. I still remember a picture he had on the boat. It was a cut-a-way sketch of the Cutty Sark, one of the fastest sailing vessels ever designed for the tea trade back in the tall ship days. It was a beautiful picture and complimented his boat perfectly. But, it had another purpose. He would take a pretty (hopefully) girl out sailing and when they got past the three mile international limit, he would turn the picture around. On the back was a sign in big, bold letters that read "EITHER SIN OR SWIM!" That's my Bob!

Bob met and started dating this beautiful, 18 year old student nurse, whom he talked about constantly. He kept ranting and raving about her to the point that I said "why don't you bring her over to the house some time?" When he finally did, I saw what all the fuss was about. Her name was Linda Marquis and she looked a lot like a young Katherine Hepburn. At first, she was a little shy, but when she began to feel more at ease, you got the full effect of her directness. It didn't seem that there was anything she was afraid to ask or anything she was afraid to answer. She seemed totally void of any fraud and was obviously infatuated with Bob.

Later in the evening, Bob got me off to the side and said he was thinking of asking her to marry him. I said "holy shit, you, the confirmed Bachelor, the guy with the neat boat and all of the freedom in the world?" He said "yeah, that guy." I told him that if it had to be, I definitely approved of her. They were married and lived happily ever-after, or at least for six or seven years.

Bob and I both went to work for Mackey Airlines, an international commuter, for a period of time. It took us about a year to get fed up with that crap, so when Bob Emmons, the President of World Aviation Services, inc, asked me if I wanted to come back as Chief Pilot for the AUTEC Project, I jumped at the chance. Bob Firth went on to other flying jobs but remained in close contact.

As time went by, (you know my story) and for whatever reasons, Bob and Linda began to drift apart. Somewhere in that gloom, Linda and I met and began to console each other. We have now been married for 34 years, have 29 year old twin daughters, Jennifer and Amanda, fight like a cat and dog and love the hell out of each other. As I often tell people, "Linda and I have more fun by accident than most people have on purpose." Not to long ago, she was reminiscing and told me "You know, Bob and I were married for seven years and you and I have been married for thirty four. So far, you're the winner!"

Linda is one of those kind of people that you could drop off in the middle of the Sahara Desert with nothing, come back six months later and she would have everything under control. "Hi. Where ya been? Can I get you anything?"

She has these cute little things she does when she's mad at me like flipping me the finger up-side-down and asking, "Can you hear this or do you want me to turn it up?" Or when she's telling me that "Men are only good for one thing, but then how often do you have to parallel park?" Her other favorite is, "Do the initials FO mean anything to you?" Now, when she is really, really angry at me, she tries to make me feel bad by doing some chore that she has been trying to get me to do for some time, like clean the garage, etc. So far, I haven't pissed her off enough to paint the house, but I'm working on it!

"The last of the last of the Great Broads," and I adore her! Of course, Jennifer and Amanda may start a new generation.

Chapter 15

We didn't get much of a break from the competition to the next phase of training. In mid June Joe Norman, John Cann (who was kind of like an exchange student from the British Special Air Service Regiment), and myself loaded up in Joe's new Chevy Corvair and headed for Orange, Massachusetts. This would be the sight of the VI World Sport Parachuting Championship, and our training camp for the next three months.

The *Team* members for training camp consisted of Jim Arender, Loy Brydon, Phil Vander Weg, Jerry Bourquin and myself for the men. Hank Simbro was the alternate, who would train with us and in the event of a bad injury, would replace the injured person. This would also be the first year that the United States would field a complete women's team. The five women were Helen Lord, Nona Pond, Muriel Simbro (wife of Hank Simbro) Gladys Inman and Carlyn Olson. There were three alternates for the women's team; Jeanni McCombs, Kim Emmons and my life long pal and soul mate, Anne Batterson. "Deke" Sonnichsen would be our head of delegation, but would run his end of the show from Menlo Park, California until the other teams arrived in Orange. Also on hand were members of the *Golden Knights* who would use this period to lend assistance and gain a little knowledge and experience.

Orange was the first Sport Parachuting Center to be set up in the United States and, except for the winter months, was ideally suited for that purpose. It was located away from any major airway so there were no conflicts with the airlines. No air carriers landed at Orange. The local population greeted us with open arms because of the added revenue the event would create, and Jacques Istel had done a wonderful job in promoting the event throughout the region. He had also bulldozed a huge arena between the triangular runways. It was a 100-meter, bowl shaped area, which was filled with soft, white sand. This provided an excellent target and landing area for the jumpers as well as a seating area for the spectators. They could bring blankets and picnic baskets and watch the activities. Which, incidentally, he charged twenty-five cents a head to come out and watch us train! If there was a penny to be made, Jacques knew how to make it. There was "The Inn at Orange" which he also owned. It had quarters that could house a few jumpers, a restaurant and a bar. The tradition was that at the end of the day, whoever wanted to participate could get on a plane and jump into "The Inn" which had a very small landing area surrounded by very tall trees. From 12,500 feet, it really looked small. Whoever landed closest to the target got a free steak dinner.

The "Inn" was a wonderful place to unwind after a hard day of training. Hell, it was the only place to unwind, but when the barley pop and wine began to flow and the "Jump Stories" began, or a guitar was brought out to sing ballads of some unfortunate jumper whose parachute failed to open, even the spectators enjoyed themselves. In those days, it seemed to be a common trait for sport parachutist to gather in any strays that wanted gathering. Basically, we were all ambassadors of the sport.

I'm getting a little ahead of myself here.

We were also introduced to a new jump platform in the form of, the Noorduyn Norseman. This was a bush plane used widely in Canada and Alaska. It was the predecessor to the De Havilland Beaver. It had a very large body and wide door, which was well suited for sport parachuting. I think the engine was a 450 horsepower Pratt and Whitney. I know it was loud as hell. You could hear it climbing twenty miles away.

Along with the Norseman came two of the craziest pilots and strangest characters in the aviation world; Nate Pond and Wiggy Richmond. Nate was from the Pond family of Good Hills Farm Connecticut whose dad, "Batch" Pond dated back to aviation in the 1920's. We tagged them after the two common vibration frequencies known to airplanes. Wiggy was "High Freq." And Nate was "Low Freq." Wiggy was also famous for a combat picture he took while flying a P-40 Warhawk in WWII. It has been used in many movies and documentaries. It is of a freight train traveling along a row of trees, under attack by an airplane. The steam engine blows up and the plane flies right through the explosion. That was Wiggy. He said, "It scared the shit out of me too".

The *Team* voted me as Team Captain and Muriel Simbro as representative of the women's team, and training began.

It was a wonderful training camp. For the first time we trained as the United States Parachute Team. In the past, the military members and the civilian members had trained separately, then met at the site of the competition and competed as a team. This way, we bonded better. We got into each other's heads. We learned from each other. We trained each other. We respected each other.

I mentioned that John Cann, from the British Army's Special Air Service Regiment, was training with us. One afternoon, he and I were talking and I happened to mention that I thought I heard something like a popping noise while descending in the parachute. He said he experienced the same thing and that it sounded an awful lot like bullets going by. Well, I had not been to Vietnam yet and didn't recognize that sound. We talked it over with everybody else but we were the only two hearing it. To play it safe, we contacted the local Sheriff and devised a plan.

The next day, the Sheriff and a couple of his deputies staked out the general area while John and I made another jump in that vicinity. Again, we heard the popping sound. About 30 minutes after we landed, we got a call from the Sheriff. Sure as hell, they found a father and his two sons shooting at us with rifles. Come to find out, they had a chicken ranch and were pissed off about the noise the Norseman made while climbing out over that area. I looked at John and said "Holy Shit"!

It was all going great! It was going wonderful! It was going marvelous! All was right with the Universe! until July 13th, jump number 890.

We were practicing the men's Team event from 4,950 feet. We all got out and fell for 20 seconds, stacking as best we could by varying our rates of descent. After opening, we wouldcontinue to get stacked so as to arrive at the target one at a time. Brydon first, me second then Bourquin, Vander Weg and Arender. Brydon landed first with what appeared to be a dead center. That gave me the incentive to be as accurate as possible. I landed 44 centimeters from dead center. The rest of the guys did as well. It was a world class average and would probably have been a World Record if it had been during the actual competition. What a great team effort, but in order to get my 44 centimeters, I was traveling forward and had to reach back for the target. Guess what my second point of contact with the ground was? My frigging shoulder. I re-broke my collarbone in the same damn place!

This was really the pits! The World Championship was scheduled to begin on August the 13th. Not counting this lousy day that only left thirty days for me to mend. Even if I did, I would have no training. We had to start thinking about using Hank Simbro, who was the first alternate. The decision didn't have to be made right away, but would keep Hank and myself on pins and needles for the next thirty days. Hank training as hard as possible and I was trying to get the days to pass quicker. We would evaluate the situation on a day-by-day basis.

I needed something to occupy my time and energy; something that would be of benefit to the Team effort. "Deke," suggested that I become the Women's Team trainer. At first, I didn't like the idea because of my background. I was a Staff Sergeant in the Army; Special Forces trained and not accustomed to working with women. But "Deke" insisted and the women thought it was a good idea, so I said OK.

I didn't plan on making a lot of changes right off the bat; instead I really watched them closely. Not just their techniques in style and canopy work but also their attitudes on and off the drop Zone. I began to see a lot of things I didn't like, but first I had to analyze whether I didn't like it because it was wrong or because it was just a man's point of view and a military man at that.

I noticed that they relied on the men's team too much in things like packing their parachutes. Closing the pack tray was sometimes difficult. If they couldn't get it closed, they would usually ask one of the men to do it. They normally let one of the men "spot" the airplane for them. And, if it was a little bit windy, they didn't try very hard to get up and around their parachute after landing. They would rely on one of the men to run, catch it and spill the air. I would try, on a one to one basis, to get them to do things more on their own, or with one of the other girls. But it wasn't catching on very much.

Another trend that I didn't like was not showing up on time for meetings and even training. I asked to see all of them in one of the tents we had set up. Hank started in with us and I said, "Hank, you better stay out here." He asked why and I said, "Because I'm about to chew your wife's ass!" Hank said, "Oh, okay" then turned and walked off.

What happened next in my training philosophy was going to either make or break my relationship, socially, mentally and professionally with these ladies. And I must point out that, in my estimation, they were the finest women athletes, "Last of the Great Broads", and ladies in every sense of the word. I dove in head and heart first!

"You guys really think you're something, don't you?" Every eye riveted on me, and it got as quiet as a church mouse. I continued. "You've been reading all of the crap that's been printed in the papers about you and looking at your pretty faces on those billboard signs, and now you think you're about the greatest creation sense toilet paper. Well, that's about what it's worth, toilet paper!"

Orange and the surrounding area was such a small community, that they really made a big production about the first United States Women's Parachute Team. Every day there was some mention about their training, or their background or their families or something in the local newspapers and some of the more prominent papers. Carlyn Olson had even gotten an RC Cola endorsement and had her picture on a number of billboards around the local area. The publicity was important to us because we relied so much on donations. Well, right now, I definitely had their attention!

I decided to go for broke. "It's not bad that they're printing it, or that you're reading it, we can use the publicity. What's bad about it is that you're starting to believe it! There are only a handful of female parachutists in the United States and most of them are right here in this room. That's all you have ever competed against. Well, I'm here to tell you that the women you will be up against in the World Meet can jump circles around you, both in Style and Accuracy!" I started to wonder how they were going to take this. There were a couple of white faces looking back at me, and a few red ones. But there was no turning back now. "I've seen these women. They're good, they're professional, but, first and foremost, they're a Team! You guys are acting like this is going to be a walk in the park, and you're all going in different directions. "I'll give you some examples of what I'm talking about. Number one; it seems like none of you can close a pack tray, you always have to have one of the men come over and do it for you. Number two; you never do your own spotting, you have one of the men do it for you. And number three; on windy days, you can't seem to get up and run around your chute, you wait for one of the men to come over and collapse it for you. Well, that doesn't cut it anymore." They seemed to be reaching a low boiling point so I figured I better sum it up.

"From now on, if you can't close a pack tray, you get one of the other girls to help. If you can't decide on an exit point, discuss it amongst yourselves. And if you can't get up and around your own parachute, you can drag from here to North Carolina for all I care! Now, I'm here to help you as much as I can, if you still want it. If you don't, it doesn't make a rat's ass to me. Training is over for today. Discuss it, and Muriel can let me know your decision!" As I turned and walked out, I felt like I did back in demolition training. There was a fuse burning on a load of dynamite back there and I just hoped it didn't go off before I got out of the tent.

None of the women would come around me the rest of the day, and I didn't blame them. That night, at The Inn, Muriel came up to me at the bar and said "You were pretty hard on us today. There were some hurt feelings and a couple of pretty pissed off ladies, but we talked it over and figured that you had just gotten a little too close to the truth! They're willing to work with you but don't expect them to be your pal for a while." I said "Thanks Muriel; you know, and I know, that the potential is there. All I ask is that they give it their best shot."

The effect was immediate, and Muriel was right. They didn't have too much to say to me for the next few days. They did listen though, and I watched as they began to help each other more. They started to click as a team and as a result, their individual performances began to improve. Two incidences really stuck in my memory. One was watching Jeannie McCombs go straight over the target and miss it by about 30 yards. She had gotten into a position that couldn't be salvaged. She was too high and too close to the target. It made no difference if she turned left or right, she was still going to miss the target by the same distance. As I walked up to her, she sat up, and with big tears in her eyes, pointed her finger at me and yelled. "I didn't know what to do, so I just didn't do anything, and don't you yell at me!" I just shrugged and walked off. She never saw the grin on my face. The other incident occurred on a high wind day. Anne Batterson came in cross wind and really hit hard. She appeared to bounce off the ground and took about three running strides in mid-air before landing on her feet and was around the parachute in an instant. I said to myself, "Whoa!"

They were beginning to show signs of becoming a very competent and cohesive Team. The better they got as a Team, the more their personal confidence built up. Just at the time that every thing was falling together, Lyle Cameron, of *Skydiver Magazine*, wrote a scathing article about the women's team. It basically said that they were rank amateurs, and didn't stand a chance in hell of receiving any kind of medal in the World Championship. It came at exactly the worst time. It totally demoralized the girls, and set their training back by at least a week.

I had always made it a point never to write an article for a magazine. Especially one stating a personal opinion, but I told the girls that if they could put it behind them and make a good honest effort, I would write a rebuttal. In the mean time, I called Lyle and told him what a rotten thing he had done and just what a "Prick" I thought he was!

Meanwhile, other developments were taking place. General Stilwell had been transferred to Fort Devens, Massachusetts, as Base Commander. One day, he made a trip to Orange to visit and also get in a couple of jumps. At the end of the day, he elected to jump into the "Inn". I had driven up there for the evening and watched the jump from the ground. The spot was pretty good, but the General's accuracy was lacking due to months of demanding Military duties and very little parachuting activities. I watched as he landed right in the very top of the tallest tree on the edge of the drop zone. As he was struggling to get his parachute free and climb out of the tree I walked up and said "Hi General Joe, loose something up there?" He said "Knock it off Fortenberry and help me get this thing out of here." It was a very pleasant evening, the whole *Team*, and a few interested by-standers sitting around chatting with General Joe. During the course of the evening, he asked about my shoulder and suggested that I drop by Fort Devens and talk to some of his medical staff. The next bad weather day we had, and training was suspended, I drove to Fort Devens.

Because it was a semi-official trip, I wore my uniform. As I walked into his outer office, I noticed two "Full Bird" Colonels waiting to see the General, so I was prepared for a long wait. I told the secretary who I was and why I was here, then went and sat a respectful distance from the "Brass". They glanced at me with some obvious curiosity, then returned to their conversation andwaited. It wasn't more than two minutes after I announced myself to the secretary, that the General walked out with outstretched hand and said, "Dick, how the hell are you? I'm glad you came by, come on into my office." Somewhat embarrassed, I walked by two stunned Colonels. We talked for a while and he asked about the *Team*. How well were we doing and what kind of chances did we have in the World Meet? I told him that the men's team had better than average chance at Overall Individual and Team Gold, but that I was particularly happy with the progress of the women's team. I didn't know if they would medal, but I felt they would make a good showing for their first time out. After a while, he picked up the phone, called the base hospital and asked to speak to the "Head Honcho." He mentioned him by name, which I can't recall, but I do remember he was a Colonel. The General told him who I was and what the situation was with my shoulder. He said, "Why don't I send him over and see if your people can make up a little cast or something that he can put over his collar bone while he's jumping." There was an obvious pause on the other end of the line, and then the Colonel replied, "With all due respect Sir, may I suggest that he not be jumping with a broken collar bone?" General Joe said, "Thank you Colonel, your point is well taken, but just let me send him over and see how imaginative your people can be." The Colonel said, "Send him over, Sir." As the General bid me goodbye outside his office door, I walked by the two waiting Colonels. They no longer looked stunned or curious; they were 'Pissed!'

The medical Chief of Staff was still not thrilled at having me there, so he explained the situation, which basically was, "Do it anyway!" and turned me over to the orthopedic staff. With the exception of one Captain, they weren't too thrilled about it either. He said, "Okay, let's see what your shoulder looks like and start from there." He x-rayed it and saw that it was mending nicely, but was by no stretch of the imagination ready to have heavy pressure put on it. I explained that we still had about two weeks before the Meet started. That would be thirty days since the injury. He said that it should have a full six weeks of recovery time. Knowing that that was not an option, he set out to devise some form of protection for it. The Captain was getting a little caught up in the challenge by now, and was curious as to how we could best protect the collar bone. He decided to go with a form fitted cast that ran the length of my collarbone and could be taped on before each jump. If I accidentally opened head down, which I had no intention of doing, it would evenly distribute the pressure over the entire collarbone instead of the two inch width of the main lift web. I thanked him and promised that I was not going to jump until the last day possible. He said, "As far as I'm concerned, I don't have access to your medical records and this was just a favor for you and the General. I hope it works, but I wash my hands of it!" I saluted him and left.

Even though we were in a hyper training mode, we were also called on, occasionally, to do some testing of equipment. One day, Pioneer Parachute Company delivered us some new pack-trays. They were equipped with what they called 'rocket jet' cape-wells. These were the two metal fittings that connected the parachute risers on each side of the harness. These cape-wells didn't have the traditional safety cover that had to be released in order to jettison the canopy. We thought of the cape-wells, mainly as a way to get the parachute collapsed after landing in a high wind. Pioneer was thinking ahead, when parachutes would shed their familiar round shape, and more resemble wings, and then it may become necessary to jettison the main parachute before opening the reserve. Anyway, they asked us to test them.

The U.S. Team had a whole new look this year. The canopies were solid black except for the seven rear gores, those were red. It was a classy look but, more importantly, from the higher altitudes, it allowed us to observe our teammates, whether they were running, holding, or crabbing. It helped in our decision of where to open. It inherited the nick named of "The Lobster Tail". Pioneer had donated these parachutes to the whole team, so when they asked us to test, we tested. The job fell on Loy Brydon.

I remember the first jump he made on the new cape-wells. I was critiquing one of the women on her previous canopy work and wasn't paying much attention, until I heard a gasp and someone yelled, "Hey, Loy did a cut-a-way!" I looked up in time to see Loy's parachute streaming behind him. At about 1,000 feet the reserve came out and Loy landed on the edge of the airport. In a flash, we were all on him asking what happened. "Why did you cut-a-way?" He said, "I didn't. During the opening shock, one side just released!" We called Pioneer and they said it was impossible. It must not have been "seated correctly." Well, this kind of pissed Brydon off. He repacked, making DDS (double damn sure), that they were "seated" right. He went back up (he had everybody's attention now) for another test jump. Not to say that Loy wasn't fearless, but he opened high enough that if it happened again, he had plenty of time and altitude to get rid of it and get the reserve parachute out. We watched in wild anticipation. The jump was uneventful. Loy said, "Well, maybe they were right."

They next day, we watched again, as "Low Freq." climbed the Norseman for altitude with Loy on board. Again, there was plenty of altitude to reach terminal velocity, which would apply maximum load on the cape-wells during opening. We heard the engine cut back and watched Loy get out. He pulled about 3,500 feet and as soon as the parachute deployed, we watched it collapse. We waited for the reserve, but he kept falling. I was getting a little concerned until I saw the reserve deploy at about 1,000. The exact same thing had happened. I asked Loy why he waited so long to deploy the reserve. He said, "When the one side released, I thought I would jettison the other side and just get rid of the whole mess, but I couldn't get the other one to release!" We suggested that he call Pioneer, but Loy said, "Screw 'em, they want a test; I'm damn sure going to give them one!"

In all, Loy made five jumps on the new, state of the art, rocket jet cape-wells. Three of them were cut-a-ways! Loy said, "Let's call Pioneer!"

Pioneer sent a company engineer out to check out the situation. After a quick glance, he said, "Ooops, they're mounted up-side-down." Loy said, "Ooops, they're mounted up-side-down?" I said, "holy shit!"

Well, for better or worse, the VI World Parachuting Championship was drawing near. We moved into the local school (I can't remember whether it was the grade school or the high school) where all of the competitors would stay for the duration of the meet. They were great accommodations. The classrooms had been emptied of desks and replaced with bunk beds. Each team would have a "his and hers" dormitory style living quarters. The P.A. system provided an excellent means of communication and each morning we would be awakened by music. As I recall, the wake up song was "The Happy Trumpeter." The cafeteria provided us with wonderful meals and tried very hard to mix them with each country's ethnic cuisine.

The competitors began to arrive. You could feel the excitement and electricity filling the air. Old friendships were renewed with handshakes, hugs and kisses. New acquaintances were established with introductions of new team members. And of course, the phsyc games started immediately. The French Team introduced me to "the next World Champion", a young man named Jerard Treves. We had never seen or heard of him before, but they said he was 'unbeatable!' He was a nice enough kid and for some reason latched onto me. Until the meet started, he followed me around like a shadow. I think it was mainly to practice his English.

August 12th, 1962, I made my first jump since breaking my collarbone a month earlier. I felt rusty and sluggish but it would have to do. The next day we practiced a style jump. The comment in my log simply says "fast but sloppy". That was it. The meet started on August 16th with Individual Accuracy from 3,300 feet, and would be plagued with bad weather for its duration. My first jump was scored at 2.48 meters. Not bad for a month layoff.

The next day was a weather day. There is nothing worse for a competitor than sitting around wondering how your next jump will score. You lose all momentum and it's very hard to keep hyped up.

On the 18th we all got one more jump in. Mine scored at 3.36 meters. This would not put me in the medals; plus, I would have five days to think about it. We had rain, drizzle and low ceilings for five solid days. We couldn't even get enough altitude to do the low Accuracy jumps. As the host team, we tried to think of entertaining things to do. One Russian team member was a medical student and wanted to tour the local hospital so we arranged that. But after a couple of days everybody lost interest and just moped around.

On the 23rd, we got our third jump in this event. At least we could call it a complete event because you only score the best three jumps. This was not going well at all for me, and the French prediction for Treves was coming to pass. I scored 3.59 meters. Loy was holding right in there in second place behind the Frenchman. The next day, I landed 2.28 meters from that little allusive 7-centimeter disc.

The final tally for the event was Treves won the Gold medal, Loy Brydon won the Silver, and I just squeezed into third for the Bronze. Our women's team never placed in the event and this concerned us deeply.

Because of the weather delays, the men's 1,500-meter Accuracy event was never completed, but "up jumped the devil!" Muriel Simbro won the Gold medal over Janina Krejewska of Poland and Nona Pond won the Bronze.

A *Team* Accuracy jump had been introduced into the competition and we had trained pretty hard for it and had high expectations. Even though on one of the Team jumps, Loy and Jerry both got dead center landings and I had 1.30 meters, the best we could do was third place. But "up jumped the devilagain," our women's team won the Gold over Poland and the U.S.S.R. Way to go girls!

Five more days of bad weather.

During every major world competition, the host country makes an effort to show off some of their countries main attractions. We chose New York City. I think it was just because it was close by. Anyway, I hope so.

A month earlier, *Sports Illustrated* magazine had sent a photographer and reporter to do a piece on the U.S. Team. They had asked to take a couple of pictures of me in front of an inflated parachute. I agreed and promptly forgot about it. Now, on our trip to New York, we stopped the busses on the Interstate to get refreshments. When we walked in the door of the restaurant, I noticed many of the competitors were grouped around something. As I walked up, they parted, began to clap and whistle. I looked past them at a whole rack of *Sports Illustrated* Magazines with my picture on the cover. It was the September addition, 1962. Inside featured Wilt Chamberlain and Casey Stingle but I had the cover. To this day, whenever I look at it, I laugh when I look at the price. It was only .25 cents. But at the moment, although I was flattered, I was also embarrassed to the point that I just went back to the bus and sat there until the journey continued.

I have no idea who picked the routing for this trip, but it took us through some of the worse areas of the City. Run down factories and businesses; poor housing, slums and the homeless. I'm sure that everyone had a number of stories to tell when they returned to their own countries. The trip was very poor planning on somebody's part.

Even though we had not completed the 1,500-meter Accuracy event for the men, when the weather broke it was good enough to start the Style event so we went for that. Jim Arender would lose his World Style title to Evgenija Thachenko of the Soviet Union but Jim hung in there for the Silver. Because the Atyle event is so lengthy with all of the preparation and those old Norseman having to climb to 6,600 feet, it took through September 3rd to complete it and we were lucky at that. Not only did the weather get nasty, but also some tough decisions had to be made. We were running out of time.

Deke asked me to meet with him and said that there was a move on to end the Championship at this point. The French had a Gold medal and was third place team overall. They were happy to go home with that. The men's team from Czechoslovakia was in first place overall. Deke laid out our situation as a team. If we voted to end the meet now, Jim Arender and Muriel Simbro would be World Champions Overall, Brydon would have a Silver in Accuracy, Arender in Style. The U.S. Women's Team would be World Champions overall and the men's team third. One more Gold and Bronze; Nona Pond and I would have Bronze medals for third overall. I told Deke that before I could vote that way, there was someone I had to talk to. Deke said, "I know."

Loy Brydon was in contention to place higher in the Overall standings, which could very easily knock me out of third Overall, and the last event would be his forte, Accuracy.

I met with Loy and confronted him with the situation. He asked which way I was leaning. I said that as Team Captain I had no choice but to look at the overall placing of the team. He said "And as an individual how do you look at it." I didn't answer. I just sat and waited. He said, "It's an easy decision for you, you're medaling overall". I just continued to sit and wait. After a while he said, "I have no choice, I agree with you and Deke. You have my vote if it's needed". As I walked out I could feel his disappointment. I always knew how big a man Loy was in stature, now I knew just how big a man he was in character. I also had my disappointment. This may well be my last World Championship, and chance to avenge the decision at Sophia in 1960.

That's the note the VI World Parachute Championship ended on, except for a drama developing that I was totally unaware of.

The voting was done and it was decided that the meet was complete and over. We had a big banquet at the cafeteria. *Sports Illustrated* Magazine had sent me about a two-foot high cover of my picture. I passed that around at the banquet and had all of the competitors and a few "special" others sign it. To this day it is one of my prized possessions.

The drama took place the next day at the awards ceremony. As each team marched off the field, they would make a right turn and walk about 50 yards, then disperse. When the Yugoslavian Team marched off, one of their members, Milan "Max" Knor didn't make the right turn. He ran straight into a prearranged police car and was whisked off. How exciting, a defection!

Max went on to marry Kim Emmons, (one of the women who trained for the U.S. Team), finish his college engineering degree and raise three wonderful children; one of which became a Doctor of Veterinarian Medicine Years later, Kim and Max would live in the next community to me in Fort Lauderdale, Florida. Max died there in 1998 of an aneurysm.

One of the biggest let downs of the VI World Championship was the swiftness in which it was over. Every other International Meet that I participated in there was the long trip back as a team. Whether it was victory or defeat, we had a chance to "Come Down" as a team. After the Adriatic Cup for example, it was the long bus ride back to Germany, drinking wine and singing silly songs. Then there was the plane ride home. Hugs and kisses at the airport, a little news media action then go home.

After Orange, everyone got in their busses and left. It was over! I remember standing there with the feeling that I was forgetting something. There must be something I was supposed be doing! When I realized there wasn't, I was filled with a vast emptiness. I just went home.

You know how some memories can be triggered by a sound, taste or smell? Well, I have always had fond memories of Orange, Mass. when I think of drinking an orange or root beer float, or hear one of two songs; "Wolverine Mountain" or "Midnight in Moscow".

Chapter 16

Upon returning to Ft. Bragg, I took two weeks off and spent a lot of time at Carolina Beach with my wife and kids, but I was so depressed about the Orange showing and the way it ended that I didn't enjoy it much.

Some of the members of the Australian team stayed over at Bragg to train with us. I took the opportunity to try a new technique of grading and training students. Instead of observing them from the ground with binoculars, I would jump with them and observe at close range. This worked pretty well and got me off of the ground and in the air more. My first student in this method of instructing was Lt. Molloy of the Royal Australian Army. Later, I would use the same method but reinforce it with a helmet camera so the student could see first hand what I was talking about when I critiqued him. This was September 17, 1962. I believe that I was the first instructor to use this method of instruction.

It wasn't long before we were back on the demonstration circuit. One of the first was at Aberdeen, Maryland. We made two demos. On the second, the comment in my jump log just says, "Exited over the bay and tracked!" Brydon and I were supposed to perform the diamond track. We both got out of the Caribou at the same time. As soon as you left the aircraft, you got an accurate picture of exactly where you were over the ground. Well, we weren't exactly over ground. We were so far out over the bay that I wasn't really sure that we could make it to land. I don't know who did the spotting, but it couldn't have been me! Loy and I took one look down, glanced at each other, and started tracking like a son-of-a-bitch. I always considered Loy and me as the two best trackers on the team and I learned it all from him. We were neck and neck from 14,500 feet to about 1,700 feet where we opened. We pointed the parachutes at the target and never turned. We just barely made it to the edge of the drop zone. I think that to this day, it was one of the longest lateral distances ever covered on a jump. He and I still laugh about it when we recall it. At least I laugh at it!

We hit a couple more demos, Ft. Eustis, Virginia and Rome, Georgia, then headed back for Bragg and more training for competition. The holidays went by and I only made two jumps in December, but would make up for it at the first of the year. It was back to Yuma to finish up what we had started in January of '62.

We had made a pretty good run on the daytime records. There were a few left to work on, but most of the night time records were there to be broken. I described in Chapter 11 the criteria for breaking these records. It remained the same, except that because most of the jumps would be made at night, there would be little time for escapades like the "Sam Spade" episode a year earlier.

From January 22nd to February 17th, I would make 50 jumps, mostly record attempts. The *Team* would break most of the existing records and a few that we had set in January of '62.

The Army sent a CV-2B Caribou to assist in the attempts. One of the pilots turned out to be Gary Williams whom I would work with years later as Gulfstream III and IV co-captains with Mobil Oil Corp. To shorten this up a bit, I am just going to cover the records we broke and point out a couple of interesting jumps that took place.

22 January broke the 6-7-8-9 man records from 6,600 ft. hanging in the harness from that altitude tended to cut off the circulation in your legs and they would "go to sleep". It was kind of tough landing with numb feet and legs.
24 January re-broke the 8 man record from 4,950 ft.
28 January broke the 5 man record from 4,950 ft.
28 January broke the 3 man record from 4,950 ft.
31 January broke the 6 man record from 3,300.ft.
5 February broke the 8 man record from 6,600 ft.
7 February broke the 4 man record from 6,600 feet.
13 February broke the 6-7-8 and 9 man records from 3,300 feet.

The main problem with jumps like these were that we all exited the aircraft at the same altitude but somehow had to get staggered to arrive at the target at different intervals. To do this, we had timed each man's rate of descent because of body weight, etc. Even then, the lower jumpers, usually Brydon, Duffy and myself would have to dump air out of the canopies to increase our rates of descent, while Danny Byard and the lighter jumpers would try to stay aloft as long as possible. Even with all of this, we sometimes came into the target rubbing canopies.

14 February broke the 5-6-7-8 and 9 man records.

That was pretty much it. It wasn't all that simple. These were only the jumps that broke records. There were many jumps in between where we missed; all in all, it was very exhausting.

With the completion of the assault on the world night accuracy records, came a lull in which we could play around, experiment or just relax. Bobby Letbetter and I began to discuss the possibility of trying a night baton pass. We had the airplane. We had the little beacons on our helmets and we had a baton. Why not? On 15 February, we waited for it to get good and dark and boarded the U-1A Otter and climbed to 9,500 feet. Bobby would carry the baton and be the anchorman. I would chase him. My biggest concern was over shooting him because he would probably never see me. We came across the drop zone and Bobby got out with me close behind. I couldn't see Bobby, but I could see the little beacon blinking away. I kept closing slowly, but the beacon wasn't getting any bigger. We only had 45 seconds to accomplish this feat and as slow as time seems to pass in these events, I felt we were running out of it. I still couldn't see Bobby's silhouette but that little beacon just kept blinking at me. I finally decided it was now or never so I folded up into a ball to increase my vertical speed without moving horizontally. All of a sudden that little blinking light became about five times larger and there was Bobby, patiently waiting. I thought "holy shit"; I'm overshooting, and flared. When I did, I was falling right next to Bobby about five feet away. He never even saw me. I closed the gap, reached and took the baton out of his hand. It caught him by surprise and I actually felt him flinch when I grabbed the baton. I pulled away and we both opened and landed on the target. Unless someone had logged a night baton pass at an earlier date, I believe this was the first in the United States.

Bobby was later killed on patrol in Vietnam. I flew a helicopter load of *Team* members to his funeral in Arlington Cemetery.

Rest in Peace Bobby.

A couple of other events took place during this period, neither of which had much to do with parachuting or the breaking of world records, but were 'events' nonetheless.

Billy Lockward's dad, besides being a skydiver, was also a Medical Doctor. During one of the weekend lulls, he invited everyone over to his house for a party. Having other things to occupy my time in Yuma, I didn't make it, but when the guys came back on Sunday, I got the story.

After partying all night, Docky Locky, as we referred to him, asked if anyone wanted a vasectomy and I'll be damned if four or five of them didn't take him up on it. I mean, hell, it was free, so the good doctor took them one at a time on the kitchen table and performed the operation. Amazingly, they all seemed worse from the hangovers than the operation. That is, all but one! I won't mention any names here but, he'll know who I'm talking bout. He had been in a car wreck years earlier in Germany and as a result, one tube was wedged between bones and Docky Locky had to dig for it. He was black and blue and sore with a capital S. They all had to make numerous jumps beginning Monday morning or were subject to disciplinary action from the Team Commander. I don't know how but they all made four or five jumps that day.

Everything was going smooth and it appeared that the Team Commander would never know what had taken place until after the second day of jumping. That night, he was in some misery. He finally said "Hey Dick, come here. I think

I'm in trouble!" He asked me to look at his crotch and see if I saw anything wrong. I said, "Hey man, I'm not touching it!" But he did seem to be in some distress so I had a look. The stitches had come out and you could actually see his testicle. I said, "holy shit", and yelled, "Hey guys, come here. Did you ever see one of these?" So, at his expense, we all had a good laugh and an interesting look at his balls that night. I washed my hands for two days!

The next day he had to go to the Base Hospital and have the stitches re-done. I guess that either because we never missed any jumps or the Team Commander didn't quite know how to write it up in a report, nothing was ever said about it again.

The other event was the brawl at a bar named "The Snake Pit", but I think I'll just skip that part. If you want more on that subject, just contact Coy MacDonald. "And the plot thickens!"

Chapter 17

We returned to Ft. Bragg and spent the next three months training. On March 25, 1963, there is an asterisk by my second jump of that day. On that jump, I became the tenth person in the United States to achieve 1,000 jumps. It's signed by "The 1st Knight", John T. Hollis.

The first week of June, right after my 25th birthday, we boarded a C-54 and headed for Germany where we would compete in the Europa Cup, an International Invitational Meet. This aircraft was the military version of the Douglas DC-6 or DC-7. Both had Pratt and Whitney R-2800 engines rated at 2,000 horse power each. Unlike the earlier version, the DC-4, they were pressurized. All of them took eighteen hours to get to Germany and twenty-four hours to get back. The time difference was because of the prevailing Westerly winds. Both ways seemed like forever. They usually refueled in Thule Greenland, and there is nothing green about Greenland. After the Europa Cup, we would remain in Germany and train for the Adriatic Cup to be held in Portoroz, Yugoslavia in August.

The U. S. delegation consisted of:
Colonel John Singlaub-Head of Delegation
Major Henry Rust-Pilot

Mr. Jim Arender-Judge
SFC Phil Miller-Judge
Lt. Roy Martin-Team Leader
SSgt. Dick Fortenberry-Competitor
SFC Gerald Bourquin-Competitor
SFC Phil Vander Weg-Competitor
SFC Gene Paul Thacker-Alternate
Sp5 Coy McDonald-Competitor
Sp5 Bobby Letbetter-Alternate
SSgt. Joe Norman-Alternate

SFC Phil Miller had been stationed in Germany as a Captain and was well known by the German Aero-Club, and they requested him as Chief Judge. Other countries represented were, Austria, Germany, Great Britain, Spain, Switzerland, Ireland, France and Belgium.

We traveled by bus to a small town tucked away near the Bavarian Alps in southern Germany named Leutkirch. It was an interesting place with a large castle overlooking a small grass airfield. That's where the meet would be held. The story went that the castle belonged to the descendents of a highwayman who took all of his plunder, invested it wisely and bought respectability, becoming a land baron.

On our practice jumps, the team average was less than 1.5 meters. It was apparent that we were the team to beat.

On the first day of practice, I met a man named Gerold Reinitzer. He was the only competitor from Austria. Gerold was there with his wife Inga and their beautiful daughter Doris. Doris was about six or seven years old with the blond hair and blues eyes you would type cast a young Austrian girl in a movie with. We have all been life long friends ever sense.

Here's how we met. I had just come off of a practice jump and was packing my parachute on the grass when I kind of had this sixth sense that someone was watching me. I slowly turned around and this little blonde haired, blue-eyed girl was standing there. I instinctively winked at her. She blushed and ran off. While packing after my second jump, I again had the feeling of being watched. I turned around and there was Doris again, but this time when I winked at her, she didn't run. She blushed, winked back and stood her ground. From that time until the end of the meet, if Gerold couldn't find his daughter, all he had to do was look for me and she would be there jabbering away, trying to teach me how to count in German. Although we couldn't speak each other's language, we had hours of conversation.

Gerold was a very good Accuracy jumper, but as was the case with a lot of jumpers in the early days, he lacked proficiency in Style. Because he was the only competitor representing Austria, there was no one to turn to except outside help. He asked me if I could help him by observing his Style practice through binoculars and then critiquing him. I said "sure". After doing this a couple of times, Lt. Martin got wind of it and pulled me off to the side and asked why I was training my competition? I said, "Because he asked." He didn't like that answer and said, "What if he beats you?" I said that as far as I was concerned, winning wasn't every thing. It beat's the hell out of second place, but there are more important things in life such as imparting knowledge, international relations and friendship. As I left, I turned around and said, "Besides, I'm just going to teach him enough to beat everyone but me," and walked off with a grin on my face.

In the Individual Accuracy event, Phil Vander Weg demonstrated the talent we all knew he had, and won First place. I was less than three points behind him in Second place. My new found friend, Garold Reinitzer, won Third place. Coy McDonald and Jerry Bourquin placed Fourth and Seventh, respectively.

From a team standpoint, we did excellent. Jerry Bourquin spearheaded our efforts with some outstanding Accuracy including a Dead Center landing. We won the event. Because of inclement weather and low cloud bases, and much to all of our disappointment, the Style event was canceled. By combining all of the Team and Individual scores together, the U.S. Team was proclaimed the Overall winner.

From Leutkirch, we traveled to Illesheim Army Airfield in Sembach Germany. This would be our training base for the upcoming Adriatic Cup Parachute Meet to be held in Portoroz, Yugoslovia the last part of August. Sembach was one of those typically quaint little German villages you might see on a post card, clean and very neat. All of the houses were well landscaped, groomed and everything seemed to be in its proper place, absolutely no clutter. There was no industry to speak of. It mainly thrived because of the U. S. Army's Illesheim Airfield nearby. The airfield was home to a small Army aviation unit flying the H-37, which was a large twin engine helicopter with a huge clamshell type door in the front of it. The large, radial engines that provided power to it leaked so much oil that the pilots used to say, "Fill up the oil and check the gas". The base had all of the amenities for a sustained training program. Nice living quarters, Post Exchange, large swimming pool, Theater and a large grassy field for a drop zone. So, we dug right into it.

We had a single engine Otter and crew assigned to us for the entire period, so when the weather permitted, we averaged four jumps a day.

Midway through training, we had a request to travel to Sywell, England and perform a demonstration at an air show. It was a welcome diversion from our daily regimen, and besides, I had never been to England. It was an opportunity to show them how one of their former colonies was progressing. During the week of the air show, the United Kingdom was going to conduct their national Parachuting Championship to determine who would represent them in the next World Championship, and requested that members of the *Golden Knights* judge it. This was a very high honor for us and we readily accepted.

We flew to Sywell in the Otter, which had a cruise speed of about 120 knots so it would be a very scenic trip. I specifically remember crossing the English Channel and seeing the White Cliffs of Dover for the first time. The weather was so clear; we could see them from miles out.

The airfield at Sywell was perfect for an air show and just flying in general. It was far from any major city or large airport such as Heathrow. There were no runways. It was a huge, level grassy field and you took off and landed any direction you wanted. But for the air show, they had specific rules and regulations on which events would take place at what time.

Although the week had many notable events, a few stand out more than others and they are what I would like to cover.

Before the start of each day's events, Bourquin, Letbetter and I would start out by dropping the wind drift indicator.

Each day, the British army assigned a soldier to follow it and mark the spot it landed with a large orange panel. We would then make another pass and jump. I remember one morning that the wind was so calm that there was a broken fog lying in patches around the fields and farms. As we opened, it was so quiet that we could hear all of the sounds from ground activities drifting up. It was like we had gone through some time warp and I could envision WWI Spads and Sopwith Camels flying up out of the fog. These were delightful moments to me.

One day, the winds were very high and we went through the routine of dropping the drift indicator. It must have drifted almost a mile. Even though we didn't see the orange panel, the three of us made another pass and jumped. We made it to the target, but after landing decided that the winds were too high to conduct any meaningful kind of an Accuracy event. So we would go on with the Style event because after the parachute was opened, the scoring was over and the jumper could just concentrate on a safe landing.

Right here, I have to say that a private is a private is a private, I don't care what Army he's in. It took about an hour to set up the arrow and shutter panels for the style event and we were lying on our backs, with binoculars and stopwatches in hand when I heard this clearing of a voice. I looked over and saw this British Private standing with the wind drift indicator in his hand. He had red hair and a freckled face and was soaked and wet from the waist down. In what sounded like a Scottish Brogue, he said, with as much disgust as he dared, "Here's your fuckin' piece of paper Sarge. It landed under a bloody bush and a bleatin' bull wouldn't let me 'ave it!" Jerry, Bobby and I looked at each other and had to bite our lips to keep from roaring. I still feel that if just one of us had snickered, he would have killed all three of us!

On the weekend, we suspended competition in order to make the airfield available for the air show. The air show consisted of mostly vintage aircraft. There were all kinds of aerobatic displays including wing walking. On the second day of the show we were watching an older airplane, like a tiger moth, which was demonstrating its maneuverability in slow flight. He must have only been a couple of hundred feet high when all of a sudden he stalled, inverted and headed straight down. I had just gotten my pilots license two months prior to this and instinctively knew this wasn't part of the show. He hit the ground, nose first and then plopped back on his wheels. There was a British Army pilot standing behind me and I heard him comment, "I say, that was a hell of a short field landing." I couldn't help but chuckle at the typical British humor. It was lucky that he was going so slowly. It didn't kill the pilot but a friend I had met was one of the first to arrive at the scene of the crash and said later that his feet went clear through the floor of the aircraft and were hanging out of the bottom. I couldn't help but remember a picture I had once seen of a cowboy going over a cliff on his horse. He was pulling hard on the reins yelling "Whoa you son-of-a-bitch, whoa!" They had to cancel the wing-walking act because the pilot was the husband of the wing walker.

Before returning to Germany and our training, the British 22nd Special Air Service Regiment (SAS) invited us to their base in Hereford, England for a visit. I had heard stories of these guys, but took a lot if it with a grain of salt. I should have known better! The Base was typical WWII era with old wooden buildings. Sgt. Mick Turner lent us his small van for transportation and I got my first taste of driving from the right side of the car on the left side of the road. It was kind of tricky to start with and took a lot of concentration, but I soon got the hang of it. Like I mentioned, the barracks were WWII vintage and the Sergeants Mess, which we refer to in our Army as the Non-Commissioned Officers Club was no different. It had these high, wooden rafters which will come into play later. After duty hours, a soldier would stand at the entrance with a pint of beer in case the RSM (Regimental Sergeant Major) should walk in. He tests the beer on his arm occasionally as a mother would do with her baby's bottle, to see if it's too warm. If so, he pours it out and refreshes it. One evening we were having a few pints with the SAS and encountered this Artillery sergeant who was a hold over from WWII, and didn't like "bloody Yanks!" He continued to refer to Jerry, Bobby and myself as "you bloody Yanks" this and "you bloody Yanks" that, until we wanted to kick his ass. But being guests, we had to bite our tongues. Well, unbeknownst to us, a couple of the SAS troops were in the kitchen making a 13 knot hang-mans noose out of a rope. When they walked in with it, the Sergeant became even more belligerent. He started saying things like, "I'm not afraid of you blokes and you blokes ain't going to do any thing with that!" The SAS guys threw the noose over one of the rafters and stood him up on a stool. They asked him if he had any last words. He began yelling "Get me down from here, let me down!" So they kicked the stool out from under him. We couldn't believe it! The Sergeant was hanging there with his hands up on the rope trying to relieve the pressure on his throat, gagging and kicking! About that time, the RSM walked in and saw what was going on. He took the pint from the soldier, tasted it, complained about it, then walked over to the hanging Sergeant. I distinctly remember the RSM taking his time. He put his swagger stick under his left arm, jutted out his chin and finally said "Let the bloke down!" The sergeants' face was pretty flushed as he slumped to the floor. He got up and left as fast as his shaky legs would carry him. The

SAS had a big laugh, and to my knowledge, nothing else was ever said about it.

On July 13th, 1963, Jerry, Bobby and I teamed up with the SAS and made a formation jump into the local soccer stadium at half time. The locals were very impressed and we spent a lot of time "mingling" and signing autographs.

One other thing that was notable during our visit was a skull that was mounted over the mantle behind the bar at the Sergeants Mess. It had a candle in it that was lit on a few occasions. We didn't think much of it until one of us, casually, inquired about it. Back in the States, when our Special Forces, or any of our military conducted live military exercises, we did it against each other. When the SAS held military exercises, sometimes it was against the Red Chinese. The skull happened to be that of a Red Chinese Colonel that was 'accidentally' killed on one of those exercises. They didn't know what to do with him so they buried the body and brought the head home. There it was, prominently displayed on the mantle behind the bar at the 22nd SAS Sergeants Mess! I had a whole new perspective of the SAS!

It was time for us to leave and return to our duties of preparing for the Adriatic Cup, but before we left, we were each presented with a pewter cup from our SAS friends. I can see mine now. I keep it on my desk with pens and pencils in it. Mine reads "SGT. Richard T. Fortenberry FROM S.A.S. Skydivers." It's one of the few mementos I have remaining, intact.

Chapter 18

There was no break back in Illesheim, Germany. We got right back to work. The first order of business was how to thread four pieces of thread through a needle at one time. By that, I mean have four jumpers leave the aircraft at the same time but arrive at the target at different times. If we had enough altitude, we could "slip" the parachutes, dumping air to descend faster, but the jump was from 1,950 feet. The comments in my log book for the first four attempts were "Oh Mother!" On the third attempt, we tried inverting the 'stick,' or order of jump. That was no good. Then we thought of something, but it involved some very precision flying from Captain Henry Rust, our *Team* pilot. We had about a 50 foot grace distance on our jump altitude. The aircraft had a barometric device to make sure that we stayed within those parameters. We asked Capt. Rust if he felt that he could fly at the bottom of the limits, and when the first jumper exited, climbed to the top of the parameter as the other three exited, he said "Let's try it." It worked. It gave us just the right stack to arrive at the target at different times. We practiced this many times to make sure we stayed within the altitude limits according to the Barometric pressure device. This maneuver made Hank Rust feel more of an intricate member of the *Team*.

Another event to be held at the Adriatic Cup was a water jump for Accuracy. We traveled to Friedrichafen, Germany to practice these jumps in the Bodensee Lake. We loved this part of our training. The Bodensee Lake was a gorgeous lake bordered by three or four countries. Large ferry boats connected them. The countryside matched the beauty of the Lake. We didn't know why at the time, but we were given a strict schedule for when we could practice our jumps.

The target was a rubber raft. You were timed from the time you touched the water to the time you touched the raft. A perfect jump would be to hit the raft and the water at the same time. One rule was that you must have contact with your parachute when you hit the water. This was for our own safety, to keep an over zealous jumper from jumping out of his or her parachute at an altitude that could harm them. Another rule was that you couldn't land on the raft thereby endangering the judges. The method we all used to shorten our swim time was to release one side of the reserve parachute, letting it hang out of the way. Then we would scoot way back in the harness saddle, release our chest and leg straps and set in it like a swing. When your feet touched the water, you just start swimming. The other fun part of these jumps was that all we wore was a bathing suit. No helmet or boots. It gave you a nice free feeling.

We only had three days of jumping at the Bodensee, so we crammed as much training in as we could. It was difficult because between each jump we had to let our canopies and harnesses dry out. We made one jump the first day, two the second and one the last. My times were 3 seconds, 6 seconds, 19 seconds and 0 seconds, which was equivalent to a dead center landing. On the last day, we found out why we were not supposed to jump out of our scheduled time frame. The weather was bad, but clearing.

We badly needed that last practice jump. The weather cleared enough for us to make the jump, but it was out of that time frame. We decided to do it anyway. It would just be one lift. Five jumpers, five passes. What could it hurt? As we made the jumps, we noticed a ferry boat going by. The passengers were all on one side of the boat watching us and almost capsized. Our bad!

Back at Illesheim Army Airfield, the weather was great and we trained every day except weekends. We would have trained then but that was when they 'mowed the lawn.' They didn't actually mow it. They allowed the local sheep herders to bring their herds on base to graze. It served a purpose. It allowed the sheep to feed and kept the grass short. On Monday morning, you really had to watch where you landed if you were off target, otherwise you would be washing sheep shit out of your jump suit and off of your boots!

We had one more side trip before heading to Yugoslavia and that was an invitation to compete in a meet at Spa Belgium, Spa was another beautiful, small European town. We were excited about the meet because it would allow us to get into the spirit of competition before the Adriatic Cup. It was a real 'no pressure' event. We were there from the 5th of Aug. to the 12th of Aug. and only made four jumps including the practice jump. Loy Brydon was the team alternate for this meet and made a dead center landing on the practice jump. This set the mood for the rest of the meet. Overall, it was just a fun period of time. I got to jump out of the Donier 27 for the first time. The funniest thing that happened was one day Loy, Coy McDonald and I were laying side by side on the DZ when a bird flew over at about 50 feet. All three of us watched as a projectile came out of its ass. No one moved a muscle as we watched it descend and hit me right in the middle of my chest! Loy looked over at me with this silly grin and said "This just ain't going to be your day, is it?"

Back in Ellesheim, we only had about two weeks of training left before going to Portoroz, Yugoslovia and the Adriatic Cup, but an event that took place prior to leaving for Portoroz would cause quit a stir with the *Team*. During our Accuracy training, Lt. Martin was beginning to tell us where to spot and where to exit the aircraft. This began to bother the *Team* as we were the best parachutist the United States could produce and he was telling us how to spot an aircraft? The *Team* asked if I would say something to him about it. I don't know why they asked me but I said I would, so after one of our meetings I asked if I might have a word with him in private. I put it as tactfully as I could, saying that as the overall U. S. Team Leader, we realized how hard of a job he had, with all of the logistics, scheduling and the many responsibilities that go along with that title. I also pointed out that he was in charge of the best parachutists the United States could field, duly selected by a U.S. National Championship process and that part of our job was to decide where to exit the aircraft. I told him that the *Team* was feeling a little 'put out' by him 'suggesting' where we spotted. He told me that he was unaware of this and thanked me for bringing it to his attention. The next day, Lt. Martin had the routine Team meeting and said "Last night I had to make an extremely difficult decision. I thought very long and hard on it. The Team going to Yugoslavia will be, Jerry Borquin, Phil Vander Weg, Coy McDonald, Joe Norman and Loy Brydon." Holy shit! The whole *Team* sat there dumbfounded. Especially me! I wasn't on the list! I was the U.S. National Champion! I had the highest Accuracy point average during our whole training period and I wasn't on the list! I finally recovered enough to ask what he had planned for me. He said "You're going back to the States Saturday with Sergeant Thacker". It's hard to recall when I have been let down so hard in all my life. That day the *Team* took off in the aircraft for their training jumps for the first time without me being a member. I cried!

For the next few days, the *Team* continued to train, but in a very solemn mood. They each, in their own way, tried to console me but it wasn't working. I tried to think of a way out of this, but there was no recourse. Even though this was the U.S. Team, he was my Commanding Officer. I resigned myself to returning to the States. I considered asking for a transfer from the Army Parachute Team upon my return. I felt that I could no longer effectively do my job under Lt. Martin's command.

In years to come, Roy and I would rekindle our friendship and he would go on to be an excellent combat commander in the Vietnam conflict.

As I pointed out, he was the head of our delegation but he didn't have total authority over the U.S. Team. That came under the heading of the President of the Parachute Club of America, "Deke" Sonnicsin, in Menlo Park, California. A couple of days before I was slated to return to the United States, Lt. Martin held another briefing. He said that he had a telegram from Deke Sonnicsin requiring him to leave me on the U.S. Team. Actually, it was a little stronger than that. It basically said, "Dick Fortenberry will not return to the United States. He will represent the United States in the Adriatic Cup!" Unfortunately, this meant that Phil VanderWig would be off the team. It took me months to find out what happened and how Deke was informed.

As I mentioned earlier, SFC Phillip Miller had been a Captain when I first met him years before in Germany. During that period, he had established a close relationship with Herr Richard Khonke, who owned the only parachute factory in West Germany. Herr Khonke was, also, the head of delegation for the Republic of West Germany's Parachute Team. Phil contacted him and asked if he would inform Deke Sonnicsin of the situation. Now it would be in West Germany's best interest if I didn't compete, but Herr Khonke had this overwhelming sense of honor and pride. If he was going to compete, he wanted to compete against the best. Deke later informed me of the content of Herr Khonke's telegram. Basically, it said, "I cannot understand the United States jeopardizing their position at the Adriatic Cup by sending Dick Fortenberry back to the States at this time."

As is customary, the *Team* votes for the Team Captain. The next day, I was voted Captain! Off to the Adriatic Cup.

We flew to Frankfurt where we met up with the rest of the U.S. delegation, Deke Sonnicsin and the ladies who made up the women's team. They were Anne Batterson, Carlyn Olson and Jeanni McCombs. We all boarded a bus and headed to Portoroz. The drive, the weather, the atmosphere, everything was wonderful. Although there was a slight feeling of apprehension because of the upcoming event, we were all so glad the training and preparation was over and we were all together again. The trip would take us through the heart of West Germany, into the mountains of Germany and Austria, down into the coast lands of Yugoslavia, now called Slovenia. Portoroz was a small, little known, tourist town. There was an American movie star staying at the same hotel we were in. His name was Guy Madison and played Wild Bill Hickok in the TV series of the same name. He was very interested in our activities and hung out with us a little. The first order of business was to recon the area and check out the competition. There were some old faces and some new. My friend Gerold Reinitzer from Austria was there but not his family. I told him that I was disappointed that I would not see my little girlfriend, Doris.

The competition would consist of four events; a team Accuracy event from 1,950 feet, an Individual Style event from 4,950 feet, an Individual Water Jump Accuracy event and a demonstration event. This would be our first time to compete in a demonstration event and the rules were very sketchy. The biggest concern was safety. There would be no low openings but other than that anything was possible. The jump aircraft was the Russian built AN-2, a large bi-winged aircraft with one huge 900 horse power engine. There were no seat belts in the aircraft, not even for the pilots!

The Russians demo was pretty unique and I thought they would win the event. They came over at about 7,000 feet. One parachute came out and opened immediately. No big deal, but then one at a time bodies started falling from the parachute. Five of them cut away and opened their individual parachutes at about 2,000 feet. I have never seen that done again. I can't remember the other demos, but Loy Brydon and I won the event with the 'Max Track.'

We activated our smoke grenades located on a bracket attached to our foot and exited at 7,000 ft. We turned 180 degrees from each other and tracked for all we were worth and opened at 1,800 ft. I don't know how far apart we got but the judges came over and inspected our smoke grenades to see if there was some kind of propulsion devices involved. We were afraid that we would be disqualified for a safety violation because when we opened, I was over sea level ground but Loy was over about an 800 ft. hill which meant he was only about 1,000 ft above ground when he opened. They never said anything and we certainly didn't mention it! The trophy was a carved wooden statue of a man with his back arched, looking at the sky. It almost looked like he was tracking.

Our technique of climbing the aircraft during the exit on the Team Accuracy event went well. We watched the other teams struggle to get separation for landing on the target while we did it with ease. Some of the other teams realized how we were getting such good separation, but it required so much coordination between the jumper spotting the aircraft and the pilot that they knew this was not the time to practice. We won the event.

I need to mention that during the weekend break in the competition a couple of things of interest took place. Number one, one of the female members of the Yugoslavian Team who had competed in Orange, Mass, during the VI World Championships had been killed in a training accident preparing for the Adriatic Cup. Deke had brought with him a bottle of sand from the "Bowl" at Orange. We boarded one of the AN-2's and flew to Zagreb where she was buried, poured the sand over her grave site and placed some flowers there. It was a very somber event. The local newspaper covered it and the Yugoslavian Team was very appreciative. During the trip back to Portoroz, the Hungarian pilot let me fly the aircraft. Number two, Gerald Reinitzer drove to Gratz, Austria and brought his daughter Doris back. I thought that was very nice. At first she was too embarrassed to see me because she had cut her hair short but she finally came around. We picked up our friendship where it left off two years earlier in Germany. She had a baby tooth missing and brought it with her. Doris gave it to me for 'good luck.' Every jump I made, Doris would rush over to see if I had her tooth. I would reach in my pocket; pull it out to show her. No spectators were allowed inside the hundred meter circle during the Accuracy events, but no matterwhere I walked out of that circle, she was right there to check on the tooth. I don't remember if I mentioned it earlier, but years later, Gerald and his family came to Virginia to visit me. My little sweetheart, Doris, is now a Veterinarian in Vienna.

For Jerry Bourquin and myself, the meet was going very well until the last event which was the Water Jump for Accuracy. We were in second and third place by less than a point. Urabel, from which country I don't remember, had 742.69 points. Jerry had 742.00 points and I had 742.03. Because the landing would be in salt water, I decided to take the sleeve off of my parachute and just accordion fold the canopy into the pack-tray. After taking the sleeve off, I realized that I didn't have any retainer bands to stow the suspension lines with so I just accordion folded them in also. The two pilot chutes were now attached directly to the apex of the canopy. In short, everything was a big glob inside the pact-tray. I also told myself to be sure and get away from the prop blast before pulling the rip-cord. Another after thought was to hook some rubber shower shoes to the leg straps of my harness so as to have something to walk with on the hard, rocky beach after the jump. Well, with the excitement and anticipation of the jump, I forgot all that as I stepped into the prop blast and immediately pulled the rip-cord. I barely got the "Oh Shit" out of my mouth when I got the hardest opening shock of my life. The pilot chute anchored itself into the prop blast, the canopy opened in a flash, I sailed the length of the suspension lines and came to an abrupt halt. I had to just hang there for a few seconds to let my "gyros" re-cage, get the stars to stop flashing in my eyes and regain some feeling back in my arms. I never did find the shower shoes. My jump would have been the equivalent of a dead center landing because I touched the raft and the water at the same time, but they docked me 50 points for leaving the parachute harness before I touched the water. They did the same thing to Jerry. The rules stated that you had to have physical contact with the harness on entering the water. A later picture taken by Joe Gonzales, showed me dragging the left parachute riser into the water with me, but it was after the Awards Ceremony and the trophies had already been awarded. Overall, the U.S. did very well. Coy McDonald won First place for the men and Anne Batterson won First place for the women. The trip home was a blast!

Oh well, that was yesterday! It's time to move on. The U.S. Nationals are two weeks away in Issaquah, Washington.

Chapter 19

Things are happening pretty fast right now. We made our last jump in Portoroz on the 1st of September and on the 9th and 10th I made three jumps at Ft. Bragg. My next jump was on the 12th of September for the beginning of the U.S. Nationals at Issaquah, Washington. In order to get in some practice jumps we made sure we arrived a couple of days early.

Issaquah was a quaint little town just outside of Snohomish. The competition would be held at the local airport. At the entrance to the airport was a small café, and on the last jump of the day, we would land right behind the café, go in and have a bit of libation and dinner. We named the café the 'Toggle Inn' after the wooden toggles on our parachute guide lines.

Upon arrival, I was also notified (I forget by whom) that there was a guy named Carlos Wallace, from Texas, that was out to beat me; not to win the Nationals, but specifically to beat me. I had never heard of him much less met him, but he had a mission.

The meet didn't start well for me and it looked like Wallace might get his wish. My first accuracy jump was

27ft. from the disc; all I wrote in my log book was "not mentally prepared." The second jump wasn't scored. The judges were off doing something else when I landed, so I got a re-jump. This was really screwing me up mentally and throwing me way off of my rhythm. The next day, I made two low altitude accuracy jumps from 2,200 ft. On the first one, I was 4.3 meters off the disc. The one thing notable about that jump was that I had my log book signed by Frank Carpenter, D-111 and Pope #12. The Pope #12 was from an old drinking game we used to play! Frank was a hell-of-a stunt man and all around good guy. The next jump was scored at 6.07 meters. This meet is just going way down hill for me. Thankfully, the next day was bad weather.

It wasn't raining; it was just overcast and gloomy, but we had to hang around the airport just in case it cleared. Other jumpers seemed to be in a little funk also. I went over to Hank Strauch, who was providing the aircraft for the meet and asked if I could borrow one of his jump planes. He looked at me with reservations in his eyes but said, "OK." I went to the hangar and found Anne Batterson sitting on the floor reading a book. I said "grab a parachute and follow me." She looked up doubtfully and said "why." I just said "trust me." And away, we went. I picked Anne because she was an adventurer and I knew she would appreciate this more than anyone else. It was September 16, 1963, a great day! We jumped in a Cessna 172 and took off. The side door had been taken off for jumping, so the visibility was great. The first thing we did was find a lake that was hosting a hydro-plane boat race. I went down and raced one of them. I didn't get close enough to the shore for anyone to get my tail number. The overcast was about 1,000 feet but only about 200 feet thick. I found a 'sucker' hole and went through. We found ourselves on top of these beautiful, white, fluffy clouds with Mt. Shasta off in the distance. Compared to the gloominess we had just left, this was a fairy land! We didn't talk, we just enjoyed. I found a small cloud lifting up about 200 feet above the others. I put my right wing tip in it and just circled it. All good things must end, so reluctantly I found the 'sucker' hole again and flew back into the gloom. I found the airport and landed. We were no sooner on the ground than Hank came running over and said "God I'm glad you back! I asked why and he said "look at the fuel gauge." He hadn't refueled after the last jump run and I didn't check it before take-off; a pilot's number one worse mistake. We were on fumes! I won't get on or in anything now without checking the fuel gauge!

That little distraction seemed to do the trick. I felt I was back in the groove and mentally prepared for whatever the next week might hold.

The next day, the skies cleared and we conducted the Style event. I made two jumps and turned 10.2 seconds on both. That was excellent in 1963. In the remarks section of my log book, on the first jump I wrote, "I felt like part of the elements!" On the second I wrote, "Shaved the heading on my third turn, but corrected and lost maybe .2 of a second." These jumps had me leading in the Style event.

On the 18th, we did the 15 second delay, Accuracy event from 5,000 feet. I made two jumps. The first was 2.92 meters and the second was 10.21 meters. This was not good! Carlos, I know you're watching!

I needed a distraction; something to take my mind off of the meet and something to relax me, mentally. It came in the form of a night water skiing jaunt. I don't remember who organized it or who furnished the equipment, but that night we found a lake and went water skiing. It was perfect. There wasn't a cloud in the sky with a full moon and not a breath of air. I remember getting outside of the boats wake and seeing the reflection of the moon following along side me on the surface of the lake. It was marvelous! I slept like a baby that night. Unfortunately, it wouldn't last long.

The next day was a continuation of the Style event. We had two more jumps to make and one of mine would have to be scored. As I mentioned earlier, four jumps were made in each event and you could throw the worst one out. My third jump was respectful, but I felt I could do better. When I got ready for the fourth jump a jumper with a helmet camera followed me to the aircraft. I asked what he was doing and he replied that he was going to film me for the TV Company that was covering the meet. I told him "no way." This opened a whole can of worms. The jump was delayed to sort this out. Chris Schenkel, the announcer for the TV Company came over and got into the fray. He said that if I didn't let the cameraman go up with me, the TV Company was going to sue me. Well, this kind of ticked me off. I hadn't signed anything to that effect. He said that I had verbally agreed a few days earlier to let a cameraman film my Style Series. I told him that I had agreed to let someone film me if I had the event won. Well, that wasn't the case. I needed this to win the Style event and the last thing I wanted was the distraction of some guy hanging around me with a camera. The discussion got pretty heated, so before I got sued for knocking someone on their ass, the suggestion was made that we go up for an extra, non-scored jump to do the filming. Maybe the confrontation was a good thing. I was so pissed off that I turned a 10 second flat series and won the National Style Championship. I went on to win the Low Altitude Accuracy event and the Overall title, U.S. National Champion; so much for Carlos Wallace from Texas. I later heard rumors that he had been killed in an armed robbery attempt.

This was the first time anyone had won the overall National Championship three years in a row. When the trophy originated in 1961, it was named "The American Cup," and an agreement that whoever won it the most times in a ten year period would retire it. Or if anyone won it three consecutive times they would keep it. I have it standing in my den to this day. I will eventually donate it to the USPA Sky-diving Museum when, and if, they ever get it opened.

The awards banquet was a blast as usual. All tension was over, old scores settled, new ones started. There were tears, laughter, elation, sadness, every emotion possible. The trophies were awarded and speeches made. As I recall, Loy Brydon and I were sitting next to each other. He was awarded his Gold Wings for achieving 1,000 jumps. About half way through the banquet, Deke came over and gave me a bottle of wine. I was kind of hiding it under the table when Hank Strauch came over and asked "What would it take to get a class of that wine?" I asked him what he had. He said "How about a check-out in my Waco UPF-7?" I gave him the rest of the bottle!

The next morning I showed up with Anne Batterson in hand, to see how good his promise was. Hank had slept in, so he suggested that we go get some breakfast. I wanted to suggest that we open up the hangar and go flying, but I kept my mouth shut. Hank had a full course breakfast. Anne and I had coffee, hoping he would rush it up a bit. We watched him put sugar in his coffee, then some milk. He put salt on his eggs and then pepper. He put butter on his toast . . . . then jam . . . . then got more coffee . . . . more sugar . . . . more milk, then a third cup of coffee . . . .! I wanted to yell "Come on damn it!" but kept quiet. He knew exactly what he was doing and was enjoying every minute of it. Finally, he finished. I paid the tab and we were on our way back to the hangar, at about 5 miles per hour! Finally, we arrived back at his house. "You want to come in?" That was the last straw! "No damn it, we don't want to come in!" He laughed and we headed for the hangar. He opened the hangar doors and, pushed up against the walls were all kinds of flying things. Spare parts scattered all over, work benches, vices, lathes, all the tools of the trade. And right in the center of the hangar, with a spot light shining on it, was the most beautifully restored, bi-winged Waco I had ever seen. It was all decked out in red and white checker 'show paint.' I almost felt that it was looking back at us wondering "who the hell are you and what are you here for?" Hank let us be amazed for a while then told us the story of how he and the Waco got together. He had found it up-side-down in a river, bought it for a song and dance, then spent some of the most wonderful times of his life restoring it.

I was starting to have a few doubts about if I should do this or not. I only had a private pilot's license and barely 100 hours flight time. Then I figured that it would probably be all dual flight with Hank there at all times. We pushed the aircraft out of the hangar and spent about an hour going over the systems and limitations, did the walk-a-round and we were ready to go. Hank went back to the hanger and came out with two seat type parachutes, two leather helmets and goggles. We chuted up and I was instructed to get in the back seat where the pilot flew. The front seat was designed for two passengers but also had a set of flight controls. There was an intercom system so we could talk back and forth. Hank yelled "Clear Prop" and on the intercom said, "Fire it up." I could almost hear the Waco say "Hank, you really gonna let him do this?" I turned the magnetos on, cracked the throttle and hit the starter. The prop started rotating; theengine coughed a couple of times and then roared into life. What a sweet sound it made and it vibrated life into the whole aircraft. First, I checked that the oil pressure was up, then the other gauges. We sat there until the oil and cylinder head temperatures were in the green operating range then taxied to the take-off end of the runway. You couldn't see over the nose of the aircraft so you taxied by zig-zagging left and right down the taxi way to make sure nothing was in front of you. At the end of the runway, I turned into the wind and ran the engine up to operating rpm's. Then I checked the left and right magnetos for the proper rpm drops and we were ready to go. On the intercom Hank said "Let's do it." I did a 360 degree turn, to check that no one was in the pattern, and took the runway. I eased the throttle up to maximum power, countered the torque pressure with the rudder and down the runway we went. I kept it in the center by looking out the sides of the cockpit until I got the tail off the ground then eased back on the stick and stepped back in history about thirty or forty years. I allowed myself a few seconds to roam the skies with Lindberg, Wyle Post, Amelia Earhart and the likes.

Then I heard Hank say "take her up to 3,000 feet." He told me the direction to fly in order to find a place where there was very little aviation activity. As we climbed out, Hank talked about what we were going to do. We would stay with the basics to start with; steep turns, and all stall series, power on and power off, full stalls and power recoveries. Hank said "Are you listening?" I pulled my head back into the cockpit (pilots will understand that phrase) and said yes. Hank would go through a maneuver and then ask me to do the same. I had done all this in training for my private license so it came pretty easy. Finally he said "all right, let's do some basic aerobatics." He went through a loop, aileron roll, barrel roll and a snap-roll, all the while explaining to me, what he was doing. Now, it was time to get my stomach back in the cockpit and go to work. I started the loop by diving the Waco to build speed, all the time watching the engine rpm and easing the throttle back to keep from over speeding it. I then eased back on the control column (joy stick) to keep a nice, constant "G" force while adding throttle on the climb side of the loop and easing the throttle off on the back side. Then I tried to finish at the same altitude as I had started. All of this went pretty smooth. Not so on the aileron rolls! Every time I reached the up-side-down stage, I would get a little light on the "G" forces and pull back on the stick, doing a "split S." Hank said we would get back to that later and had me do the snap-rolls. The snap-roll is just a spin on the horizontal plane. You pull full elevator and push full rudder at the same time. Then he had me do a double snap-roll. We could only do this to the right because we had to use the engines torque. After completing the first snap-roll, just hit full throttle and the engine torque would do the second. Then we did a loop with a snap-roll on top that was my favorite. Back to the aileron rolls. No luck. Still split S-ing it. Hank said "Let's head back to the airport." I figured he was fed up trying to teach something to someone who, obviously, couldn't hit his ass with both hands.

We landed and went back to the coffee shop. Hank spent the better part of a half hour trying to explain basic physics to me. As many hand signals as he was using, people must have thought I was deaf. More coffee, more cream . . . . more sugar . . . . and me sitting there with my knee pumping up and down impatiently. I didn't know if he wanted to pursue what looked like trying to teach a guy with no legs, how to jump rope, but back to the airport we went. We took off again and headed for the unrestricted area.

This time things went a lot better. Soon, I was doing loops and aileron rolls almost like I knew what I was doing. Hank was pretty quiet. I figured that either I scared him to death or I was doing fairly well. Whichever the case, I was in heaven. Finally, Hank told me to head back to the airport. I was disappointed that we couldn't continue playing forever but what could I expect for a bottle of wine! After landing, Hank told me to keep it running and stay in the cockpit. He climbed out, looked back at me and yelled "three times around the pattern!" Oh My God! He was letting me solo it. I made two touch and go landings and a full stop, being careful not to betray his trust in me.

When I taxied back to the parking area, I noticed Anne standing there with a parachute and helmet on. I figured that he was going to give her a ride. She climbed up on the wing and got in the front seat. Hank yelled "You have about an hour and a half of fuel. Take it up and wring her out!" I couldn't believe it! Anne and I spent the next hour looping and rolling and snapping all over that beautiful Washington sky. In my life time, I would accumulate about 17,000 hours, flying everything from combat in Vietnam to corporate jets all over the world, but that hour was one of the most memorable ones!

"And now here is my secret.
It is only with the heart
That one can see rightly.
What is essential
Is invisible
To the eye.
Antoine de Saint-Exupery

Chapter 20

Back to good old Bragg. I'm beginning to feel like I was born and raised here. In a way, I guess I was. Six years ago I was a snotty nosed kid working in a shirt factory, sweeping up scraps, in Banning California. Now, I'm a three time National Champion with 25 world records and his mug on the cover of *Sports Illustrated*! Fate sure has a way of handing it to you.

We hit the demonstration circuit again for a short while, jumping in Charleston, SC, Elkins, WV, and Ft. Belvoir VA. Then on 14 October 1963, Columbia Broadcasting Systems gave me a camera to mount on my helmet and the next twenty-eight out of thirty-four jumps I was filming the *Golden Knights* doing some weird things.

I sent the camera to Bell Helmet Company in Bell, California and asked if they would mount it on a helmet for me. The President of Bell at the time was Frank Heacock, who had donated helmets to the U.S. Team the year before. He remembered seeing the Bell helmet on my head on the cover of *Sports Illustrated* and said "Sure!" They did a great job. They put it on a very sturdy mount that would eliminate any possibility of vibration. They also mounted a sight in front of my right eye with a bull's eye in the center.

If the helmet shifted on my head, the bull's eye would shift inside of the sight so I would still be on target. It sure beat the hell out of the old cloths hangar I used to use.

The director of CBS Sports was Bob Dailey. He wanted to feature a thirty minute film of the *Golden Knights* and he wanted about twenty minutes of it to be air to air photography. Although Jerry Bourquin assisted in some of the filming, it was my project. The problem was we would not get to review the film until it aired on television. We would shoot the film, send it immediately to New York where they would look at it and tell me if it was any good or to re-shoot it. The filming was done in black and white at 64 frames per second, which meant it would be in slightly slow motion. The narrator was Bob Whitaker.

My plan was to shoot everything at least twice and if I had any doubts, shoot it again. Hell, they were paying for the film and besides, if it came out good they got the credit but if it was bad, it would be my fault. Needless to say, I spent a lot of time on the phone to New York!

We started by filming the normal Air Show routine. The four man formation, the baton pass and the diamond track. The team members would wear white uniforms and carry red smoke grenades. Jerry and I would wear black and no smoke in order not to detract from the subject. Ft. Bragg dedicated Nijmegen Drop Zone to us so as not to be interrupted by other military operations. This gave us quite a drive to work every day, but we didn't mind. After about a week of filming and no word from CBS I was getting a little concerned so I called Bob Dailey. He assured me the film was "fantastic" and to keep doing whatever we were doing. As I recall, out of all the rolls of film we took, they never asked us to re-take anything. Although they did augment some of it with ground located cameras.

Let's talk about some of the trickier shots we took. We put a 'reefing line' on Sgt. Jerry Babb's parachute. The reefing line was designed for big cargo parachutes to allow them to open slower. We sewed the small reefing line rings onto every suspension line on his 'chute where they connect to the bottom of the canopy. On two of those we attached a cutter, which is like a small guillotine that is operated by a .22 caliber bullet, activated by Jerry pulling a line attached to it. A reefing line was threaded through each of the rings effectively tying the parachute shut, so as to enable it from opening until Jerry activated the cutters. This was referred to as a "Streamer." Got it? We always said that Jerry Babb wasn't as smart as most kids his age! Jerry would pull his rip-cord about 3,000 feet and allow the parachute to streamer until 2,000 feet at which time he would pull the reefing line cutters. If at least one of the bullets fired, his 'chute would open. The tricky part about filming this was that after he 'streamered' his parachute it would create about 10% more drag than I had. This meant that for 10 seconds or so, before his parachute fully deployed, I would be falling faster than he was and would have to go vertical to keep him in the camera lens. This would allow me to get open between 1,800 and 2,000 feet. I had briefed all of the jumpers that I had to rely on them to open their parachutes at the prescribed altitudes because, with the helmet camera, I couldn't be looking back and forth at my altimeter. This all worked well until . . . . drum roll . . . . and the plot thickens!

He knows who he was and I know who he was. We'll leave it at that! I was going to film him doing a competition style series. He would open his parachute at 2,200 feet which would allow me to film his opening and for me to get open at about 1,800 feet. He was doing a nice series and the filming was going good until he finished. All of a sudden he took off tracking. I took off after him. It was hard keeping him in the frame but I was holding my own. Finally, he flared, stopped his track and pulled. I filmed his opening as long as I could stay stable and then look down; "Holy shit!" All I could see was large trees coming up at an alarming rate. I made a split second decision to pull the main ripcord instead of the reserve. The main parachute normally takes about 150 feet to open; the reserve takes about 75 feet. I was so low that if I didn't see a pilot chute immediately, I was going to activate the reserve. When the main canopy opened, I was about 600 feet above the ground. He told me later, much later, that he had spotted short (left the aircraft too soon) and forgot that I was filming him. In order to land closer to the target, he "adjusted' his opening altitude to about 1,500 feet. That almost put me in the dirt! When he saw my parachute below him, he realized what had happened, steered his over to his car, got in it and left. He didn't even bother picking his parachute up. He also stayed away from me for the remainder of the day!

More calls to New York. "Wonderful, keep it coming". Damn! It can't be that good.

Another sequence that I liked, we accomplished in one take. It was done by Captain Chuck Mullins and SFC Harold (If the army wanted me to have a wife, they'd issue me one) Lewis. They had only done it five or six times and we had never filmed it. We went to 12,500 feet for this one. Harold had two main parachutes, the same as I used on the double cut-a-way demonstration. In addition, he had another "D" ring attached to his harness. Captain Mullins had the normal parachute and reserve, but he had an additional harness with a hook on the end. Harold left first, followed by me, then Captain Mullins, in quick succession. I positioned myself just above Harold and waited for Mullins to come into view. They made contact and Harold held Captain Mullins stable while Mullins hooked onto Harold's parachute harness. That accomplished, Captain Mullins pulled Harold's first main ripcord and they both opened under the one parachute at about 5,000 feet. I filmed their opening then opened my parachute. I looked back up and got them in the camera's sight and waited. Captain Mullins cut away from Harold and began falling again, still trailing smoke, and opened about 2,000 feet. I looked back and captured Harold just before he released his first parachute and began free-falling again. He opened his second parachute right beside Captain Mullins. Wow! If I got that entire action in frame it would be a terrific sequence. Off to New York it went! We continued filming other events, then a couple of days later Bob Dailey called. "It's fantastic. No need to make another take. It's marvelous." I was still skeptical but let it go.

The first time I saw the film was on my television at home. I was impressed with CBS's presentation and their editing of everything we sent them. The shot of Harold Lewis and Capt. Mullins was great if I do say so myself. Years later, I tried to get a copy of it but never could. I even called Bob Dailey who was retired in Boca Raton, Florida. He said that to his knowledge it was probably not saved. Chuck Mullins passed away in the late 90's. One day, I got a call from his son, Kevin. He said "Mr. Fortenberry, I was going through my dad's stuff and found something you might be interested in." "Holy shit!" He had found a copy of the film. Kevin had it made into a DVD and sent it to me. I Love that kid!

Well, all that fun jumping, and it was fun, didn't help my Accuracy at all. None of my next three jumps were less than 3 meters. I would have to improve on that.

On the 22nd of January, 1964, I had another very memorable jump. I did a double baton pass over the Main

Post Parade Field. It was to be presented to General William C. (Chesty Westy) Westmorland upon his departure from Ft. Bragg. It was jump number 1,213 in my log book and he took the time to sign it for me. After landing, we stood in formation while he passed amongst us. I remember that SFC Bill Edge was standing next to me. The General stopped in front of him, looked at his name tag, and said "Sergeant Edge, you were with me in the 173rd Airborne Brigade in Korea weren't you?" Bill said "Yes Sir." The General said "Nice to see you again." What a great memory.

There were two more jumps of interest on this page of my log book and then we'll move on. I think both were illegal but what the hell, half of the crap we were doing was experimental anyway. The first one was a 'daisy-chain' with SFC Barker. I don't even remember why we did it. I just came upon it in my log book. In the remarks section it says, 'anchor man on daisy-chain w/Barker. 20 foot static line. Barker had a Mae West. Translated it meant we each replaced the rip-cord with a 20 foot static line. We boarded a UH-1 Huey helicopter and climbed to 2,500 feet. I hooked my static line on to the helicopter and Barker hooked his onto me and when we jumped the helicopter would activate my parachute. When it opened, Barker would continue falling for another 20 feet. When he reached the end of his static line, the pins would be pulled out of his pack tray allowing his parachute to open. If my parachute failed to open, we would both have to rely on my reserve parachute. You may ask yourself, "Why would they do that?" Who the hell knows; it seemed like a good idea at the time. Every thing went according to plan except Barker had a 'Mae West' on opening. A 'Mae West' is caused by one or more suspension lines getting looped over the top of the canopy creating what looks like two small canopies or two big boobs; hence, the name 'Mae West' of Hollywood fame.

The next, I believe, was the first ever accelerated free-fall, (AFF). I took a Major Robinson for a 20 second delay on his first free-fall. We rigged his main parachute with a Russian KAP-3 automatic opening device. I instructed him to hold onto my harness and I would hold his. I would keep him stable until 3,000 feet at which time I would slap his right hand. That would be the signal for him to let go of me and pull his ripcord. Everything went well until I slapped his hand. He wouldn't let go! I started pushing and shoving but I couldn't get rid of him. I looked at his face and his eyes were as big as saucers. I didn't want to open my parachute because he would most certainly go unstable and I wanted him in a face-to-earth position when the KAP-3, which was set for 2,200 feet, went off. Like clock work the KAP-3 fired, activating his parachute. At that point, he was history. I opened my parachute and we lazily drifted to earth, living happily ever after. We scraped that idea for a while!

Chapter 21

A lot of interesting things happened in 1964 that affected the rest of my life. One was that in April we made another trip to Rio de Janeiro, where we made seventeen more jumps with our Brazilian Special Forces buddies. All were made out of vintage aircraft; C-82's, C-119's and C-45's. It was fun to visit with our friends and to once again set on the roof top bar at the south end of Copacabana Beach with a beer in hand, and watch the four lane traffic switch from one-way to two-way traffic. Ah, the small pleasures in life!

Now an interesting life altering decision. Because I had won the National Championship it automatically put me on the U.S. Team; but in the meantime I had sent in an application for Army flight school and had been accepted. A couple of things I had to think hard about were; I was twenty six years old and flight school was pretty hard to get into. If I declined the appointment, I would probably never get another chance. The other concern was that I had already had two chances to win the World Championship and came up short. The younger parachutists were getting harder to compete against and I would probably come up short again, so I gave up my position on the U.S. Team. I felt a real emptiness when I notified the Parachute Club of America; I didn't have to feel bad for too long. In about two weeks I received a letter from the Pentagon. It was an order from the Department of the Army (DA) stating that I would remain on the United States Team. I called DA and told them that flight school was very important to me and that, to them, I was just a number. If I didn't show up on my assigned date, I would probably never get another chance. They gave me three starting dates of classes and told me to take my pick I chose the first one after the World Championship, which would be the first week of September, 1964. They said "OK, you're in. Now go give it your best shot!" Man, what a relief! I would get another shot at the title and be guaranteed a flight school slot to boot. Plus, the pressure was off. By that I mean that up until now people expected things from me. I was the U.S. Champion, Team Captain and on the cover of *Sports Illustrated*, I was "America's Dick Fortenberry." How much pressure is that? Now I was ordered to participate. I was just one of the guys.

The VII World Championship was scheduled from 30 July thru 17 August, 1964. Our training site would be Fresno, Calif. The whole U.S. Team contingency arrived there on the last week of May and our first jump was on 1 June. It consisted of: Deke Sonnicsen, Head of Delegation, Menlo Park, Calif., Captain Charles Mullins, team trainer, U.S. Army Parachute (USAPT), Dick Fortenberry, USAPT, Rudy Peterson, Issaquah, Washington, Coy McDonald, USAPT, Phil Vander Weg, USAPT, Jerry Bourquin, USAPT, Bill Berg, Snohomish, Washington, Ron Sewell, Seattle, Washington and Loy Brydon USAPT.

The women competitors consisted of: Anne Batterson, Bloomfield, Connecticut, Tee Taylor, Dallas, Texas, Gladys Inman, Spokane, Washington, Maxine Hartman, New York City, Carol Penrod, La Canada, California, Susan Clements, Oakland, California, and Jeanni McCombs, Los Angeles, California.

Deke Sonnicsen had made arrangements for the Drop Zone to be located on a farmer's property outside of Fresno. Dave Steeves was contracted to do all of the flying with his two aircraft. He had licensed two vintage aircraft, a V-77 Gull wing Stinson called the "Mule", and a Fairchild 71 which was rumored to have been the sister ship to Adm. Byrd when he flew to the South Pole. The 220 hp. engines were replaced with 650 hp. engines and were wonderful jump platforms but the Stinson was the main work horse.

Dave Steeves was a colorful, outspoken guy with as colorful of a background. As a Captain in the Air Force he had an engine failure in a T-33 Jet trainer over the Sierras and had to eject. He broke both ankles on landing and spent days crawling out of the mountains. The main thing that helped him survive was that he came upon an abandoned hunter's cabin that had some cans of food left. After reaching civilization, the Air Force praised him for his feat but then began to question it. They accused him of faking it and selling the aircraft to a third world country. He resigned from the Air Force, settled into the Fresno area and spent all of his spare time flying those mountains looking for the crash site. Years after his death in a crash of the "Mule," some hikers found a crash site and with the serial numbers, identifying it as the one he ejected from.

On the first day of June, we made a demonstration jump at the Towne and Country Motel where we were staying in exchange for reduced priced rooms. It was time well spent because they sure put up with a lot of our shenanigans for the next two months.

We officially started the elimination process on 3 June, 1964, a day before my 26th birthday. Our day would start about 4:30 am. As soon as the restaurant opened we would have breakfast then head for the Drop Zone (DZ).

There we would do our daily workout which included a mile run, be chuted up and climbing for altitude when the sun came up. The first day we made five Style jumps from 6,600 feet which would be the altitude used in the World Championship. We would make between three and five jumps a day if the weather was good. Looking in my log book, jump Number 1,259 is signed my Maxine Hartman and in the remarks section she wrote "Happy Birthday, Fink." I have no idea what that was about, but I don't think she ever really liked me. After a few days of this routine we talked it over and decided to modify it because of the heat. After 1:00 pm the thermal activity created by the heat was so bad that accuracy was an oxymoron. From then on we would do all Accuracy Training in the cool of the morning and Style during the heat of the afternoon.

During this period, each jumper was judged on his or her proficiency in Accuracy and Style. As a result of this, the Executive Board and Captain Mullins would select the five men and one alternate and four women and one alternate for the 1964 U.S. Team. The final selection was posted on Saturday, June 13. They were; Dick Fortenberry, Loy Brydon, Jerry Bourquin, Coy McDonald, Ron Sewell and Bill Berg as alternate. Anne Batterson, Tee Taylor, Susan Clements, Gladys Inman and Carol Penrod as alternate. However, three days into training Susan badly sprained her ankle and was replaced by Carol Penrod.

Another interesting note is that we were practicing our Accuracy jumps with the 7 gore TU which would probably not be the parachute we would have for the competition. Manufactures were designing new canopies and harnesses for us to consider using. One of the designs was the Para-commander by Pioneer Parachute Company. Another was called the Crossbow. The new harness would have both parachutes on your back with the reserve on top of main.

At first this was strange because we were so accustomed to having the reserve hanging on our stomach with the altimeter and stopwatch mounted on it, now we had to wear the instruments on our wrists. It also meant that if we had a malfunction of the main parachute, we would have to jettison it before activating the reserve. In order to do this the cape-wells that connect the main parachute to the harness, were modified. The safety latch was removed so it only took one action to get rid of the main. One day we would jump the Para-commander, the next day a Crossbow and the next day the old TU. Some days we would jump a combination of the three. This was playing havoc with our Accuracy training but it was as good a time as any to learn new techniques. (It appears in my log book that on the 23rd of June we decided to go with the Para-commander (PC) as the main parachute and the Crossbow reserve, because all my jumps after that date are with that combination). I wanted to mention that for historical purposes. It also shows that my Accuracy increased dramatically.

A technique I used for canopy stability was to stop my turns by countering with the opposite guide line. By that I mean if I made a left turn by pulling the left toggle, instead of stopping it by letting up on the left toggle, I would counter it by pulling down on the right toggle and then ease up on both. This would create a braking effect and gradually start moving forward, thereby, eliminating any oscillation. By having the reserve parachute mounted on your back instead of on your belly, it allowed more flexibility during Style practice, especially in the loops. I was now consistently turning in the mid-nine second range. After settling into the new equipment, training got down to a routine and was going smoothly. The weather was good, morale was high and everyone was getting along with each other wonderfully.

Besides the training jumps, we would, on occasion, make demo jumps or publicity jumps. For some of these, we hired a guy named Doyle Fields, who owned a lucrative hair styling salon in Venice, California, but his passion was aerial photography. He had been a motorcycle racer but found out that he had a heart condition so he gave that up for sky-diving. Go figure! Doyle was one of the nicest, most unassuming people I had ever met, but had a wicked, sometimes, evil sense of humor. If he pushed someone into the swimming pool and they started to retaliate, he would grab his chest and yell, "my heart, my heart." We always fell for it because you never know! Some of the jumps we made would be photo ops for *Parachutist* magazine or the local news media and Doyle was great at that. For these pictures we would usually jump from 7,000 feet. Sometimes we would make individual jumps and sometimes group jumps. Doyle would buzz around us taking pictures from all different angles. Most sky-divers are pranksters by nature and would, on occasion, pull the others' rip-cord handles, prematurely opening his or her parachute. One night at poolside, after a couple of beers, Doyle made the comment that no one had ever gotten his rip-cord and never would. As Team Captain I very seldom got involved in that sort of thing and had somewhere picked up the nick name "Fortunecookie," I think from Anne Batterson. A few days later I was doing a photo jump with Doyle and he took pictures from all different angles then we joined up for a close-up. Now, if you don't know what's coming next, as my friend Saul would say, "You're one beer short of a six pack." I can still see the look on Doyle's face as we separated about 4,000 feet and I had his rip-cord! He managed to land somewhere on the farm without hitting high line wires, barns or the likes. That night, at the bar, he said "Fortunecookie, I expected that from anybody else, but not you." I said "Hey, Life's a bitch, and then you die."

No one was designated as "team trainer" because we were all pretty much equal to the task. We more or less trained each other and kept close records on our progress. If asked by another team member to observe and critique them on their performance, we would. I remember doing so with Tee Taylor on her Style technique. By observing a number of her jumps and discussing them with her we were able to decrease her Style times dramatically. Anne Batterson noticed the change and asked if I would assist her. I watched a couple of her jumps and noticed that her upper body was creating the turns nicely but she had little control of her legs and this was slowing her down. We discussed it and suggested that she keep her legs closer together. I watched a couple more of her jumps but to no avail. Finally, I said lets try something. I got a piece of suspension line and tied her ankles so that they wouldn't come apart for more than about a foot. She said "No, no, no, give me another chance." I told her it was no use. We had to do something. I watched her hobble out to the aircraft and her team mates help her aboard. Obviously, they were having some fun at her expense. As they were climbing for altitude, I began to have second thoughts. What if she opened head down and the pilot-chute got tangled in the suspension line. I began to sweat it out. Finally, out she came. I was on my back with binoculars and a stopwatch. She fell through terminal velocity, and began her turns. Wonderful! It took a full second off of her normal series time, now we just had to get through the canopy deployment. I have to admit that I was very relieved when it blossomed normally and I vowed to never try that training method again. When she walked off the target she was grinning ear to ear and never had that problem again.

We were making four and five jumps every day. After a while, the early mornings, the vigorous training and the heat of the day began to take its toll. To relieve my tension,

I asked Dave Steeves to check me out in a small airplane he owned. It was a two person monoplane built by Navion and had tandem seating. Sometimes, at the end of the day, I would take off and just fly around looking at the beautiful country side and let the tension melt away. One afternoon I noticed that Anne was in a funky mood and asked her if she would like to go along. She agreed, so we went flying. It was almost sunset and the sky was crystal clear; one of those days when the visibility goes on forever. I climbed to about 3,000 feet and leveled off, the sun was about to go down so I put it just off my left wing and told Anne to watch. The atmosphere was so crisp that the sun was a perfect orb and we could watch its progress as it began to sink below the horizon. Just as the sun sunk out of sight, I gave the little airplane full power and pulled back on the control column. The sun began to rise again! In the back seat, I could hear Anne screaming and clapping her hands. When the sun again disappeared we flew back to the airfield in silence, deep in our own thoughts. It was one of those special moments that you never forget.

For the remainder of June and the first part of July, training progressed normally except that on the 25th of June, I had a malfunction of my main parachute. I had just completed a Stylejump from 6,600 feet and when I pulled my rip-cord I felt an opening shock, unlike a normal one. I looked up to see that the top of the parachute was tied up in a knot. I prepared to jettison it by pulling the cape-wells to the 90 degree position. All I had to do was to further pull them to the 180 degree position and the canopy would release, but then I felt another jolt. I looked up to see that the malfunction had corrected itself and I had a perfect canopy. I tried to position the cape-wells back up into the locked position but couldn't. The dilemma now was, do I ride it in this way or get rid of it. With the cape-wells in this position they were really exposed. Mistakenly hitting one would release the parachute. If this happened too low, I wouldn't have enough altitude for the reserve parachute to deploy. I decided to get rid of it. Just before pushing down on the cape-wells the thought crossed my mind that "You've always had that reserve. If it malfunctions, you're going to hurt like hell!" I pushed them. I watched as the main let go and the reserve started out. It worked as advertised except that I had very little control over where I was going. I landed in the middle of the farm and they sent a vehicle to pick me up.

Sometimes we would get little competitions going on the side to break up the monotony. It actually got us out of the training mind set and gave us a little competitive adrenaline rush. One day, Loy Brydon, Coy McDonald and I bet Carol Penrod, Gladys Inman and Anne Batterson a beer that on our next round of Accuracy jumps, our average distance to the target would be much better than theirs. That night, they said it was the best beer they ever had. Damn!

Fourth of July weekend, 1964, was the start of the "Powder Puff Derby" from the airport in Fresno. This was an all female trans-continental air race. The first race took place in 1929. It started at Santa Monica, California and culminated in Cleveland, Ohio for the Cleveland National Air Races. Emelia Earhart, Poncho Barnes, Louise Thaden, Bobbi Trout and other women brought national attention to women in aviation with the Derby. This year someone requested that the U. S. Parachute Team put on a demonstration. We readily agreed. It would be good publicity and maybe some more donations. The whole team participated, including Captain Mullins. We used both aircraft, the "Mule" and the Fairchild-71. As usual, it was a hot day with many thermals. We took off together and would get as much altitude as possible; at least 12,500 feet for a sixty second free-fall. I was in the "Mule" and we virtually ran off and left the Fairchild until about 8,000 feet, then here he came. With the thick camber of its wing, the Fairchild had much better lift at higher altitudes. He could have gone higher but he leveled off at 12,500 and waited for us. We did the normal Air Show, the diamond track, the max track, the formation and the baton pass. Loy, Jerry and I did a three-way max-track. When we left the aircraft, I went straight ahead and each of them turned 120 degrees from each other and took off. We opened way passed the boundaries of the airport. I found my own little audience that was observing the activities from afar so I headed for them. A thermal caught me right as I was landing and I made a one foot standing landing right in front of them. I got a thundering round of applause, or as thundering as about ten people can get. I shot the breeze with them for awhile, mostly about what the *Team* was all about then I asked if someone could give me a ride back onto the airport. They all volunteered.

I have to say that about this time in our training things were getting a little testy. Too much of a good thing can be a bad thing. I noticed that the team members would occasionally snap at each other; nothing serious, but just enough to make the situation tense. I was as guilty as anyone else. I mentioned it to Captain Mullins and he asked for suggestions. I said, "Why don't we take the weekend off and go to Yosemite National Park?" He said "Let's do it!"

I let the *Team* know that it wasn't just a weekend off but that we were going as a team activity. There wasn't too much grumbling so we packed in the cars and set out. It was definitely the right move. As soon as we rounded the corner and saw half dome mountain I could just feel tension draining out of me. We went to the local stores and purchased picnic stuff. Included in that was beer, wine and watermelons which we placed in a cold stream. Swimming in some of those streams would take your breath away but it was extremely refreshing.

We picnicked at the base of El Capitan Mountain. The mountain is 3,600 feet high; the top two thirds of which is concaved and the bottom third convex. I think the whole team was thinking the same thing. We could jump off El Capitan and do a ten second delay before opening. This was way before "base jumping." There was a waterfall next to it. We watched the spray from it. Sometimes it was blowing away from the mountain and some times into it. You just had to pick a calm day or the right wind. All of a sudden a voiced boomed out "Forget it!" It was Captain Mullins. Everybody chuckled, but the thought was still there.

The next day, some of us climbed to the base of Bridal Veil Falls. I stood at the base of it and watched the spray as the water hit the rocks at the bottom. I knew it was against park regulations but I couldn't help myself. I climbed over the fence and went as close to the falls as I could get and still stand up against the force of the spray. The wind must have been forty or fifty miles per hour. I just stood there with my arms out stretched and let that icy cold spray cleanse me. I must have stood there five minutes. When I turned to leave, there was Anne Batterson standing next to me with her arms stretched out, her eyes shut tight and a look of serendipity on her face. Years later, in the heat and turmoil of Vietnam, I would often close my eyes and use that memory to get me through. When we got back to Fresno and our training routine, you could feel a whole new freshness and vigor in the *Team*, but the adventures had not yet come to a halt.

In the middle of July, July 18th to be precise, jump number 1,372, we heard that there was a group of Explorer

Boy Scouts on an outing in the Sierra Mountains and they were running short on food supplies. It was suggested, by whom, I have no idea, that the men's and women's National Champions re-supply them by parachute. That would be myself and Anne Batterson. Somewhere we came up with some small, cotton, cargo parachutes. Again, we have to think publicity and donations to the *Team* fund as a lot of these Scouts were from parents of local businesses. We loaded the Stinson up with the needed supplies, put on a parachute for safety, and headed for the Sierras. We found the scouts by the side of a lake and buzzed them. Not knowing we had supplies for them, they were still very excited to see us. Once we started dropping the parachutes, they were ecstatic. They jumped up and down and waved like crazy. I have to admit, it was exciting for me too. It took two or three passes to get everything out, then one more buzz job and we left.

During some idle conversation on the way back, Dave said "I know where there is a nudist colony if you want to fly over it." We told him not to fly out of his way but he said it was right on our flight path, so we agreed. It was called "The Eucalyptus Grove Nudist Colony" andDave made a low pass over it. The thing that popped out at us was a guy standing by the pool with nothing on but a red baseball cap. That cap really stuck out (no pun intended). Dave said "If you guys want to jump in, I won't even charge you for it." I looked at Anne and asked "What's the craziest thing you've ever done in your life?" She said "I don't know, I haven't done it yet!" We said "Why not," but we didn't have helmets, jump boots or reserve parachutes so we headed back to the DZ to get them. When we got there Anne couldn't find her helmet so she grabbed Gladys'. Our helmets had U.S. Flags painted on the sides and our last name on the front. We got back on the aircraft and headed for an "adventure!"

We didn't have a wind drift indicator with us so we would have to "wing" it. We climbed to 3,600 feet on the way back to the colony. We decided not to land inside for fear of hurting someone or landing in a tree. On arrival, I guided Dave over our opening point and said to Anne, "Last chance to back out," she said "Go!" I stepped out and looked back to see if she was going to leave me "hanging", but there she came. We did a ten second free-fall then opened and headed for the fence that surrounded the camp. As we approached, I noticed the guy with the red hat standing just inside. We landed and started gathering our parachutes then I noticed Dave on a low approach. Holy Shit! He intended to land out here. I looked at his approach path and noticed four strands of telephone wires in front of him. He saw them right at the last minute, hit full power and went right through them. For about fifty yards you heard the wires zinging and pinging as the prop tore through them. Needless to say, he didn't make a second pass. He headed back to Chandler Field. Anne and I were definitely committed now.

We walked up to the red hat and said "Hi." He said "Hi" and parted the fence so we could get in. He said "Well, that was exciting." I said "Yeah, a little too much." He asked if we were nudist and we answered "No." He asked if we had ever been to a nudist colony and again, the answer was "No." He said his name was Otis, I told him mine was Dick Fortenberry. He said "We only go by first names here." I told him that she was Anne Batterson, she wasn't going to be the only person here with just a first name! He explained that this was a family colony and enlightened us on some of their ways. When we arrived at the pool area, Otis, who was an attorney out of Los Angeles, introduced us around. Among others, there was a Navy Commander and his family. Everyone was swimming, playing volleyball and in general, having a great time. Otis asked if we wanted to take a swim. We looked at each other and said "Sure." He said he would have to get permission from the owners so we walked over to the main house. The owners were sitting there, naked, having lunch and didn't seem none to happy to see us. Otis vouched for us and they said OK, but we would have to pay a $4.00 visitors fee. Luckily, Anne had some money on her, I didn't. She paid the $8.00 and away we went. Otis said "You can undress any where, so we did. The only thing I was self conscious about was that everyone there was tan all over and I had one big white stripe and Anne had two.

We fell right into the program and sat around chatting. We were interested in their activities and, after finding out that we weren't just a couple of pranksters (which, actually, we were) but members of the U.S. Parachute Team, they were enthralled. They asked what it was like to jump out of an airplane, how was a competition run, what were the events, where was it going to be held and what were our chances of winning. All in all, it was quit pleasant. A couple of the kids wanted to know if I could teach them some dives off the diving board. I agreed, and male readers should take note to ever do a full gainer dive without a bathing suit!

We visited for about two hours and then the loud speaker stated that "Dick and Anne have visitors at the main gate." We figured that it was our transportation but didn't know who. We said our goodbyes and dressed by the poolside, at which time I couldn't find my wrist mounted stopwatch I used to time my free-falls with. Otis said that honesty was a very big thing at a nudist colony because "We don't have pockets. If it's found we'll get it to you." Dave Steeves had gotten a friend of his who belonged to a local Parachute Club to come get us. When we got into the car he started calling us all kinds of names. I asked him what his problem was and he said "I've been planning to do that for two years and you beat me to it." I told him "You snooze, you loose!"

Brydon and I used to try and better each other on occasion. When he heard about this, he swore that he was going to jump off El Capitan the next weekend. Captain Mullins had to order him to stay out of Yosemite the rest of our stay in training camp. I told him that that wouldn't top it anyway!

I don't know what it was about that adventure but it sure helped my Accuracy jumps. On the 23rd of June, I made my first back-to-back dead center jumps. Then I had a 0.40 cm jump and backed it up on the 24th and 25th with five, straight dead centers. I think that was the first time anybody in the States had done that. I thought I had six in a row but Coy McDonald said I missed by a finger width.

About a week later, Anne and Gladys came over to where I was packing my parachute and was laughing until tears ran. Anne had a box in her hand with my stopwatch in it. Because our red hat friend remembered seeing Inman on Anne's helmet, it was addressed to Anne Inman. Along with the watch was a hand written card that stated, "We found this poolside and thought you would like it returned. We enjoyed your visit and if you are ever in the area again, by all means, drop in!" It was signed "Your friend in the Sun, Otis."

There was one other interesting thing that happened before leaving Fresno. Do you remember the Cadet from Annapolis that we trained during his summer break? Well he showed up. He was now a Lieutenant in the Navy flying A-4 Sky Hawks off of carriers. He said that after all of the training we did with him that if he ever had to eject that he could "beat the seat." That meant that he could separate himself from the ejection seat and open his own parachute. Didn't happen! Because of a fowled deck on the carrier, he was doing an aerial refueling. He said the fuel nozzle was leaking fuel all over the nose of his aircraft, when he heard an explosion and every red light in the cockpit came on. He just pulled the throttle back, banked left and ejected. He said when he woke up he was hanging in the harness; he really woke up when he hit that cold assed Pacific Ocean.

We closed down our training camp on the 26th of July 1964. It was one of the more memorable camps I had ever attended. I felt really good about my own personal ability and that of the *Team* as a whole.

Look out Leutkirch, Germany! Here we come!

Chapter 22

I thought we were never going to make it to Germany. We had fallen short on our budget to get the team back East. Somehow Deke (who we had dubbed The Great White Father) hustled the money. When we got to the East coast, PCA national director, Bill Ottley had arranged for busses to take us to New York, but a mix up in luggage and the team being split up into different hotels resulted in us missing our flight from New Jersey's McGuire AFB. Now they had to put us on whatever flights they could find space available. Joe Crane flew alone on one airplane, Jim Arender, U.S. Judge, flew on another with the women. The Army members flew on the third aircraft and Deke was alone on the fourth which broke down and was delayed for hours waiting for a part.

At Frankfort the team regrouped and boarded a U.S. Army bus which promptly broke down, I was hoping this was not an omen of how the meet was going to be, but we finally arrived in Leutkirch.

The town had not changed much, it was still a beautiful little country town with absolutely no clutter about it. All of the firewood piles were stacked as if they had used a tape measure, every house had well tended gardens, and the flowerbeds were beautiful. It was obvious that an event was to take place because of all the banners and decorations.

Two tents were set up for each team at the airport. These would be to store our equipment and to get out of any bad weather. We would stay in a hotel in town, with the exception of the Australian Team, they would stay in the tents. Just like the U.S. Team, they relied on donations to finance their trip. When the time came, they didn't have enough money for airline tickets for their women's team so the men gave up their hotel money for their tickets. Gotta love those Aussies! We spent a lot of time with them.

When we arrived at the airport there was that old familiar feeling of anticipation. The first thing I did was to start sizing up the competition. There were a lot of familiar faces but some new ones also. Klima, my Czech nemesis was there. The older faces had looks of quiet confidence while the newer ones were filled with awe and eagerness. We spent the day renewing old friendships and acquiring new ones. That night we had a team meeting to discuss the days activities and what to expect. We all agreed on whom, of the old faces, would be the main competition, but didn't have a clue about the new ones.

Another psych job was what kind of new equipment everyone had. We were pretty sure they didn't know much about our Para-commanders (PC's). August 3rd was, 'You show me yours and I'll show you mine' day. The Soviet Team and The Czechs were our biggest concern, but then anyone who brought a parachute could be dangerous. We spent the morning watching as competitors began to make their practice jumps. By the way, we were jumping from U.S. Army U1-A Otters. How we got that approved I don't know but the pilots were having a ball. One of them, Ray

Bowers, signed my log book a couple of times. I told him I was headed for helicopter flight school when this was over. He told me to have fun now because there was going to be hell to pay.

On Friday, July 31, six Army Otters loaded up for practice jumps. The weather was perfect and the last jumper floated to earth as the sun set over the horizon. So far there had been no big surprises in equipment but we hadn't jumped yet and the topic of discussion was the secret weapon we had stuffed in the duel purpose Security Parachute Company "Crossbow" pack tray. When asked, we would only reply "can't tell you." One Irishman said "Hey mate, don't you think we read American magazines? I can probably draw you a picture of the damn thing!" Finally, it was our turn to show them what we had.

It rained all day Sunday washing out the entire opening ceremony.

Finally, at 8:30 on Monday morning, the women's team marched out of their tent all chuted up. You could tell that everybody was wondering where the reserve parachute was. We said nothing and the girls got aboard the Otter and took off. As they climbed for altitude, everyone gathered around the target area with binoculars and cameras. As we had preplanned, the aircraft passed the normal target about 800 yards and the girls jumped, along with cameraman Doyle Fields. They all landed within 2 meters of a predetermined target, about a half mile away. Some thought this cloak and dagger stuff was a little much, but some thought it was brilliant. I thought it was a little too dramatic and it could have gone terribly wrong if it weren't for the Aussie's. After the initial shock of the U.S. Women's Team jump had passed, the Australian Team performed their version of it. Four Australian girls put their parachutes in carrying bags. Four of the Aussie men put on sun glasses and donned raincoats, and strung suspension lines with a make-shift picket fence around the girls. They hung a big sign on the fence saying "TOP SECRET!" Then they paraded around the drop zone, reprimanding anyone who got too close. A Canadian voice boomed over the public address system; "We ask that no pictures be taken of the Australian Women's Team, especially by the American Team!"

On opening day, a German military band marched onto the field followed by the Australian team, wearing green jump suits lead by Team Leader, Allen Jay. They marched passed the bleachers and onto the drop zone followed by twenty-five other Nations including ten complete women's teams. The teams stood in a wide arc and listened while Jacques Istel, President of the International Parachuting Commission, formally opened the Championship comparing the five nations in the 1951 championship with the twenty-six nations competing thirteen years later.

"The differences are obvious," he said. "Great progress has been made in techniques, equipment and performance. A competitor in 1951 would be non-pulsed by the standards of 1964, but it is the similarities, not the differences we should dwell on for our tradition is short but proud. The noble aims of peace, fellowship and friendship are present today as they were in 1951. The difficulties of organization have been overcome by the German Aero Club as they had been by the Aero Club of Yugoslavia. The hard work and dedication of championship staff and supporters of parachuting have remained unchanged. So has sacrifice. Time and energy have not been spared and many participants are here only at considerable cost and effort. This too, is part of our tradition, of the tradition of aviation sports, of the tradition of the F.A.I. To the participants, we give best wishes, tinged with envy known only to former competitors."

At this point, Meet director Arndt Hoyer came to the mike, grasped the F.A.I. flag and spoke the parachuting code. "We solemnly pledge that we will compete in a sportsman-like manner for the furtherance of our sport and the honor of our country." In many languages, 270 sportsmen answered; "We pledge." In the next two weeks this pledge would be tested many times! This was the Cold War period and no matter how much you tried to avoid it, politics rears its evil head. For example, Phil Miller, assistant meet director, received a phone call from the Pentagon wanting to know how the military aircraft situation had been resolved, rather than how the U.S. Team was doing.

After the speeches, heads of delegations, team leaders and contestants traded pennants and good wishes. I told Erill Meagher, Irish team leader "Lots of good jumping." I winked and gave him a copy of the July issue of the *Parachutist* magazine saying "this tells all of our jump secrets." He grinned and replied, "Thanks, but I had rather have one of those Para-commanders."

Young German girls then came out on the field with bouquets of flowers for everyone. One touching scene was Herr Richard Kohnke, West German head of delegation, who had worked tirelessly for two years for this event to take place. One of the young girls approached him with her flowers in hand. She handed them to him then someone lifted her up to kiss him on the cheek, His eyes welled up and tears just gushed down his cheeks. This from a man who jumped out of flaming observation balloons in World War I!

Monday afternoon, you could have cut the tension with a knife when the U.S. Men's Team loaded on the aircraft for their first practice Accuracy jump. Every person on the DZ had a camera waiting for what the Frenchmen called the "Super Commander." We climbed to 1,000 meters and made individual passes. Loy was first; he was pretty much our most consistent Accuracy man, but this wasn't his day. He came in stretching like mad for the target and landed almost prone, but missed it by a few meters. I was next and had a very good approach. I landed 23 centimeters from the disc. Ron Sewell came in on an oscillation and almost knocked himself out. Bourquin had a fairly descent jump. Coy McDonald, who was jumping on a bad ankle, landed close but really hard. Deke, head down, headed for the team tent. Close to the tent, a reporter asked him what he thought of the PC now; Deke lowered his head, thought for a moment, then raised his head with a great big grin and said, "Marvelous, Absolutely Marvelous!"

On Tuesday we began the meet in earnest with the 1,000 meter Individual Accuracy. There would be no more secrets. Everything would hang out in the open to see who the main competition would be. Ron Sewell made the first jump and scored 2.04 meters, followed by Loy Brydon who tore the target up with a 32 centimeter landing. McDonald was next with a 4.18 meter landing. I came in next and had one of those "golden" approaches. That's one in which you make your final turn for the target and only have to make very tiny corrections with steering toggles. I scored a dead center landing. I would make three dead center landings out of eight Accuracy jumps during the meet. Jerry Bourquin finished the first round of jumps with 2.64 meters.

My first dead center was matched by Frantisek Jindra of Czechoslovakia, and a 1962 Orange, Mass. Veteran, Evgeny

Kazakov, a Russian who had his name painted in large red letters on his white canopy.

Another thing that was proven on this first event was that the chalked off 100 meter circle was a thing of the past; only two jumpers of the 279 made landings outside the circle. It was obvious to everyone that the Accuracy competition was going to be very close. On the next round of jumps, six jumpers hit the white, six inch round disc. Romano Fortarel from Italy hit the target so hard he bent it, it was his first and he was overjoyed. East German, Heinz Schall made his first dead center, but French national champion Pierre Arrassus and team mate Francois Lemoigne both got dead centers putting the French team in the lead.

The sun was about to go down but we had time for one more lift. We got to altitude and started our Individual jump runs. Coy McDonald smashed the disc with his bad ankle for a dead center but had to be assisted off the field. Bourquin followed with a 21 centimeter landing. Compared to the rest of the guys, I blew it with a 2.13 meter landing. In the remarks section of my log book, I wrote "Good grief!" But we took back the lead. The scoring dropped off a bit on the last round of jumps, with Jaroslov Jehlika of Czechoslovakia making the only dead center. Schall of East Germany won the event. I was fifth with an average score 0.92 with 0.00 being the best. That's how tough the competition was going to be.

The next event was the Ladies 1,000 meter Accuracy. Anne Batterson hit for 3.65 meters; Gladys (who was mother of three boys) landed 3.29 meters. The New Yorker, Maxine Hartman, hit at 7.72 meters, Tee Taylor was right on with 32 centimeters. The only dead center was made by France's Nicole Bera, only the second woman in history to make one.

Gladys landed outside the 100 meter circle on her second jump. She shrugged it and said "I guess I'll have to throw that one out." The women picked up on their following jumps with Anne having the most constant average. Tee Taylor finished Fifth for the event. Valentina Seliverstova from Russia was First. Erzsebet Stanek of Hungry came in Second, followed by France's Nicole Bera.

In the middle of the week we spent two days on the Style event. I didn't perform my best on the two jumps I made. I had a time of 10.1 seconds on the first one and 10.5 on the second one. In the remarks section I wrote "like turning in peanut butter!"

We were scheduled to finish the Style event on Sunday but the crowd was so huge that they decided to go with Team Accuracy instead because it had more spectator appeal. All jumping was delayed for a few hours because of a weather front that moved in with heavy wind gusts. When they died down, a German paratrooper, known as a "wind dummy" for obvious reasons, went aloft. He came over the target at 1,000 meters and exited. He opened a white, flat circular canopy with no steering capability, held his arms out to his side and let the wind take him where it would. Where he landed a marker would be placed for us to judge our opening point. This was the old fashioned way of doing it and for tradition purposes adopted it for this meet.

First up were the East Germans. Once again, Schall nailed a DC, indicated by the judges not moving to mark it, but to throw their hands straight up in the air.

The Czechs were next, and two of the four jumpers scored dead centers. The competition was really getting heated.

We were next. Myself, Sewell, Bourquin and Brydon, but only three of us hit the target area. From the ground it appeared that Brydon was having trouble controlling his canopy. One of his steering lines had broken on opening so about half way down he stretched his arms out to his sides indicating to the judges that he had no control of the parachute. He landed about 60 meters from the target. This confused the judges and it took them some time to decide to mark it. Deke typed up a request for a re-jump stating that Brydon was one of the world's most accurate parachutists and it was obvious that he had little control. What control he had was used to direct himself and the parachute away from the crowd for safety reasons. When he was certain that it was safe, he put his arms out to his sides as a signal to the judges.

Jumping continued with Schall scoring his fourth consecutive dead center. It was clear that he was going to be the man to beat. I was getting that sinking feeling of being a bridesmaid for the third time. The French team also scored two dead centers. The U.S. would make the last jump of the day and break a World Record. We came charging in with a four man average of 90 centimeters. The Russians re-broke the record two days later. That night in the gymnasium, where many of the jumpers and friends were drinking beer and relaxing, Sonnichsen learned that his request for Brydon's re-jump was voted down, ten against one, with Arender casting the only pro vote.

Deke conferred with Steve Groff, Captain of the Netherlands team, and Dave Jansen, an ex-West Point instructor and now Leader of the Norwegian team, on how many votes they could count on if a further appeal was submitted to the F.A.I. jury. There were too few, so the subject was dropped.

Monday all of the teams took a boat tour on Lake Constance on the Bavarian-Swiss border. It was beautiful and relaxing but you could still feel the pressure of the competition.

Tuesday morning jumping continued with the completion of the men and women's Team Accuracy.

Wednesday was literally a wash-out. It rained all day and nothing was accomplished. Those types of days really worked on my nerves and I didn't have an airplane in order to go flying and relax.

Thursday and Friday, we completed the entire Style event. My best time was 9.2 seconds. Russia's Tkachenko, the 1962 style champion, turned an unbeatable 8.8 and 8.5 series to retain his title of World Style Champion. Klima finished Third and I Finished fourth, always out of the medals. Tee Taylor poured it on with two series of 10.8 seconds and one of 10.7 seconds to win the event and set a women's World Record. On Wednesday, all team leaders got together and decided that upon completion of style jumping, the men's 1,500 Men's Individual Accuracy would continue and that the women were finished. This was great for the United States. It meant that Tee Taylor was the overall World Champion and the Women's team won overall gold!

Friday was a very hectic day. We got started late and in the afternoon low clouds canceled jumping. Also, the Bulgarian team said the drop zone was too packed down and hard, so there was another delay while they dug it up and raked it. The Bulgarians finally made the last lift of the day.

I went to bed that night knowing that the next day was 'do or die' for me, and it had come down, once again, to me and my old Czech friend, Klima. It was hard to sleep at all that night. I think every jump I made in Sofia and Orange went through my mind.

I was a little tired when I woke up on Saturday. Klima and I both had two more jumps left in the 1,500 meter Accuracy event. Climbing to altitude for the first one gave me a chance to clear my head and concentrate on the task at hand. I came across the exit point and jumped. Nothing fancy, just a stable fall for seventeen seconds and pull the rip-cord. The spot was good. I made a few turns testing the winds and the parachute; always watching the smoke on the ground. About 300 feet I made my final turn to the target. It was going to be a golden approach; holding the toggles down just a little for breaking so it appeared that I would land about a meter short, and then ease up on the toggles and wham! Both feet on the disc for a dead center!

On his last jump, Klima made a Dead Center. More so than any other championship I had ever been in, this last event was really turning into a spectator sport. It was as if they sensed that the competitive struggle between Klima and myself was an overlapping thing.

Before my last jump, Sonnicsen called me over and told me that I needed 1 meter and 32 centimeters to win the Overall Championship. He wasn't aware of my competing philosophy. I said "Deke, I didn't want to know that." I always competed against myself, not someone else. Know what my personal best is and try to beat it. Now I had a number in my head that I didn't really want.

I don't recall anytime in my life that I felt this much pressure. I boarded the plane and took off for the most important jump of my life. As we came across the target, toward the exit point I noticed an unusually large crowd around the 100 meter circle. It appeared to be every competitor at the meet. I exited, fell for seventeen seconds and pulled. The opening spot was perfect. I went through my usual routine and at about 300 feet made my final turn to the target. People later said that at that point, Klima just threw his hands up, turned around and walked off, never looking back. The approach was golden. Then about 100 feet something happened. "Holy Shit, what now." Either the wind picked up or I just misjudged, but I was going over the target. I would have to make one desperation turn close to the ground. I did and landed hard. I jumped up quickly to watch the judge's mark. 1.43 meters! Damn! I was a bridesmaid again. I noticed the crowd was very quiet. They said my face was white when I approached the team at the 100 meter circle. Deke said, "Well?" I whispered "a meter and 43 centimeters". It was deathly silent for a couple of seconds, and then Anne Batterson said "for Christ's sake, somebody tell him." Deke said, "Congratulations, you are the new World Champion. All you needed was less than 2.00 meters. If you had gotten 1.32 as I said, you would have won this event also for two gold medals." I about passed out. I didn't walk off the DZ. The team picked me up on their shoulder's and carried me off.

At the Awards Ceremony the next morning, there was a crowd of about 15,000. They were there to watch the Ceremony, but mainly to watch the fun jumps to be made later in the day when we would all swap parachutes and make the Jump of Nations.

As I walked out to receive my gold medal, someone began to clap. Then all of a sudden it turned into thundering applause, whistling and yelling. I was receiving an ovation from all the competitors. The older ones remembered Sofia in 1960 and had apparently told the story to the younger ones.

For the jump of Nations, Klima and I grinned at each other. He handed me his parachute and I handed him mine. He was a little shorter than me so we both had to do a little adjusting of each harness. He and I boarded the same aircraft and climbed to 7,200 feet for a thirty second delay. We exited one after the other, and then came together in free-fall and shook hands. That's what it is all about!

The next day, there was a picture of me in the local news paper. I couldn't read it, but I got the gist of the caption. "DEM WELTMEISTER." The World Master.

The trip home was festive to say the least. We were a little disappointed that the men's team finished 4th but we had the Men and Women's Overall World Champions. The overall women's team World Champions, and Tee Taylor, had a gold medal for style.

Upon arrival in New York, Pioneer Parachute Company put a PR man named Tony Furman onto us. He got us on a number of talk shows (Barry Gray), Tee had to leave early but I stuck around for a couple of days for the TV shows, "What's My Line" and "To Tell the Truth."

Three weeks later I was at Fort Wolters, Texas for primary flight training in helicopters. Before arriving, the *Army Times* news paper printed an article; "World Champion Seeks Warrant Officers Wings." They were waiting for me! A Captain walked up to me in our first formation of "hell week" and asked, "Are you Dick Fortenberry?" I yelled "Sir, candidate Richard Fortenberry sir." He asked "Are you THE Dick Fortenberry?" I yelled, Sir, candidate Richard Fortenberry sir." Then he screamed, "Are you the skydiver

Dick Fortenberry?" I meekly replied, "Yes Sir." He put the bill of his cap against the bill of mine and yelled "Well, your hero days are over. Skydive down here and give me 20 pushups!" It was like that for thirty-eight weeks, but that's a whole other book.

When you know it's the
End of a phase
Of your life,
Recognize it,
Accept it,
And move on.

THE END